Don't Let It Break You, Honey:
A Memoir About Saving Yourself

Don't Let It Break You, Honey:

A Memoir About Saving Yourself

By Jenny Evans

ROBINSON

First published in Great Britain in 2025 by Robinson

1 3 5 7 9 10 8 6 4 2

Copyright © Jenny Evans, 2025

The moral right of the author has been asserted.

All rights reserved.

No part of this publication may be reproduced, stored in a retrieval system, or transmitted, in any form, or by any means, without the prior permission in writing of the publisher, nor be otherwise circulated in any form of binding or cover other than that in which it is published and without a similar condition including this condition being imposed on the subsequent purchaser.

A CIP catalogue record for this book
is available from the British Library.

ISBN: 978-1-47214-899-5

Typeset in Adobe Garamond Pro by SX Composing DTP, Rayleigh, Essex
Printed and bound in Great Britain by Clays Ltd, Elcograf S.p.A.

Papers used by Robinson are from well-managed forests
and other responsible sources.

Robinson
An imprint of
Little, Brown Book Group
Carmelite House
50 Victoria Embankment
London EC4Y 0DZ

The authorised representative
in the EEA is
Hachette Ireland
8 Castlecourt Centre, Dublin 15,
D15 XTP3, Ireland
(email: info@hbgi.ie)

An Hachette UK Company

www.hachette.co.uk

www.littlebrown.co.uk

'Above all, be the heroine of your life, not the victim.'
Nora Ephron
Speaking at Wellesley College, Massachusetts, 1996

'The country and the British public deserve to know the depths of what was happening. We will be better off for it.'
Prince Harry
Witness Statement, 2023

For
Mum, Deb, Jasp, Leo
and
Cwtch the cat
With profound love and thanks.
And
for anyone who is at the bottom of a well.
This is for you.

Author's Note

I wrote this book because I believe in the power of stories. Good storytelling invites deep thought and can provoke much needed conversations. It can challenge power structures. It aims a light into the dark.

I have long known that I wanted to expose the corruption I describe in these pages. That, after all, is the job of a journalist: and I have been a journalist for twenty years. Doing so means sharing parts of my personal life, which has at times been an uncomfortable process, to say the least, but one I decided, on balance, was necessary.

If we cannot hold the people who harm us directly to account, we can at least tell the story of that harm. The voices of those who have been marginalised or dismissed – particularly women – are too often buried under layers of legal obstruction, societal shame, or deliberate erasure. By sharing my own story, I hope to honour the courage and resilience of my sources and of all survivors of bullying or violence.

La honte doit changer de camp. Shame must change sides.

For legal and ethical reasons, I have altered some details of the story. Certain individuals' names and identifying characteristics have been disguised, either because they spoke to me in confidence or because what I know about them would be considered libellous and all but impossible to prove. Sources who spoke on condition of anonymity appear as composites, to protect their identities without losing the essence or impact of what they had to say. Quoted conversations between us are reproduced in order to illustrate the information I was receiving, and the investigative path I was following, rather than to hold out the contents of those quotations as absolute truth.

This book draws on a wide range of primary sources: personal notes and memories, email chains, news articles, official records, and the voices of those I encountered along the way. I have done my utmost to remain faithful to the accounts given by these people, and many of those who were directly involved have confirmed the accuracy of my recollections. I am grateful to them.

It has been a privilege to write this book. Thank you for reading it.

Jenny Evans, 2025

Prologue

'I want to report an assault.'

The first thing that happens when you utter those no-going-back words at a police station front desk is that you are taken into a side room and asked to wait. A senior officer then comes to meet you, in my case with a notepad, and asks you to tell them everything you can. I had a woman officer, who was kind and patient and who, once I stopped talking, said, 'I believe you; that is the first thing you have to know.'

She asked if I had any corroborative evidence at all – the dress I was wearing at the time of the assault, any witnesses, anything like that.

As it happens, I had kept the dress.

I agreed to do a filmed interview. To give more detail, with a view to pressing charges. At that point, five years after it happened, I was still so shocked I couldn't remember everything I remember now. Or, I remembered, but I couldn't pull focus. I couldn't look. Trauma does weird things to your brain.

I had not spoken about what happened before.

The Famous Man had held my face during the assault. He had done that to silence me, and it had worked.

So, it was like being hit by a truck, when I opened the *Sun* newspaper, four days later, to see my story in print. Not my name, just my most deeply held secrets.

They held her down . . . a violent ordeal . . . penetration.

I snatched the newspaper away from my boyfriend and paced the room, my mind racing with phrases that would, over the years, become a roar of frustration.

How is this happening? What the fuck is going on here?
Eventually, I became determined to find out.

Part One:
The Breaking

1

Before my parents split up, we lived in a big house in a small town in South Wales, all stairs and corners, silver birch and fir trees, raspberry bushes and spider webs. The house was on the same street as our infants' school and within walking distance of an old-fashioned sweet shop, which sold penny chews and sherbet lemons in paper bags. At the other end of the road were the woods, where our cat ran away to and came back pregnant. The council soon chopped down the woods to house an estate, and we always wondered what had happened to her boyfriend.

Life on Park Street was not as idyllic for my parents, who were trying to protect me and my big brother, Will, from noticing their failing marriage, but they did a good job; we had no idea. We were told Dad slept in the spare room because he snored.

Will was only eighteen months older, but to me he was everything. The brightest star in any room. In part, this was because he was an encyclopedia of the not-very-useful knowledge that drives kids wild. He taught me, aged six, that there is a word for 'to be turned into a worm' ('vermiculate', if you are interested) and what 'pathetic' means; how to use it and how to spell it. He had heard Mum say it about Norman Tebbit.

In those days, both Will and I were blond, his hair thicker and glossier than mine (how unfair). His shy smile, the same shape as Grandpa's, beamed when he caught you in a practical joke. Will's eyes, a startling cobalt, put my pale blue to shame. We had attic bedrooms to play in, with a landing between them on which we first built an elaborate shop, then created a never-ending soft toy and Action Man Olympics, which could be returned to by either one of us, or both, to advance whichever race was being run at any one time. Hilary, a bear with no eyes, was a particularly good hurdler. I can't remember what we used for hurdles.

Will's room had the 'sliding cupboard' at the back: a creepy, pitch-black cubbyhole of horror filled with an enormous, inky water tank. His walls were navy, his bed frame red metal (hello 1980s), with a grey and red 'graffiti' bedspread he chose himself. His carpets were strewn with *Star Wars* figures and Transformers, as well as books. Hundreds of books. If you retrieved Will's old bunk-bed ladder from the sliding cupboard (deep breath, crawl in forward, back out as fast as you can), you could balance it precariously against the edge of the deep windowsill and watch the kids in Park Street School playground at the back.

Too young to attend myself when we moved into the house, I was often to be found with my nose pressed to that window, waiting for Will to return. Then, we could sip Dad's cocoa from mugs with our names on and get on with building Lego lands across the floor. Calm in peaceful companionship, at home with one another.

My bedroom was yellow. The bedspread (pastel polka dot), Edwardian chest of drawers and vanity desk had been chosen by Mum – she transformed the entire room one birthday, as a surprise when I got home from school. My room overlooked the street, so I could watch the neighbours come and go in a dance of different coloured front doors. A bonus was to catch Benjy the dog being taken for a walk from the newbuild right at the end. At night, I talked to Glow Worm under the duvet, his bug-eyed face smiling back at mine. Nothing got to Glow Worm; he was always happy with the world and so was I. My favourite thing was night rain, amplified by the attic. Even now I get a childlike thrill when I hear the sound of raindrops on a roof.

Mum delighted in her kids in a way I know now is very lucky. We always felt enjoyed by her; cherished. As soon as I was old enough for school, she took a job as manager of a Citizens Advice Bureau (CAB) and also became involved with the local Campaign for Nuclear Disarmament (CND) group. She took me to the Greenham Common Women's Peace Camp in Berkshire for weekends of mud and singing, as hundreds of women protested a government decision to store nuclear weapons at the Royal Air Force base there. I remember dolls, paper hats and a woman called Marion playing the accordion with gusto. One Saturday, on a CND march through Abergavenny, our home town, we all had to lie down on the ground outside Woolworths as if a nuclear bomb had destroyed everything. Truthfully, I was a little freaked out as we were loaded into trucks next to people dressed as skeletons, but Mum's mate Lyz gave me a wink and held my hand.

Summer in Park Street meant picnic breakfasts in the garden: peaches from the peach tree, warm baguettes, noses sticky with strawberry jam. On Saturday afternoons, Dad might take Will and me for a walk by the river, throwing sticks for Teggy, our little black and white dog, teaching us how to skim stones and spot kingfishers. Mum might take us to the park, laughing as we bounced out of the rocking rocket, shouting, 'Higher! Higher!'

It is a certainty that the safety and security of those early years, which gave me a core belief that the world is essentially good, essentially happy, essentially safe, helped me navigate later aspects of my life that have felt like an absolute shit show. I can draw on Park Street to this day; all I have to do is think about the garden, or my bedroom, the Saturdays, or the Christmases, to feel my heartbeat begin to slow and be able to remind myself of the somewhat unbelievable truth that I live in the same world now as I lived in then.

Friends I have known since that time, whose home lives were perhaps more chaotic than my own, also remember the Park Street house with the same halcyon glow. It was the playing, I think. We were encouraged to play, and we had such good toys and games and dens. It was a sanctuary for us all. Though I, of course, didn't know any different. Not yet. I was lucky then.

2

I once asked a therapist, 'Is your dad dying when you are thirteen particularly bad timing?'

She shook her head. 'It's a fucking disaster.'

Dad died.

He had a new wife by then – a younger woman he'd married just two weeks earlier, and who he'd known for six months. His death was sudden and unexpected, a heart attack while under general anaesthetic. It was a minor operation, and it was extra shocking because he hadn't told us he was having it; he didn't want to worry us.

Dad was fifty when I was born, twenty years older than Mum, so uniquely among my friends, I had a War Dad. A make-do-and-mend, knows-how-to-patch-an-elbow, corned-beef-hash-for-tea-again kind of dad. He grew up in Cardiff, the son of a traumatised First World War veteran who worked for the council and a teetotal Baptist who worked at the Post Office. His mum, my nana, was born in 1898. Nana always kept the butter and the Bible next to the fire and made sure the Welsh cakes were warm when you walked through the front door.

Dad's first job, when he was saving for university, was as a bus conductor. For the rest of his life, instead of saying 'Excuse me', when he needed to pass you, he always went for, 'Mind your backs, please. Move right down the bus.' I adored him. He had green eyes, crested with the same laughter lines now emerging in the soft skin around my own. His cheeks were round like mine too, but he had dark hair and a salt-and-pepper beard I liked to stroke. He was a storyteller, seeing poetry everywhere. He loved kids and he loved dogs.

Dad was in his late teens when the Second World War ended. He told me it was the changes he witnessed the Attlee government make – an extensive social housing building programme, the expansion of the welfare state, the establishment of the NHS – that saw him, like many of his generation, became 'dyed in the wool' red. When we moved to Abergavenny, he became a local Labour councillor. A few years later, he moved again – out of the Park Street house, to a littler one round the corner.

'Is Councillor Evans at home? It's my drainpipes.'

Will and I were instructed to let all the Mr Drainpipes in, offer them tea, then retreat so *Councillor Evans* could listen to their problems. Will, eleven, and I, nine, would stand behind the door listening to complaints of tree roots damaging foundations, a dog causing a nuisance, dance music 'ruining everything for everyone on the whole bloody street, Mr Evans'. Rather than follow due process, Dad would typically grab a ladder and go out and fix things himself if he could, his fingers forever flecked with cuts from 'doing a little job' for someone. His house had two videos in it, *Carmen* and *Educating Rita*. When there was nothing on telly we would watch those films on rotation, while I sat on his lap and kissed his chapped hands.

In the lead-up to elections, I was promoted to campaign assistant and found myself trailing the streets behind Dad's brown slacks, knocking on doors to hand out posters. I could identify voters easily. Labour were pleased to see us, even just to enjoy a good rant about the Tories, who had been in power for a long time, 'cutting every public service we've got, Mr Evans', 'Oh, I know it. I know', Dad would smile, warmly, 'Please call me Keith'. Very occasionally someone in a tight, pastel-coloured jumper would come to the doorstep just to tell Dad how much they loved Mrs Thatcher. He would smile, make a few carefully placed political points about our mining communities, still decimated, then back away with a 'Cheerio now'.

Any door that remained unanswered, I pushed a leaflet through, hating the spring-loaded letter boxes that trapped my fingers. Dad and I would listen for the soft swish of it landing. A moment of pause in a dark street. Then he would take my hand in his, and on we'd go. Sometimes he pretended to limp, and I pretended to mind, laughing as I tried to stop him.

Within a week of Dad's death, his new wife had sold his car. He had told me, as we walked the river meadows at dusk, that he was marrying her because she needed to change her surname, 'so that her ex-husband won't abduct [their child] and take her back to Turkey'. I picked buttercups and thought about his reasoning. It felt like a noble thing to do, a kind thing, a Dad thing. But my insides had dragged with sadness. I didn't sense from him any joy. 'Do you love each other?' I had asked, knowing only that marriages should involve love. 'Oh yes,' Dad had replied. 'Oh yes, Jenny Wren.' He had put his hand on the back of my neck, an act of reassurance. Perhaps neither of us believed it.

After the car went, the new wife locked us out of Dad's house and started selling everything he owned, item by item. Mum and Deb, my big sister (twenty years older) from Dad's first marriage, managed a couple of times to talk their way in, each time shoving ornaments into their pockets. Deb negotiated getting my 'memory box', a Victorian collar box that had belonged to Dad's dad, which we had filled with little treasures: extra-flat stones for skimming, thimbles, old coins. Mum got me one of Dad's jackets and a shoebox full of his poems. That was it. Within months, Dad's house and everything in it, including my toys, my clothes, the poetry books he and I read aloud to each other over breakfast, disappeared.

We were bereft and, without Dad, skint. Mum had resigned from her day job, now a community education officer. It required her to work evenings, and she didn't want Will and me to be alone after school in the kind of shock and grief you wish children never had to know. The first few mornings after he died, she crawled into my bed before the alarm went off; strong arm around my middle, warm hand on my forehead. We lay there in silence, staring at my wall, breathing as one. Then the bell began to sound, and we got up to face the day.

Without an income, Mum began making hats to pay the bills. She was determined not to lose the house and floppy velvet hats that could be pinned at the front were a) a big deal in the 1990s and b) easy to make. Every night after dinner she sat at the kitchen table, nimble-fingered and determined, rat-a-tatting at her sewing machine like her life depended on it. It did. I was the hat model. On market day, I'd swap colours every few hours, drinking tea, stomping my Doc Martens, painted with flowers by Will, to keep warm. Mostly we sold at the craft markets dotted around South Wales, but any stall would do, and the ends just about met. Though we regularly stuffed the car with other bits from the house and hawked it at car boots for extra cash.

Clothes came from charity shops. Pocket money came from child benefit. Sue, two doors down, worked the markets as well and there was a steady flow of tenners between our families. In that way, week by week, hand to mouth, we got by. There was a junk shop called Trash and Treasure at the end of our road and sometimes, on a Friday night, Mum would pawn the big brass fireguard to get food, then buy it back after the Saturday market. On those Fridays, we had a chippy tea.

As we reached our mid-teens, Mum gave up her evenings once more to study to be a therapist. For a short while, our belts became even tighter. Bone-tired, she once burst into tears because Will had eaten an entire pasta bake when he came home stoned and there was nothing else in the cupboards. 'What am I meant to feed Jen?'

Outwardly, I blossomed, by which I mean, I grew up (grew tits?). I became tall and thin, my face changed, wavy hair hung to my shoulders. Within a year of Dad's death, I was already a different person from the girl he had known. I trod a different path; people – men – responded differently to me. I wore this new power lightly, with a flick of the hair and a knowing grin (I knew nothing), but I was grieving and fragile; a paper lantern of a person, fuelled by fire, so easily crushed. My mates and I coated the brave and bawdy mask of all teenage girls – cheek, sentimentality, self-deprecation – with thick mascara and Body Shop bronzer. We wafted around town in Charlie perfume and lip gloss, in search of fun and more fun, and more and more. We gulped cider, smoked weed and carried on.

I seemed untouchable, but I was scared, of everything.

Most of all, I missed my dad.

3

'When the Holocaust visits your life,' a pause as she surveyed the room, waiting for her words to bite, 'try not to lay the blame at your own front door.'

Maya Angelou, actor, activist, author, poet, had been asked by an audience member how she walked so tall having survived such pain. All of us in that room had read Angelou's memoir, *I Know Why the Caged Bird Sings*. We knew she had been sent away from her parents aged four to be raised by her grandmother. A Black girl in the Deep South, in the 1940s. We knew that when she was returned to her mother, aged eight, she was raped by a stepfather figure. We knew he was then beaten to death and, believing her voice had killed him, that little Maya did not speak for five years.

What we were not prepared for was the power of her presence. It is a cliché, but I could not take my eyes from her. Angelou was six foot but seemed taller. Straight-backed, stoic, her hair close cropped, gold hoops dangling from her ears. Her lips were blood red, her dress, silky black. She was a goddess. As she removed a white blazer and surveyed us once more, her quiet strength triggered within me the deep and bewildering grief I had learned to suppress. *Dad*. Fear of the world's sharp edges crept across me like a shadow and I began to weep.

Since 1988, the Hay-on-Wye literary festival has drawn Pulitzer Prize winners, American presidents, authors, musicians, comedians and philosophers to our quiet corner of Wales. It is a summit of art and deep thinking, radical ideas, excellent ice-cream and average wine. There is a particular kind of magic to bagging a deckchair on a sunny weekend at Hay and having nothing to do but loll and people-watch and read, as music thrums across the ley lines into the night.

Maya Angelou had come to talk about her latest book, *Wouldn't Take Nothing for My Journey Now*. The title is a line from a civil-rights-era song, 'Keep Your Eye on the Prize'. It is about holding on despite pain. About living with hope.

The week that Dad died, we decided as a family to view his body in the hospital morgue. It is recommended you do that after an unexpected death, to help you process the shock. On a Saturday afternoon, when my friends were out on their bikes, I stood in a small room, dark with drapes, contemplating the spongy yellow skin of Dad's face. It reminded me of the bottom of a crumpet. I wanted to hold his hand, but he had been swaddled in red velvet and I couldn't reach him. I was staring at the crush of his mouth, silently begging him to look at me, and smile, 'Don't worry, Jenny Wren.' But Dead Dad couldn't smile. Dead Dad couldn't enjoy the buttercups and kingfishers. Dead Dad couldn't do any more 'little jobs' for people. Dead Dad was there, but he was not there. Where was he? *What* was he?

I felt a deep pang of longing for the freedom of friends and bikes. For fresh air and distraction, a world away from here. When I sought them out, I did my best to be like those friends, but I soon became aware that I was not. I had one foot in thirteen – bikes and boys – and another in contemplating life and death. Dead Dad.

The capricious nature of an indifferent world. I imagined it was a relief for my friends not to have me and my intense experience around all the time, and to withdraw. I began to become the alone that I felt.

Two years later, in the marquee at Hay, I leaned forward, wide eyed, straining to absorb every inch of Angelou's presence. I wanted to soak up her wisdom, her sadness, her calm. I wanted to never stop listening. But then, applause. She was standing. She was being led away, across the stage, through the tent towards the exit. Right past me. When she saw me, sniffing into my cuffs – a willowy fifteen-year-old in denim shorts, those painted Doc Marten's, a ripped jumper two sizes too big, she beckoned me to her. 'Don't let it get you down. Don't let it get to you,' she said, then wrapped me into a deep embrace, pouring warm words into my ear. 'Don't let it break you, honey. Don't let it break you.' She held my face, looked into my eyes and smiled.

That day in Hay, quite by accident, Maya Angelou became my guardian angel.

4

Twice a week, from around the age of ten, I could be found in our town's drama centre, a community building in a former school, dedicated to theatre and education. It was free, or I wouldn't have been able to go, and I don't know what I would have become without it. A Victorian greystone, it had a garden with a stream, an old gymnasium with wooden bars and ceiling ropes, a green room, painted green, with photos on the walls of performances past. The drama centre was run by Julia, a stressed-out-by-funding-issues, deeply kind woman with dangly earrings and a three-legged dog called Sid. There, in a well-loved studio space, my friends and I read poetry and plays, improvised, performed. We practised emotion at the safe distance of pretending to be someone else.

I was eighteen when, one Saturday morning, the drama group was told that Nina Gold, a casting director from London (*London*), was coming to Wales looking for a 'young person' for *Twin Town*, a feature film about crooks set in Swansea. Nina, who would go on to cast *Star Wars*, *Games of Thrones*, *Slow Horses* – you name it – was our golden ticket: perhaps a route to paid acting work. At the very least, a trip to London.

The first audition was held at a youth theatre in Cardiff. I opted to wear a floor-length skirt – a charity-shop find in dirty cream, formerly a Victorian maid's petticoat or something. It was covered with thin blue vertical stripes. I looked like a circus tent. I topped it with a black minidress and a man's brown corduroy jacket. I'm surprised Nina didn't call security.

Despite this, I somehow managed to get a second audition. This time, the address led to an old redbrick building in the centre of Swansea, a few miles west of Cardiff. Will came along, chain-rolling joints with his long, thin fingers in the passenger seat of his girlfriend Emma's car. Emma was cool: silver tights, tiny miniskirt, blue hair.

Nina was an altogether different kind of cool. She was *London* cool. It was the first time I noticed it. It is worn lightly but it is evident in a sophisticated kind of 'knowing', a sharper cut of hair, real jewellery, clothes not made of nylon. She smiled a warm welcome, rubbed her pregnant tummy and showed me into a side room to meet the director.

The room was small, tiled, with one of those chunky old radiators stuck to the wall that have been painted so many times they give out no heat. It had high windows. There was a large camera on top of a desk. Once I could take him in, I saw that co-writer and director, Kevin, in red T-shirt and jeans, was very Welsh looking: small, olive skinned, dark eyes and hair. His nose wrinkled when he grinned and I liked him. He reminded me I was reading for the part of Bonny, the unfortunate daughter of a lead character and, together, we read every scene she was in. It meant imitating having sex, which I masked acute embarrassment about and limped through. When Kev laughed as I read the lines, I grew an inch or two. I was doing this. With London people. They liked me.

I can't remember how many more auditions there were but a short while later, I answered the phone in my bedroom at home to Nina's voice: 'It was really lovely to see you again the other day, Jenny. We wanted to thank you so much for coming to the audition. Can you hold the line? I have Kevin for you.'

Kev told me I had got the part. I didn't know what to say beyond 'Oh, thank you'. Were there questions I was supposed to ask? He seemed amused and said he was looking forward to working with me.

Working with me.

I hung up and the boys I had been smoking weed with said things like, 'Fair play to you, Jen,' and patted me on the shoulder as they headed home for their tea.

In disbelief, I opened the window and stared at the purple and green mountain that overlooks Abergavenny. She had been the backdrop to my entire life. She had seen everything. What lay beyond her? I had struggled with school since Dad died; dropped out of doing my A levels, twice. I loved reading and writing and drama, but in the shadow of grief, nothing felt important. Now, the excitement of possibility, of promise, began to bubble up in my chest, as a pathway formed in my mind.

5

I caught the train to Swansea alone. Rehearsals were held in the same redbrick building I had auditioned in. Creeping towards the rehearsal room, I could hear the cast laughing at someone reading her lines. I slid in at the back, hoping not to disturb anything, and was soon laughing myself. Rachel was not just funny, she oozed warmth and charisma. Her dark, bobbed hair framed the biggest smile and longest eyelashes I had ever seen. *Welsh Snow White*, I thought. Spotting me standing shyly near the door, she beamed and gave me a wink. Then, when Kev called a break, she came straight over, swept me into a fierce hug and declared, 'Who's this? I'm adopting this one.'

Another wink. I was hers.

Kev is Kevin Allen (uncle of Lily). He had a bit-part in *Trainspotting* and used it to pitch Danny Boyle and Andrew Macdonald *Twin Town*, which he had written with his friend, Paul Durden. Boyle and Macdonald agreed to executive produce the film and as a result the press dubbed it 'The Welsh *Trainspotting*'. In reality, the two films are very different: *Twin Town* is far sillier and, if you can believe it, swearier. It is neon colours, caricatures and high comedy, and that's why people love it. Even today, its most ardent fans can spot me – *Oi, it's Bonny* – and start spouting lines. Mostly, in a thick Welsh accent, they go for the immortal, 'You fucking twat', something my character's dad says. If I'm lucky, they shout, 'Dad! Fatty's boys are at the door!' – one of my lines. Then they ask me if it was real piss I was soaked in, in the scene with the karaoke. I can't explain. You'll have to watch it, I'm afraid.

The cast of *Twin Town* had a lot of fun that summer. The late, wonderful Brian Hibbard, formerly of pop band The Flying Pickets had a role. I have a lasting memory of the cast singing his a cappella hit 'Only You' one morning as the sun came up, conducted by him, in the hotel bar. Most of us were wearing tights on our heads. Again, I'm afraid I can't explain.

The film catapulted Rhys Ifans and Dougray Scott towards Hollywood and, though I have some thoughts now on how welcome an intimacy co-ordinator would have been for my more challenging scenes, it must surely be remembered very fondly by all involved.

Friendship with Kev, Rhys and Rachel led to invites to parties in London. I'd only been to London a couple of times before; once on a primary school trip and a second time as a kid with Dad. I had a lot to learn. Invited to meet up with some of the cast in Soho after a photo shoot (*Soho*), I changed out of the denim mini and T-shirt I had travelled in and zipped myself into a hastily purchased vintage ball gown (*Camden Lock*), because I thought Soho was posh. On arrival, shoving my London *A–Z* into my tiny, purple, *furry* backpack, I realised everyone else was wearing jeans. Before anyone saw me I snuck into the pub kitchen (closed for food, thank goodness), found a pair of scissors and hacked off the bottom of the dress. I was the sort of grown-up who blithely wears a grungy minidress with lace sleeves to Tuesday drinks, I decided. I was becoming an expert at thinking on my feet. Of masking how out of my depth I was.

Or so I thought.

6

On the day of the assault, I was at a barbeque at a crew member's house in west London. It was *perfect*; the floorboards were stripped, the walls white, there was a vintage mirror in the living room and funky framed art. Portishead played on the CD player. I ran my hand along the furniture, marvelling at The Crew Member's taste, wishing I was her. French doors in the dining room led to a wisteria-covered pergola, which in turn shaded a shabby-chic garden table. I looked out at a garden full of proper grown-ups I didn't know, some of whom I recognised from TV. How was I going to get through this small-talk bit? Readjusting the tailored minidress I had bought specially from Miss Selfridge, I selected a spot on the lawn, folded my legs beneath me and shyly but determinedly smoked my way through a packet of Marlboro Lights, lighting each new one from the end of the last.

I had become close to The Crew Member during filming. We had spent long hours chatting on set, sharing our life stories, our philosophies. We had deliberately remained in touch, but she was maybe fifteen years older than me. I wanted to be her, but I couldn't fully relax with her. She wasn't Rhys or Rachel; we wouldn't be dancing on the tables by the end of the night. We might be sitting under the wisteria setting the world to rights, though, which I would have loved. I just needed everyone else to go.

Rachel hadn't come to this party. How I wished she had. I made multiple trips to the bathroom to whisper affirmations in the mirror – 'If you just relax, you can be yourself', 'If you just relax, they will like you' – and considered slipping away to catch the next train home to Wales.

Returning to the garden after one of these trips, I felt the gaze of a man I recognised from magazines and music videos follow my path. He was a musician. Famous. I quite liked his band. Smirking, he watched me sit down on the grass alone and sip my beer, but he didn't come over. I shrank under the scrutiny of this man; I felt he knew I didn't come up to scratch. It was as if he could see the smalltown girl I was trying to hide.

When I stood once more, my napkin fell from my lap, revealing my legs, 'Oh look, she has got some personality after all,' he said to his friends.

They laughed.

I smiled and rolled my eyes. Like I was in on the joke. Like it was funny. Never has a girl who cared so much pretended so hard not to care. In that moment I became determined to show this man and his friends just how likeable I am. They would see just how much fun I could be. I would have *them* dancing on the tables. I would stay until I had turned this evening around.

It was a decision I would deeply come to regret.

7

I first thought I might be in danger when The Famous Man grabbed my throat. No, that's when I first thought I might die. I first thought I might be in danger when he pushed me backwards over his coffee table; I lost my footing and fell. I had been driven to his house by a new 'friend' I had made at the barbeque. The last few stragglers decided to head to a pub, and she had linked her arm through mine and encouraged me to come. The Crew Member I was staying with approved – she couldn't join us, but her friend was an excellent chaperone. She would see me back at hers later.

When it was decided by someone that we should finish the evening at The Famous Man's house, I smiled and tagged along. It was all the same to me. More drinks. More music. More expensive sofas. Then I realised my chaperone had gone: I was in a house, by myself, without any way of getting back to my room at The Crew Member's house. I asked The Famous Man and his friend, just the two of them left now, to call me a taxi. I didn't yet have a phone of my own. The Famous Man offered me his mobile. I extended my arm to take it, but he hid it behind his back. His friend laughed.

The Famous Man took a step towards me. I took a step back. My throat tightened with tears. I asked for a taxi again. The Famous

Man again offered his phone. I again tried to take it. He again pulled it away. This time no one laughed. Tension flooded the room. The Famous Man took a step closer. I took a step back. He knew I would soon hit his coffee table and have nowhere else to go. I was only just realising how far into the deep, dark wood I had accidentally skipped.

It is a myth that all sexual assaults result in visible injury. Visible injury does not denote a more serious crime or a worse experience. It is important to say that. I did sustain visible injury from this assault, though it took me many years to allow myself to remember and be able to accept this.

The Famous Man raised a large hand, put it to my chest and pushed me backwards, which happened both in slow motion and in a flash. Then the other pounced, like a wolf.

I saw what happened next from above. Looking down. As if I had died of fright. In the intervening years, it is what I understand to be residual trauma; remnants of images, certain sounds, a sense of fear, that anchor me in the reality that I suffered this at all. Because straight after it happened, a steel trap of denial slammed shut in my mind, telling me it did not. Or that maybe something happened, but really, it wasn't that bad. So I carried on as normal.

For me, in the first hours and days after the attack, the scratches on my thighs, the bruises emerging on my breast and legs, the pain I felt inside my body, felt like a contradiction. Nothing that bad has happened, so how can these injuries exist? How efficiently the mind switches to minimisation and denial.

It was this that stopped me going to the police, of course. This, and a bodily memory of fear, I think. On a base level, I was frightened.

Every time The Famous Man tightened his grip on my throat, I thought he might kill me by mistake. When I felt the edges of my vision darken, a pixelated kind of dizziness, I became terrified that I might pass out and no longer be able to fight them off.

Then, The Famous Man said he was bored. So, they let go.

Boringly for him, I had not stopped crying. Tediously, I had pleaded to be released. I had tried to stop them removing my clothes, fought to keep my legs closed, struggled even harder when I felt something forced inside me. I did not know what it was. It hurt. There was spit. There were tongues. There were teeth.

On a good day, I tell myself I fought them off. On a bad day, that I bored them so much they decided to give up. Whatever the reason, suddenly, and with a disgusted final glance, The Famous Man pushed me away and declared he was going to bed. The Wolf, breathless and sweating, sank into a huge sofa and began to smoke.

I crawled around the floor, trying to gather my things and do up my dress. My heart soared when I found a landline phone. In those days, only a handful of people I knew had mobiles. Rachel had one. I had memorised her number.

She was in a bar.

'Speak up. I can't hear you.'

I asked if I could come to stay at her house. She said of course and that she would send a taxi. 'Where are you? Where are you, Jen? I'll send a cab.'

I froze as I realised, I didn't know where I was. She couldn't help me. She demanded to speak to the men in the room, and somehow negotiated that The Wolf would call me a taxi and send me to The Crew Member's house, as arranged.

Outside and alone, I gulped down air, then began to wretch.

The mini-cab driver told me his name was Ken. He told me he thought I had been raped. He asked me to let him take me to the police. I looked at my mascara-streaked face in the wing mirror, lipstick spread across my chin like a burn. 'Do you have a cigarette?' He handed me a packet of Benson & Hedges and tried again. 'My name is Ken. I think you have been raped. Will you let me take you to the police?'

It wasn't that I wasn't grateful to Ken, I just couldn't think straight, I couldn't speak. I tried to knock the ash from my cigarette, but the window was open only an inch and I was shaking so much I knocked the end off and it flew back into the car, burning a hole in my dress. I didn't move.

Ken pulled over. He told me we had to get out of the car to look for the burning tobacco. He came round to my side, opened the passenger door, asked very gently, 'Can you stand?' He took my hand and helped me out of the car, then he found the end of my cigarette and asked if I needed help to get back in.

Ken wrote his name and phone number down on the back of a taxi receipt. He asked me to let him take me to the police.

I told Ken I needed to sleep.

8

I had to knock on the door of the house where I was staying. When The Crew Member opened it, I could see she was angry; I had breached etiquette by keeping her up. I had shamed her by getting into trouble. By making things messy. I had broken an unspoken rule about how to be cool – my greatest fear. More than anything, as she passed me a glass of water, sighing, running fingers through glossy hair, it seemed to me that I was a *huge* inconvenience. As I miserably climbed into bed, feeling like a naughty child, it dawned on me that she, like everyone else I had met that day, was actually just a stranger. Unable to look at my body, I turned my face to the ceiling, allowing hot tears to run into my hair.

The following morning, I caught the Tube to Paddington and called Will from a payphone. 'Something bad happened.'

Will told me to buy a hot chocolate and drink it slowly. He said he and Teggy would meet my train and walk me home. 'Don't worry, Onejen [his nickname for me]. Please don't worry.'

As the train chugged out of the station, past graffiti'd sidings and the backs of houses, I sipped my chocolate. The city and everything that had happened in it was receding. Soon I would see trees and the purple and green of our mountain. Soon I would see Will. The world felt in balance when he was there.

9

I took a room in a basement flat in Maida Vale, found a job in a bar in Soho and sank to the bottom of a well. It is dark and lonely at the bottom of a well, but most people don't realise that's where you live. You can drink and smoke and take too many drugs. You can avoid physical contact almost entirely and develop eating issues and give up all your ambitions. You can splash around in a pit of fear and bewilderment at who you've become, because the cold walls around you protect you from having to properly engage with anything-the-fuck-at-all.

After a couple of excruciating auditions, it became clear to me – and every director I met – that I no longer had the self-confidence to perform. I didn't want to be looked at. In truth, I had mostly stopped showering and brushing my teeth. I wore no make-up; I barely brushed my hair. When I wasn't waitressing, I smoked weed in bed and hoped I might die. Just one year before I had been a teen actress facing a world of possibilities. Now, I was a teen dropout who no longer recognised any aspect of her life, nor any part of herself within it. And just at that moment, just when I needed him most, Will, who had always been there, but who had himself been slowly, invisibly unravelling, hit the rock bottom of a well of his own.

It's hard to pinpoint where Will's mental health problems began. He was always shyer and more cautious than me; he hated school, I loved it. He hated parties; I danced like a lunatic. Perhaps I saw his vulnerability and went the other way to compensate, because I didn't want to be vulnerable, and because I wanted to be able to protect him.

Children in the same family often have conflicting versions of family life; our individual relationship with parents and siblings has a profound impact on how we relate to the world. My family was loving, kind, supportive. I always thought Will and I experienced the world as broadly the same; we had Park Street, the garden, Teggy, the Christmases. But we were very different. On top of Will's naturally quiet and more watchful nature, perhaps because of it, came bullying when he moved from primary to secondary school. He encountered humiliation and cruelty. His world was coloured dark with betrayal.

They tripped him up in the corridor or pushed him over as we walked across the school field towards home. They told him outings weren't happening, then had them without him, gloating about it the next day. They made it clear he was unwelcome at their parties, but when Will had a party, someone got the message out to all the pubs in town and our house was trashed. Morning and evening, he sought comfort from our desolate mum, banging his head against the kitchen cupboards, demanding, 'Why, why, *why*?'

Nothing she said touched the pain he felt.

'What is wrong with me? Why is this happening? Why me? Why me?' BANG BANG BANG.

'There is nothing wrong with you. You are good. They are unhappy. *They* are wrong. You are wonderful. My boy. My boy. The world's most wonderful boy.'

BANG BANG BANG BANG. The three of us, helpless.

I put my watch to my ear at night so that I couldn't hear him sobbing through the bedroom wall. In the mornings, I watched him throw his lunch into the bin in the garden before he left for school.

Within a year the plump blond cherub we had known was replaced by a spindly anorexic. Now, Will had black shoulder-length hair, PVC trousers, massive boots. He wore rings and earrings and eyeliner and developed a sneer that could wilt gardens.

Sticking two fingers up to his bullies, he found an older girlfriend, a younger following of 'alternative' kids from school, kudos for the amount of weed he could smoke. But at home, he cut his arms in savage rage, drank too much, loathed himself. He responded well to the child psychologist Mum found to support him and I began to pride myself on the different ways I could find to make him laugh, despite the darkness he couldn't shake.

Then Dad died.

Will was fifteen. He gave up school, moving out to stay with various family members and try his hand at work. Living with our big sister, Deb, in Bristol, he attempted A levels. His tutors seemed to love him, recommending 'in the strongest terms' that he apply to Oxbridge. But he did not have the self-esteem. The isolating shame left by his bullies did not shift. So, he took his pain and confusion to addiction's front door.

For a while, only I knew how much he was drinking and smoking. Then, I walked unannounced into his tent at a festival and found Will and his best friend on their backs, surrounded by drug paraphernalia that frightened me. Distraught and furious, there was no argument I could make that he would listen to. Although it was clear – always – that he loved me, and was on my side, slowly and shame-facedly, Will folded in on himself as if he had been boxed, and disappeared.

I might have told Mum what was going on sooner. I needed her help. But one January morning: 'Jen?'

A flatmate woke me and directed me towards the phone. 'Mum's had a car crash on the way to work, it's serious.'

Will was distracted – shocked. He didn't know much but was on his way to the hospital. I called Deb, who told me, 'What you have to remember, darling, is that we don't know how serious it is. This is what you are going to do: call your work, tell them what has happened. Tell them you can't come in for your shift. They need to replace you for at least a week. Worry about nothing else. Get to Paddington, get the train. I will pick you up when you get home.'

I couldn't see Mum at first. They were operating; one of her ribs had punctured a lung. She would die if they didn't remove it, but they weren't certain she would survive the operation. They said it could take twelve hours. Will and I sat in silence in the living room at home, staring into the open fire, Teggy at Will's feet. Will's girlfriend Emma came round. Sue from two doors down brought food.

This was January, eight months after the assault. I was still nineteen.

Will answered the phone call when it came. He listened, nodded, said, 'She's alive.'

Mum was in intensive care. Only two people were allowed in at a time.

'She broke every bone in her face,' the nurse told me. Her beautiful face. 'And her right arm and her left leg. And her rib punctured her lung, as you know. But she's alive. She's alive.' She looked dead.

Granny was stroking Mum's arm. 'Indy,' she said, using a pet name from childhood. She patted my arm. My turn.

'Hi, Mum,' I said.

Mum stirred, her eyes shifting to look at me. Suddenly she was agitated, tapping the breathing tube in her mouth, trying to say something. The nurse removed the tube and leaned towards her face. 'Tell her I'm OK,' she was saying. 'Tell her I'll be OK.'

We celebrated my twentieth birthday in the hospital. Mum could see I was upset with Will, but she couldn't work out why and I couldn't tell her. He had given up his job as an auxiliary nurse, lost his flat. He was living in a hostel. 'Don't worry, Onejen,' he wrote – we often sent letters to each other. 'It's a relief to give in to this, just for now.' In what world would I be able not to worry? *What good is saying, 'Don't worry,' to anyone, ever?* I thought when I read it. Pissed off with him. Pissed off with the world.

If I wanted to hang out with Will at this time, I had to help him sell the *Big Issue* magazine. We would stand at the end of one of the tunnels that run towards the 'Bear Pit', an apex of underground walkways in central Bristol, shouting '*Big Issue?*' at passers-by. We'd vary the tone, sometimes go high, sometimes low, trying to make each other laugh. For every magazine he sold, he received a percentage. With every sale, my heart sank. How had this happened? Who were we now? Where was Will when we weren't together? He wouldn't tell me.

I would get the train back to London with leaden feet: metal boots of sorrow. When Mum was discharged from hospital, Will and I would visit her at home together. He could no longer hide his state of mind, nor his lifestyle, so I told her what was going on and how far down a well he seemed to be. We shared it with Deb, who gave Will a key to her house in Bristol and told him he always had a room there. How lucky we have always been to have Deb. She looks more like Dad than me or Will, with thick dark hair, bobbed, and glasses. She loves literature, cricket, rugby – all the Dad things. They were very close and I have always adored her. As a kid, I thought she had the softest skin of anyone in the world and would hold her hands to my cheeks. Deb always has incredible stories to tell, good ideas for mountain treks, surprise theatre tickets.

It was a relief to share the burden of Will's addictions with Mum and Deb, but it did not take away the sadness, or the fear. Every day, we expected to get the worst phone call in the world.

This was a very dark time. I was so low, so far down my own well, I did not have the energy to pull myself out. I needed proper mates, but I did not feel worthy of the attention of others. So, it was astonishing to me to realise that some of the people I worked with appeared to like me. They invited me for drinks when our bar shifts ended. They seemed interested in what I had to say.

I think of these as my 'True Colors' friends. Cyndi Lauper's poetry describes better than I ever could how they made me feel. It is not an overstatement to say that these friendships – the raggedy, truthful, soulful love of this handful of somewhat mismatched but somehow perfect group of mates – kept me alive.

10

Five of us moved into a shonky basement flat in Stoke Newington, north London. The bathroom was mouldy, the windows draughty, I slept on a futon so thin you could feel the slats against your back. We lived on supermarket-brand quiche that cost £1.50 and ate it without salad, dipped in ketchup. But coming back to whoever happened to be in, in that grotty apartment with damp on the walls, was always to come home.

Lucy – Lu – was a singer and musician. She had bobbed sandy brown hair, her thin frame hidden beneath a chunky jumper, a guitar on her back. We made each other laugh. Lu busked on the Tube and we went to her open-mic nights. She was a straight-thinking, straight-talking, not straight, golden-hearted and excellent friend. Lu seemed to have an instinct for the pain I was in and kept me close. She was comfortable with pain. On nights off from the bar, we'd take home some wine, sing to her guitar in the kitchen and very often sleep in the same bed, finding comfort in the platonic warmth of the shared space. Lu introduced me to Ani DiFranco, Fleetwood Mac, North Devon, where she was from and where we went for adventures one Christmas. We'd dance to Fatboy Slim and Daft Punk, sing Tracy Chapman and revel in the exquisiteness of finding each other.

One night, as we lay together in her bed, in those intense few moments your brain goes crazy before you sleep, she whispered, 'You like him.'

Tears immediately spilled from my eyes. I couldn't speak. We both stared at the ceiling.

He was a South African barman with a wide smile. We had become close, sharing cod philosophy and amateur psychology in the quiet hours of the day shift. We'd have a drink after work sometimes, maybe eat our staff meals together. His name was Martin.

He tried to hide it, but he was smarter than most of the lads he hung out with. Funnier. More empathetic. He saw more than them, and he thought deeply. I had been telling myself, and Martin, and everyone else who noticed our closeness, that Will's absence from my life meant I was looking for a brother figure. There was some truth to that. I sought out many male friends in the years Will was, if not missing, then not present. The real truth was that I was paralysed. The younger, thinner, more confident me might well have been interested in a sexual relationship with Martin. He might have been interested in one with her. But neither of us could see past the anxious, asexual frump, in baggy Adidas joggers and a grey hoodie, who seemed to have eaten her.

'I can't,' I whispered to Lu in the end. 'I can't.' I think she might have cried too.

My flatmates could see I was not behaving like them. I felt no love for myself or for my body, no connection to it at all. I could not imagine being so exposed as to be naked with someone. To close my eyes. To trust them to be nice to me. To trust them at all. When I slept, I dreamed of my skin as blackly frostbitten, filled with maggots. I felt disgust. I was disgusting. Deep fear pierced my chest. A sensation of choking made me grasp at my throat as I woke. I was hiding and anyone who spent any time with me could see that.

Charlie was a dark-haired, dark-eyed fashion student. She eventually left the bar we worked in to become a stylist for a satellite TV show. Then she moved on to *Cosmopolitan*. But while we lived and worked together, Charlie, four years older than me, with a huge smile and even huger heart, taught me how to make London life less daunting. We'd dance on the bar at work then go dancing again afterwards, drinking cocktails at Madame Jojo's, the Astoria or Freedom, in Soho. If we could be bothered with a taxi, we'd head to Bagley's in King's Cross or the Aquarium on Old Street, which had a swimming pool I once found a friend joyfully topless in, alongside half a rugby team.

Charlie, who always wore Buffalo trainers and a pale blue Baby-G watch, VERY cool at the time, could see that I wasn't buying any clothes for myself and would come home with 'free samples' of tops and trousers that she gave me without asking any questions. We'd coincide our breaks on night shifts at the bar to share cigarettes on the fire escape, tell each other anything that was on our minds, marvel at the purple of a Soho night sky. Then, with a 'Love you', 'Love you', head back to earn our tips.

It was Charlie and her boyfriend who witnessed the one and only outburst of anger I allowed myself about The Famous Man. I didn't know they were home, or I might not have started throwing books at the TV in my room when he appeared on it. A sofa interview with a flirty presenter, in which he flogged his new album.

'Fuck OFF' – wham, *Pride and Prejudice* – 'FUCK you' – *Slaughterhouse-Five* – 'Fuck fuck fuck fuck!' – *Tess of the D'Urbervilles*, *The Rattle Bag*, a Jilly Cooper, my French dictionary.

'Fucking cunt fucking cunt fucking cunt.'

Ornaments were swept from the mantlepiece, notecards and pens from the desk, the open wardrobe door was kicked closed. I flung neatly lined-up shoes at the cunting wall one by cunting one, 'CUNT CUNT CUNT CUNT!'

I threw myself onto the bed, heaved and sobbed, screamed into my duvet, scratched at my neck and face, pulled at my hair.

'Babe?' Charlie's lovely, concerned face appeared in the doorway. I froze, contemplating some kind of breezy response.

But as Charlie's eyes took in the havoc I had just wreaked, I abandoned myself once more.

'He's a cunt.' I wept, wiping my face with my sleeve. 'He ruined me. He *ruined* me. I am *ruined*. I have lost everything. And he just fucking struts around being on fucking telly. Being fucking false and charming and he's actually just a cunt and I am so much of nothing.'

'You are not so much of nothing.' Charlie was putting my room back together. 'You are everything.' She sat down on the bed, smoothed hair from my sticky forehead and wet cheeks. 'You are everything, Jen.' She hugged me very tight. 'Come on, are you late for work again? Me and Toby will give you a lift into town. We've got bagels from Evering Road. I'll share my smoked salmon with you.'

As I tied back my hair and looked at a face I no longer recognised, I allowed myself to feel relief. How lucky I was to have these friends. Charlie seemed so unfazed by the intensity of my feelings. She betrayed no shock or alarm. When you are isolated by the kind of deep pain and confusion and self-hatred I was feeling, it can seem that the rest of the world isn't real. Or that it might be real, but you can't access it. Charlie and her boyfriend's breezy, loving acceptance of me losing my shit – followed by a quick tidy, a quick hair brush, bagels and Bowie in the campervan – dangled a rope ladder down to me at the bottom of the well.

Katie – blonde and with the world's best dimple – I met on the only acting job I managed post-*Twin Town*, before I fell away from the world. The night we finished filming our scenes, we drank nearly an entire bottle of tequila in shots at the hotel bar and ended up playing a kind of tag-hide-and-seek hybrid around the corridors. Katie won; thinking I'd get to the next floor faster if I took a lift, I ended up stuck with two strangers as they made their way to their rooms. Katie cried with laughter when I told her they were Bruce Grobbelaar (a famous footballer) and 'Hunter' from *Gladiators*, and that I could only focus on them, as on her, by closing one eye.

Katie and I stomped the streets of London together for years, mostly having a lot of a fun. 'Come and live with me,' she had offered when I told her one day my first London flatmates had taken my wet work clothes from the washing machine and put them in a plastic bag, so that I stank when I put them on. I went to look at the flat she lived in in Hackney, with a woman called Budgie and a cat called Pig. Katie watched me survey her double mattress on the floor, the piles of books and clothes, the ashtray by the bed, and saw what I was thinking: 'Oh right. Yeah, there isn't a spare bed. But I thought you could share with me.' She smiled. 'Better than living with people who make you feel like an arsehole.'

I moved in the next day.

It was winter. Katie and I put on thick socks, propped ourselves up with pillows, smoked rollies, ate crumpets in bed. We would read to one another to pass the time, choosing Penguin Classics – *The Mill on the Floss, Crime and Punishment, Wuthering Heights* – which we'd find in charity shops and reveal with genuine excitement. I'm not sure we ever actually finished one – we just looked for the best paragraphs. Like when you sought out the rude bits in *Forever…* by Judy Blume when you were a kid. We'd dance in her room to whatever was on the radio: 'Avenging Angels' by Space'; 'Got 'Til It's Gone', Janet Jackson, 'Ain't That Just the Way', Lutricia McNeal. We watched Eddie Izzard videos and often left shops doing their running giraffe impression.

Katie and I sometimes played the 'restaurant' game. I would like to make clear that I am not proud of this. If we were out and saw a table neatly laid for dinner, we would run into the restaurant and try to steal everything on it before we could be stopped. I have an abiding memory of Katie legging it past me laden with knives and wine glasses, shouting 'Sorry' over her shoulder to a bemused waiter. I have a photo of her on the Tube with a wicker umbrella stand on her head.

I once went back with some of the loot we'd stolen, to an Italian in Maida Vale. When I got there, inelegantly depositing napkins, cutlery, a single salt cellar onto a table in front of the owner, apologising and trying to explain, he had no idea what I was talking about. That story made Katie laugh too.

'Dance with me, Jen! Dance!' The fifth member of the Stoke Newington household was Evan, an Aussie a few years older than us. Tall, tanned, brown hair, blue eyes, glasses. Rejecting the more testosterone-fuelled culture among the male bar staff, Ev wore flowers behind both ears and danced with whoever was nearby like joy flowed from his core.

One 'lunchtime' – the 3 p.m. break after the lunchtime rush, when bar staff eat and set the world to rights – conversation turned to a report of sexual violence in a newspaper.

'What was she doing walking home alone in the dark?' came the predictable response from one of the younger men.

'What would have been your preference,' asked Evan, 'for her method of travel?' The barman was wide-eyed. 'Skateboard?' Ev offered. 'Clown car? I believe she had already caught a bus; we can assume that she was as close to her home as she could get via public transport.'

Still no response from the barman.

'Stilts?' Ev kept going. The rest of us stared, chicken baguettes halfway to our mouths.

'Don't be a dick, Evan,' came the eventual, self-conscious reply.

'I don't mean to be a dick, Callum.' Ev continued. 'I do apologise, I really do. I'm just curious as to why this young woman seems to be at fault, in your mind, for exercising her human right to walk this earth, and daring to hope to do so safely, and the man who raped her, the fucked-up fucking weirdo who stole her humanity, is not.'

Silence. I felt like standing up and cheering. Ev caught my eye and seemed to understand in an instant what all this meant to me. Then others piled in, both to question Callum and to save the atmosphere, which was rarely anything but jovial. Callum backtracked – 'clarified' – and the conversation moved on.

Ev, the good ally, became a friend for life.

11

The fifth time I was late for work – insomnia, sleeping through my alarm – the deputy manager of the bar took me aside to warn me that I would lose my job if I was late again. I don't know why I decided to tell him what was going on. Perhaps I wanted him to understand that I wasn't intentionally being disrespectful. Perhaps I needed sympathy. Perhaps I thought he might offer some support or understanding or help. I took a deep breath.

'Something bad happened to me last summer, and I am struggling with it. I can't seem to hold the pieces of my life together.'

I thought saying it – saying something – aloud would feel like a relief. Instead, a hum of fear vibrated through me, and I began to feel dizzy. *Mistake. Mistake.*

He understood what I meant – people always do. But he didn't offer sympathy, or support, or anything remotely close to that. He looked at the vulnerability in me with the same sort of disgust as The Famous Man had and said, 'You can't blame everything on that.'

He had been the manager on shift the day I pulled my stinking clothes from the plastic bag my first flatmates had put them in. He sent me home with that same look of disgust, shouting 'Pig' as I closed the staff-room door.

'Please . . . um . . . please can you keep this private?' I asked, unable to meet his eye. He said nothing, perhaps he nodded, but I suspect he told the other managers of the bar. Not long afterwards, as I slept on a sofa after a night shift, I woke up with one of them having sex with me. Raping me. I wasn't frightened this time. I was asleep, so I didn't have much chance to be. There were no physical injuries. He stopped when I pushed him off.

The next morning, we all went out for breakfast before work and the manager tried to hold my hand under the table. I was confused. Was he acknowledging what had happened? Was this an apology? Was he saying he wanted to do it again? I couldn't believe that would be true. I did not have enough status within this group for any of them to have been proud to have been with me. I was fat. I was ugly. I was a joke.

I should have pulled my hand away and left. Perhaps I should have informed the police the moment I pushed him off me the night before, though there can be no rules, no 'should's for how we respond to violence, because we are not in a logical headspace. I now understand much more about the way trauma works; when our brain senses danger, particularly if we have experienced a similar danger before, our survival system overrides any capacity for rational thought. Like an animal in a trap, we fight, we flee, we freeze, we flop or fawn – we do what our brain thinks we have to do to survive: all instinct, no reason. My reaction in that moment, as has so often been my response to danger since, was to fawn – to make him my friend. Hope he would let me live. So, I let him hold my hand.

In fact, there *is* a logic to this response; my manager had more power than me, both physically and socially, just like The Famous Man. Fighting him now, after the event, was a huge risk for me. The steel trap of denial had already slammed shut and my priority in that moment was to keep my life, work in the bar with my best friends, not have yet another pathway destroyed by male violence. I needed to pretend this hadn't happened to escape with some semblance of my life intact.

So, an hour or so later, when he called me into the office and said, without looking at me, that what had occurred was probably a dream and I shouldn't tell anyone else, I agreed.

I didn't risk telling anyone about The Famous Man again for a very long time.

12

The phone rang.

'Aaah, Onejen. Can I move in with you please?'

Will had spent two years wrestling addictions. Eventually, after multiple attempts to kick his demons' asses, he had booked himself into a Buddhist retreat in Scotland and remained there, alone and speaking to no one, until he was sure he would leave drug free. No longer would he be 'the only person in the *Big Issue* queue reading Dickens', as observed by the manager of his hostel. I was sceptical – there had been many attempts at living drug free, but this time, he did it. Will was back. *Will*. Addiction Free Will visited old friends, he got fit, he started sunbathing. He applied to study philosophy at a university in the North of England and got in, spending a year hanging out with kids a few years younger, having a relationship, working out what to do next. When he returned to live with Mum during the summer holiday, his ambition was to leave the course he was on and finally apply to Cambridge, as his teachers had long ago recommended. He had at last found his feet and his self-worth. Will had returned. And he wanted to re-find me.

'Can you get me a job in your bar? I want to do a bit of London. I want to see the life of the Squirt [his other nickname for me].'

I was working in a different bar now. I had a boyfriend, Nick, whom I loved deeply. We'd had an immediate connection, a whirlwind affair, and moved in together fast. It should all have been easy, but my ability to relax with him had allowed me to kid myself that I was 'better now'. In fact, I was nowhere near recovered. I thought he was beautiful and that I was ugly and that everyone could see that I was not good enough for him. I began to behave strangely; I was uptight with his friends and family, I expressed jealousy about exes I knew were no threat. I did nothing but push him away, deliberately sabotaging the happiness I felt I didn't deserve. That I, on some level, could not tolerate.

What is heartbreaking is that I think that Nick really did *see* me. Despite my cacti forest of defences, he 'got' me, and he loved me. But all I ever did was push and push until, finally, he left. And my heart broke in two. He hadn't done that quite yet, when Will made this phone call, but it was on the cards. I think he had met the waitress he would leave with.

This was just a couple of years after The Famous Man and The Bar Manager. I was overeating and drinking too much, taking too much coke, all of which, for me, symbolises a state of deep self-loathing. I had missed Will so much when he was addicted and hadn't had a chance to reconnect when he went to uni, so the gift he was giving me, of carving out some time and space just for us, felt exciting. It felt precious. I hoped he might help me shift back towards myself; we had always calmed each other so well.

I told Will that between Nick and me, we could probably find him a job.

'Can I come on Monday?'

I laughed. 'OK, keeno. You can stay with us while we work something out. Where are you?'

'I'm at Deb's.' He'd left some of his belongings in her attic, so he'd gone back to retrieve them before the London adventure. I could hear him chewing. 'What's for tea?' I knew that he was going to say, 'Spaghetti hoops on toast.'

He was heading out to meet an old college mate, Stan, then going back to Mum's, then coming to me. I told him I couldn't wait.

Deb and her family had gone to a country cottage for the weekend, so it crossed my mind that Will might be tempted to score, back in Bristol, with no one watching him. He knew what I was thinking. 'There is nothing I would rather do less, Onejen. Honestly. *Honestly*. Hon. Est. Ly. Wait till you see me. I am a picture of health.' I could see in my mind's eye the grin he would be pulling as he nodded to himself, self-consciously, bottom teeth set slightly to one side.

'I'll meet you at Paddington on Monday,' I said. 'Let me know the time.'

'OK, Dick,' Will said.

'Dick,' I replied.

At lunchtime the following day, Nick and I had just ordered a bottle of champagne to celebrate our anniversary when I saw I had a voicemail. It was Mum telling me that Deb was coming up to London to pick me up and bring me home. I didn't understand. I told Nick to hang on while I just called her back.

It had taken a full year for Mum to recover from the crash. She now had metal rods in her arm and leg, which Will joked he'd turn into jewellery when she died. Her face had been rebuilt and almost looked the same, though it wasn't quite symmetrical until many years later, when she had her jaw looked at again. She had lost some feeling in her bottom lip and chin, but by and large, considering how catastrophic her injuries had been, she was now well.

My first thought when I heard her message was that Teggy, our beloved little dog, may have died. Then, that something might have happened to Granny or Grandpa. Mum picked up after just a couple of rings.

'Hello?'

'Hi, Mum, it's me.'

'Oh God, it's Jen.'

'What's happened?'

'Where are you?'

'I'm in Soho with Nick, it's our anniversary.'

'Deb is coming to London to bring you home.'

'I know. Why? What's happened? Is it Teggy?'

'I don't want to tell you.'

'Tell me what's happened. Tell me what's happened. Tell me what's happened. Mum, tell me what's happened . . .'

She didn't want to tell me on the phone. But I made her.

'There has been a fire at Deb's house. Will has died.'

The champagne cork popped and my mind fizzed. I shook my head, then began to repeat 'No, no, no' as I groped my way out of the restaurant, pinballing off furniture, leaving a very confused Nick behind.

Not Will.

My spiritual and moral and intellectual guide. My cynical, awkward, funny best friend. An electrical fire had started while he slept. No one knows why. It had released deadly levels of carbon monoxide and then it had combusted. The heat was so intense the fire crew couldn't get in because their thermo-imaging equipment kept melting. And Will had died. Will had died.

Deb's friend Jaine drove us back to Abergavenny. I can't remember that journey, but I do remember that I quickly requested a visit to Deb's house. I wanted to see the room that had killed Will. I needed to look at the room.

I could smell it and feel it as soon as she opened the front door. Burned timber. Cold air. Death. The room was black with a big hole in the floor. Will had been reading *Northern Lights* by Philip Pullman. I picked up the front cover, which had somehow made it to the bottom of the attic stairs. I found a small hoop earring Will wore and put it through my ear. I still wear it – mostly because it won't come out.

At the inquest they told us that the fire didn't burn Will. It kind of raged around him. He was lying on his side. He had some 'skin slippage', which means he melted a bit, I think. The heat had been so intense that his stomach had burst, and remnants of his last meal had been found in his chest cavity. *Spaghetti hoops on toast*, I thought. When they read out a description of Will – large feet, muscular arms, an *Alien* tattoo – my mum sat on her hands.

When they asked her if she had any questions she whispered, 'Can't speak.'

That might have been the worst day of my life.

Will's funeral overflowed with young people, *Reservoir Dogs* smart in black and white and sunglasses. We buried him in a beautiful graveyard just outside our hometown, beneath the Blorenge, the mountain of purple and green.

I had organised for the *Blackadder* theme to be playing on a loop as people came into the funeral; Will and I watched *Blackadder II* endlessly in the Park Street years. I wanted these people who loved him, who were so bone-wearyingly sad that day, to also have a little laugh. He had known pain, but he was always very funny.

It was my idea to bury him. They'd cremated Dad and I'd struggled with that. But you can't win because when you bury someone you are plagued with thoughts about what stage of decomposition they are at. Or, I was. I could think about nothing else, for weeks. We bought a few plots either side of Will because I wanted him to stand out; I didn't want him to be in a factory line of graves with others.

Rather than a coffin we got him a biodegradable silk pod in bright red, which had an Aztec sun embroidered on the front. It was the first of its kind in the UK. That felt right. And Teggy, our adored little dog, died of old age that summer, so we organised that she was in the pod with Will. It felt easier putting them in the ground and walking away knowing they were together.

Every day for the first two weeks, friends and neighbours brought food and wine; women caring for women in the best way. We sat around Mum's dining table. Sometimes we laughed; often we sobbed until our chests hurt.

Will. How could we exist without him? How would our little family survive?

After a few weeks, I returned to London, where, to my astonishment, everything looked the same. Gripped by a sense that I had to make my life matter, because Will no longer had a life, I became determined to recover. I could not be broken. When we had emptied Will's room in halls at uni, a fragment of a magazine article had fluttered out of one of his textbooks. He had cut it out to keep, so I had pocketed it, and read it to myself as I travelled across London.

> *This is the true joy in life, being used for a purpose recognized by yourself as a mighty one. Being a force of nature instead of a feverish, selfish little clod of ailments and grievances, complaining that the world will not devote itself to making you happy. I am of the opinion that my life belongs to the*

whole community and as long as I live, it is my privilege to do for it what I can. I want to be thoroughly used up when I die, for the harder I work, the more I live. I rejoice in life for its own sake. Life is no brief candle to me. It is a sort of splendid torch which I have got hold of for the moment and I want to make it burn as brightly as possible before handing it on to future generations.

George Bernard Shaw.

Will had had big plans. I was determined to live for both of us now. To re-find my path.

Part Two:
The Fight

13

When I wrote to Sally Mackey, head of the prestigious drama and education course at the Central School of Speech and Drama, I didn't expect a reply. I had no A levels – I had left school when my friend Ross had died (I know, it's too much) then I had jacked in college for acting. It was Lu, a 'True Colors' friend who, armed with pizza and beer, had sat down on the floor next to me one day in my empty flat, when Nick had gone, and pushed a prospectus for Central towards me with her foot.

'Apply. Have you kept any essays you wrote at school or anything? Show them you're clever . . .'

Clever. The word landed like a brick.

Grief affects your self-esteem; not only has someone you loved disappeared, which is the thing that guts you first, but someone who was going to love you for ever has disappeared too. There is less love for you in the world. That bit hits you later.

I didn't feel clever.

Pizza in mouth, as Lu opened another beer, I sat up and scrabbled beneath my bed for an essay on Stanislavski I knew I had kept from college. The following morning, I posted it to Sally Mackey at Central, with a cover letter saying I knew I didn't have the grades and asking her to meet me anyway.

Astoundingly, a few weeks later, an embossed envelope landed on the doormat inviting me to interview.

We met in Sally's office, on the top floor of the old part of the building. It had a heavy dark-wood door, lighter walls, another of those hefty, paint-encrusted radiators. Every surface was piled with books.

Sally – sandy haired, middle-aged, warm but unflinching – took in the trembling young woman before her, clasped her hands together and said, 'Why should I give you a place on my course?'

'I just know I can do this,' was my weak opening gambit.

We talked about poetry and theatre and what they had meant to my life. I told Sally it had been a rough few years, and that I regretted giving up my education, because it was always in the power of words, in the end, in which I found solace. 'And now I want to use words, in education, or maybe in drama, in theatre, to offer solace to others too. To find connection. Something like that.'

I looked at my feet, thinking, *Twat.*

For reasons unknown, Sally offered me a place on her course there and then. She took a chance on me, as I understand she has many others before. And thank God she did. In that course I found purpose. Another path.

Central is located in north-west London, where the avenues are wide and tree lined and the cafés serve halloumi, which I had never heard of. As I made my way home from the interview, I marvelled at the majesty of the place. I couldn't believe that I was going to spend the next three years of my life there.

I thought about the thousands of theatre people, training either for the stage or behind the scenes, who had also made the pilgrimage to this building, including Dame Judi Dench, Sir Laurence Olivier, Vanessa Redgrave, Carrie Fisher, Riz Ahmed, Andrew Garfield. I no longer felt able to act, but I knew I wanted to focus my life on theatre in some way, if I could. Could I direct? Could I teach? . . . Could I write?

Day one. Sick with nerves, I reminded myself over and over again, *You're doing this for Will, you're doing this for Will*, and pushed aside the quieter voice whispering, *You're not good enough. Go home.* I was twenty-three. Five years older than most of the bouncy young tracksuits that poured through the doors around me. So busy was I being intimidated by their energy, as we made our way into the studio space to hear an introductory lecture, I nearly missed the huge smile immediately to my left.

'My name's Lizzie.' She had long brown hair tied back in a messy bun, exactly like my own, a camouflage shirt, blue jeans, grubby Converse.

I smiled back. It wasn't long before we moved in together. For the next nine years, before Lizzie moved to Cambodia to teach, we barely left one another's side. Soulmates from that first smile. And so, life as a student began and with it my recovery. With every warm-up, drama exercise, in-school performance, even with every essay, my confidence grew. I had assumed everyone would be better than me. I had assumed I would not be able to remember how to write, to critique, how to analyse text. I was wrong. I could do it all. This was going to be OK. To be back in the realm of rehearsing and reading, using theatre as a filter on the world, was to come home.

14

Year Two. Sticky-soled in the student bar, probably high and definitely drunk, I spotted Joe coming through the door and waved him over. I'd first met Joe when we were sent on placement together in Year One, tasked with running drama classes at a primary school in east London. He was always late, minus a notepad, definitely without a pen, but he was charmingly brilliant with the kids.

We chatted on the way home about what we were reading, or about the news, even sometimes about psychology or philosophy. I found him endlessly interesting and thought-provoking, and I thought he was very funny. 'You remind me of my brother,' I told him one afternoon, shouting over the noise of the Docklands Light Railway.

'Do I?' He seemed pleased.

'I mean, you look nothing like him' – Joe is bald, broad shouldered, he wears glasses – 'but you remind me of him.'

'Is that good? Oh no.'

Oh no. I was crying.

'I'm so sorry,' I squeaked 'He died. I haven't even got used to telling people about it yet.'

Joe put an arm round me. He has ever since been a surrogate Will.

He did not join me on the dance floor, but pointed to a table in the corner instead, so I made my way over to meet him. 'Cider?' I asked, offering to go to the bar. 'Cider,' said Joe.

Taking off his coat, he dropped the late edition of the *London Evening Standard* on the table. I just caught the headline.

[The Famous Man] accused of rape

Blindsided, I couldn't breathe.

I staggered to the disabled toilet cubicle, the only place I could think of where I could lock the door and be alone. The mirror was smudged. Seeking connection with something cool, I put my head against it. Then, I grabbed some loo roll and tried to clean it. I wanted to see my face. Not for the first time since the attack, I wasn't sure the sad girl staring back was, in fact, me. *Is that my face? Did this thing really happen to me?*

Joe was outside when I opened the door. He was smiling, then he wasn't.

'Are you all right, Jen? You've gone green.' I nodded. Then, I vomited.

I had assumed the attack on me was opportune. I had thought I'd 'got myself' into a dangerous situation. Suddenly I saw in technicolour that The Famous Man, and possibly also his friend, was serially violent. Now, I realised that *not* reporting my attack, because I had been pretending it didn't happen and wasn't that bad, may have meant that other teenagers had been lured to his house. Other women may have been hurt while I was hiding.

Suddenly sober, I went to find Lizzie. 'I need to go home' – we had rented a little house with Katie, my actress friend from the 'True Colors' crew – 'I don't feel very well.'

In the taxi, Lizzie leaned over me to open the window. 'Get some fresh air. You'll feel better.' My mind flashed back to the cab ride after the attack, my ghostly face in the wing mirror, shaking hands, burned dress. Deep breath. 'Something happened to me. A few years ago, when I was nineteen.'

She knew. I didn't have to say more. 'Oh fuck, Jen. No.'

I handed her Joe's copy of the *Evening Standard*. 'I thought I had got myself into a dangerous situation. But the man who did it has just been accused again.' We read the article together, then she looked at me, '*Him?*'

I nodded. 'What should I do?'

Lizzie's big brown eyes were wide with fear. 'I don't know . . . Tell the police?'

'Does it say which force is investigating it?'

We scanned the article again. I wondered if you could just walk into any police station to report something like this. Or did you have to know the specific one? How did you find out things like that? We were scared. Lizzie gave me a long hug and said, with tears in her eyes, 'I'm so sorry.'

Katie, who knew about the attack already, took one glance at the headline when we got home and said, 'I'll sleep with you.' We grabbed our PJs and thick socks, like the Hackney days, but sleep did not find me. I spent the night watching shadows creep across the ceiling of my bedroom, as night turned to dawn, turned to day and, somewhere, I found the resolve to tell the police what I knew.

How will I describe what happened to me? Will I be able to find the words?

Lizzie was already dressed when we came down for breakfast. The nod I gave her answered any questions she had about whether I had decided to report. She gave me another bear hug and left early for Central. 'I'll make your excuses. This is more important.'

Katie and I headed out to the newsagent's – the newspapers might tell us which police station to go to. We bought one of everything, made a pot of tea and spread the papers across the kitchen table, taking each in turn. The story was tabloid gold, splashed across front pages in a cascade of gleeful melodrama. The *Sun* even had a tip line you could use to phone in and report your own bad experience with The Famous Man – it was a shock – *his reputation was well known?* Why hadn't anyone at that barbeque that day warned me? My chaperone? The Crew Member?

A tight fist of anxiety formed in my stomach as I read The Famous Man's name, over and over, each new sighting making me light-headed.

She: Date. Hotel. Rape. Pain. Fear. Silence.

He: Relationship. Consensual. Confused. Refutes. Denies.

I poured milk into the tea and whispered to Katie, 'Neil doesn't know . . .'

Neil was my boyfriend. Relatively new. Our relationship had mostly been based around laughing and dancing. It was light and silly, which, in the year after Will's death, was exactly what I needed. Introducing The Famous Man and all he meant to my life brought a sledgehammer to that.

'I don't want to tell him.' I wiped my cheeks with the back of my hand, took a deep breath, allowed the sunshine streaming through the kitchen window to find my face.

'Why don't you just report what you know about The Famous Man to the police and ask to join, like, a group action, or something?'

asked Katie. 'There's safety in numbers. You can just add your name to a list, kind of thing.'

'Yes. Yeah! Maybe enough other people will come forward that they won't need me,' I croaked hopefully, reaching for the sheep-shaped tea cosy Mum had bought me for Christmas.

Mum. I decided not to call her yet.

The papers told us nothing about which police station to go to, but I knew there was one in Angel, north London. So, with a vague idea of a class action (something that mostly only applies to American criminal litigation, it turns out), I left the house to report what I knew.

Train, Tube, fifteen-minute walk. Police station front doors. Lino floor. Musty smell. Queue for desk sergeant. Inhale.

'I want to report an assault.'

15

had kept the dress, in a bag at the bottom of the wardrobe. I kept it for ages, wondering if I would ever have the guts to report what had happened to me. But as my self-esteem sank lower and my weight crept up, I began to feel too disgusting for it to be believed that I was sexually assaulted.

I have to say, I *know* how desperately sad that is. I know that violence and particularly sexual violence is about the inadequacy of the violent person, not the victim. That it is about power and not ever about looks or clothes or even sex. There is not ever anything about an innocent person that invites violence.

I know that now. I knew it then, too, intellectually, but I didn't feel it. I felt disrespected because I had been disrespected. I felt easy to ignore because I had been ignored. I felt that as The Famous Man and his friend had seen disrespect and disdain and . . . violence . . . as the correct way to treat me, then that is what I clearly did deserve. Somewhere in my core, no matter what I 'knew', that was how I felt, because that was how I had been treated.

For a long time, then, in addition to the denial, I was no longer a confident enough person to report my assault and expect to be believed. And in the end, I took the dress out of the bag I had stored it in, washed it and wore it to my waitressing job. I was too fat to wear it as a dress any more, it was too short, but I could wear it over trousers and at least reclaim it. My apron hid the cigarette burn.

The weight I carried was another means of hiding. I had spent most of my teenage years deliberately restricting calorie intake, writing down everything I ate, working on honing a very slender frame. I was still a teenager when the assault happened. Afterwards I hated my body so much that I couldn't even look at it. I felt sullied and I felt that my body, somehow, had let me down. It had enticed them. It had worked against me.

So, to punish it, to ward off male attention, and for the dopamine hit, I expect, I ate. I ate to feel something, to taste something – sugar and salt – and to stop thinking. I had periods of control of my eating, when I didn't think about it – a blissful state – and then had periods of feeling out of control of my eating and deep self-loathing. At those times, the voice in my head was particularly vicious. *You are so fucking weak. You are so fucking disgusting. Why do you never get your shit together?*

Behind metal Venetian blinds, in a side room at Islington Police Station, I finished describing, in broad terms, my experience with The Famous Man and The Wolf, and handed over my old Filofax and the taxi receipt with Ken's name and number scrawled on the back. Reporting violent crime is not for everyone, there are no rules, but to me, making this formal statement felt like getting a little of my shit together. Like taking back a modicum of control.

The officer smiled; '*I believe you*; that is the first thing you have to know.' Relief flooded my body.

'I understand the Met Police are already investigating [The Famous Man]. That's why I'm here. I'd like to add my name to the list.'

She nodded. She said she would get back to me. In fact, someone called the following day, asking me to meet different officers at a different station and to go through my allegations again.

I agreed.

This interview room was beige, with a faux-wood coffee table at its centre. A ceiling camera whirred inside a black dome. There was what was very evidently a two-way mirror running the length of one wall, which was disconcerting, but which I tried to ignore.

I was offered coffee and asked for tea. The liaison officer said she preferred tea too. We both had sugar. She brought us water.

She told me we would go at my pace, and we could take a break at any time. She asked me to describe how I ended up at The Famous Man's house that night.

I tried to remember the order of things.

I was at the home of a friend I'd met on the film set. There was a barbeque. Afterwards, we went to a pub. The crew member who had invited me, whose house I was staying at, could not join for the drinks because she needed to wait at home for someone. She sent me off with a 'chaperone', one of her friends. I was nineteen, so didn't really need one, but everyone else was more than ten years older and it was known I didn't live in London. That I still lived at home with my mum. The chaperone, whose name I couldn't remember, had long, glossy brown hair. I remembered thinking, *I want to be like her*. The Famous Man liked her too. He sensed my vulnerability and it seemed to repulse him, but he flirted with the chaperone, making me the butt of his jokes. At one point, he spotted that I had a Filofax in my handbag, plucked it out and encouraged everyone to laugh, 'Who still has one of these?'

'People who can't afford a phone yet,' I said, trying to grab it back.

He held it aloft and flicked through the pages. 'Let's see who you've got in here. Oh look – just your mum.' I could have cried when I saw Mum's number there. How I wished I was at home, watching telly.

Various people came and went from the pub, some of whom were famous. Feeling out of my depth, I did my usual trick of disappearing to the bathroom to whisper affirmations to myself.

I wasn't party to the conversation in which it was decided that we would all go back to The Famous Man's house. I remember being in a car, but I can't remember whose. I remember that The Famous Man kept putting his hand on my chaperone's leg and that she kept removing it, at one point saying something like, 'If you do that again, I'll bite the fucking thing off.' I thought she was cool.

I remember being somewhat overawed at The Famous Man's house; two plush sofas sat at right angles to the biggest TV I'd ever seen. I said something like, 'That's bigger than my mum's whole house,' and The Famous Man laughed.

I was absurdly pleased.

I hung out with 'the friend' while The Famous Man and the chaperone went to mix drinks. Then, suddenly, she stormed out. Or, she stormed towards the front door and en route stopped, momentarily, to say, 'I'm leaving now, are you coming?'

I didn't have time to collect my thoughts.

The Famous Man's friend encouraged me to stay.

I said, 'I think I'll be OK,' and she left. I had changed my mind before she closed the front door and shouted, 'Wait!' But even though I ran straight after her, delayed only by grabbing my bag and shoes, all I saw were the rear lights of her taxi, or maybe it was her car, as it sped off into the night.

Feeling nervous again, I asked where the loo was. The light bulb blew, or I couldn't find the light, I can't remember. I peed in the dark. When I opened the door, The Famous Man was outside. I jumped. He put his hand between my legs. My head fizzed. I was wearing a pair of my mum's tights, and they were too big, the gusset was loose. I felt embarrassed.

He spoke. I think maybe he went for, 'You know you want it' – how unoriginal – but I can't fully remember. I still have no notion of whether I had taken stairs to this bathroom or not. I didn't reply but made it back (downstairs?) into the light. He followed. I asked for a taxi, The Famous Man held out his phone, I tried to take it, he pulled it back . . .

For reasons I don't fully understand, there's a myth that women invent claims of rape and sexual assault. It is surely mostly expounded by the perpetrators, or those working for them, but it persists . . .

> *As a general matter, Harvey Weinstein and his attorneys have refrained from publicly criticizing any of the women who have made allegations of sexual assault against Mr. Weinstein despite a wealth of evidence that would demonstrate the patent falsity of these claims . . .*
>
> *Watching the 'performance' by Rose McGowan as she looks to promote her new book however, has made it impossible to remain quiet as she tries to smear Mr. Weinstein with a bold lie . . .*
>
> Statement by Harvey Weinstein's lawyers
> prior to his trial.

This myth takes no account of how difficult it is to make those claims in the first place. It is the thing you least want to talk about, the part of you you most want to protect. Yet you must allow it to be picked apart minutely by strangers in a disconcertingly formal atmosphere. These strangers are supposedly on your side, but they have to interrogate your story in order to find any perceived weaknesses in it, ostensibly so that they can account for them if you are challenged, but also to try to find out if you are lying. Something that is not common to reports of other types of violent crimes. It is so exposing. You are so vulnerable: the frog in the high school chemistry lab, split down the middle, spilling your guts.

When you have been through the second interview, a team of detectives go away and take what feels like a very long time to interrogate everything you've said, to find out if there is verifiable proof. If you have been making stuff up, at this point I imagine you're pretty screwed. Even if you haven't made it up *and most people haven't*, finding enough evidence to bring a rape or assault case, especially an historic one, is eye-wateringly difficult. The process takes months.

A slick of shame, which until this point you have kept inside, seeps out and coats you, as detectives track down everyone you ever told what happened to you, anyone who might remember you were there that night; those who were at the pub, the chaperone who fled, Ken the taxi driver, the one friend you showed the bruises to when you got home. Your mum. My poor mum. Enabled by the steel trap, I had downplayed it all to her when it happened. Of course I had. How do you tell the person who has tried to protect you all your life that in the end she couldn't?

Once the detectives have gathered evidence, if there is any – so often these cases come down to one person's word against another's – they submit it to the Crown Prosecution Service (CPS), but only if they think the CPS will conclude there is a reasonable prospect of conviction. If not, your case is closed at this early stage, by the police. 'No further action'. A devastating result for someone who has dared to speak.

If you do get to the CPS, your case is then re-evaluated by specialist prosecution lawyers, based on the guidelines to which they are working at that time. These are determined by the Director of Public Prosecutions (DPP – you get used to the acronyms).

When Alison Levitt KC was the principle legal adviser to the DPP she set out clear guidelines for prosecutors, based on 'delivering justice to vulnerable victims'.

A CPS lawyer who worked with Levitt described how well her approach to prosecuting sexual crimes challenged the myths that exist around them. Myths that can have subliminal influence over the attitudes of police, lawyers and juries. In a statement this lawyer gave, as an anonymous whistle-blower, to legal charity Centre for Women's Justice and the End Violence Against Women coalition, she described Levitt's approach,

> *[Levitt stated that] prosecutors must recognise the distinction between a difficult case and a weak case . . . sexual offenders often target vulnerable victims such as children, people with disabilities and people with chaotic lifestyles because they know it is unlikely that they will be believed by a jury. Such cases will often be challenging but that did not mean they were evidentially weak cases. It was crucial that prosecutors were striving to achieve justice for these victims.*

Levitt was willing to accept a short-term increase in the number of cases the CPS brought but didn't win so that all victims were treated *as* victims,

> *First because it is morally right, secondly because it is the intellectually rigorous approach . . . thirdly because by clever and sensitive prosecuting we can actually change attitudes.*

In 2016, two years after Levitt moved on from the CPS, the director of legal services, Gregor McGill, and the director's legal adviser to the DPP, Neil Moore (gold star for recognising their gender), delivered training sessions to solicitors in which her approach was reversed,

> . . . the fact that an increased number of rape prosecutions were going to trial proved that the CPS was prosecuting a greater number of weak cases . . . if we were prosecuting the right cases 'we would be winning more cases than we are losing'.

Their preference was for higher rates of successful prosecutions, rather than higher rates of court hearings. It was more important to them that it was made to look like the CPS was 'winning', than that all victims and survivors were given a shot at justice. Thus, only what might be considered 'slam dunk' cases began to be put before juries and more complex cases (which is most cases) were not brought. Post-Levitt, between 2016 and 2019, the number of rape cases the CPS agreed to put before a court decreased by more than 50 per cent, which is a record decline.

In her first annual report, in 2020, Victims' Commissioner Dame Vera Baird said that Britain was 'witnessing the effective decriminalisation of rape'. In 2022 she had not changed her view: 'The distressing truth is that if you are raped in Britain today, your chances of seeing justice are slim.'

It could be contended that the emotional toll on a victim of enduring a case they most likely won't win precludes any moral or intellectual argument. But the point is, these cases become more winnable when attitudes change. Those who have been raped or sexually assaulted have had their autonomy removed from them in the most brutal of ways. They should be returned some control over the paths their lives take, and if they want to seek criminal justice, they should be able to choose to work with professional prosecutors to try to achieve that.

The whistle-blower statement was made to assist an application for Judicial Review (JR) of the change in prosecution guidelines imposed by the two men after Levitt left. The JR was denied on the basis that the changes were not 'substantive' enough to deserve review.

It is hard not to see this tussle as matriarchy vs patriarchy. How different would the world be, and respect for the female experience within it, if women consistently held more positions of power?

Depending on the guidelines the CPS is working to at the time you report, then, your case might be prosecuted, and your attacker charged – or it might not. Decisions which can bear no relevance to what happened to you.

I'll say it again. If you have been lying and the detectives and prosecutors a) don't find that out and b) think you have enough evidence to cross the charging threshold, when most victims and survivors do not, you've got to have balls of steel to then agree to press charges against someone you know to be innocent. That is, to face the horror of a criminal trial, when a second set of investigators – this time in the form of a hostile legal team intent on painting you as a liar – once again interrogate your story and seek to discredit you. Who would put themselves through that for a lie?

How would it even get that far? When you think about it logically, this 'women lie about rape' myth makes no sense at all.

'How do you feel?'

The second interview had been at a police station in the centre of London. Katie had come with me. We stomped the streets for a while afterwards, as was our way, talking everything over. In honour of Will, we decided to get hot chocolates to calm our nerves.

'I'm sorry you had to hear all that' was all I could think about, so all I could say.

'Don't be sorry.' Katie was tearful.

I felt in some way I had made an effort to protect her. Perhaps also myself. Because I had answered all the questions – I had given the police the facts – but I had not articulated the extent of the fear I had felt at the hands of those men. Nor of the horror, nor the injury. It would take me years to locate and find words for those memories. But I hoped I had given the police enough. It was as much as it was possible for me to give at that time.

'I think I feel relief,' I eventually said. 'And I feel scared. I don't know what I have unleashed.'

On balance, it felt good to have finally removed this heavy secret from my chest; to be heard, and to be believed. But a few days later my jaw seized up and I couldn't fully open my mouth for many months; the stress of speaking an unspeakable thing had manifested in my body, which in the end it always does.

Still, I had put my experience into the hands of the professionals. I believed they would look after me, in a world that my childhood taught me is essentially good, essentially happy, essentially safe. Katie and I found ourselves in Trafalgar Square, so we sipped our chocolate at the edge of one of the fountains, guarded by lions.

16

Four days after I reported the attack, my boyfriend, Neil, went out for the papers so that we could read them in bed. The cheapest way to pass a cosy few hours that didn't make us feel like we were doing nothing was to turn on the radio and read; tray, toast, tea, tabloids. I plumped pillows and hummed to myself as I waited for him to return, thinking about uni. I had been chosen to direct fellow students in our year group's next play, alongside a tutor we all respected. I was excited.

I had told Neil that I had been to the police and the reason why – downplaying it, as I always did to those I love. I did not want to upset people, nor did I want them to assume that because bad things had happened to me, I could not handle them, or must in some way be hysterical or unstable. I took great pride in not being those things. In not being a victim.

Neil had been sombre for a few moments, as he took the information in. He expressed anger and then became protective, but before long he was cracking jokes and dancing me round the kitchen. At that moment, in that time, his natural propensity for living in the moment was exactly what I needed.

I heard the door go and shouted, 'I've done the tray', smiling as I listened to Neil's long legs skip every other stair to the bedroom. He kicked off his trainers and jeans, grabbed some toast and the *Sun*. I poured tea and let him warm his cold toes on my leg. I was reaching for the quick crossword in the *Guardian*'s *G2* supplement when Neil's face dropped.

I went cold. 'What? Oh God, what is it?'

Turning the paper around, he showed me an article by a crime reporter about The Famous Man. Three paragraphs in came mention of me, with details of what I had told the police. I wasn't named; by law you can't name a survivor of sexual violence – the editor of the newspaper would go to prison for that. But to my shock and shame, it contained an accurate description of some of what happened to me at the hands of those men. Things I did not want anyone to know.

What the fuck is going on here? How is this happening?

It is hard to describe how vulnerable it makes you feel to see your most closely held secret, one you spoke about in detail for the first time just a few days before, in confidence, to the police, printed in a national newspaper.

How do they know?

I wondered if our house had been bugged. I looked over at Neil. Would he? Could he . . . sell me out? He seemed to know what I was thinking and shook his head in disbelief. 'I didn't know there were two of them,' he said. He looked so sad. So sorry for me. Sometimes you keep secrets to protect others more than yourself.

Later that morning, I rang the senior detective on my case, the man who stood behind the two-way mirror during my interview. He seemed old to me at the time, but he was probably in his mid-forties, tall, slim, brown hair, London accent. Kind of like every detective you've ever seen in a TV drama. I would have rather had a woman, but the liaison officer was a woman, and she was always with him. He seemed to be very much on my side, I trusted him completely. I had to.

The senior detective hadn't seen the article, but he assured me that only five people in 'the Gold Group' (the *what?*) knew the details of my case. He said he would buy the paper immediately.

When he called back, he was solemn. He said he would look into what had happened, but he never mentioned it again, and I was too timid to push it. I didn't even ask him what a Gold Group was. I now know it is a group of senior Met officers with specialist relevant experience. If someone accused of a criminal offence has a public profile, or the crime is in some other way of interest to the public, Gold Groups give advice, both strategically, in relation to the case, and with a view to protecting the reputation of the Met. They were established in the wake of Stephen Lawrence's racist murder and the criticism of the force for police corruption that followed.

It wasn't clear to me at the time how focused the force was on protecting itself as well as me. That it was playing two games. If I had been aware, what followed may have come as less of a shock.

Later, I would reflect that of course Neil couldn't have sold my story – I'd resisted telling him all the details of what had happened to me. The only person who knew everything was Katie. She had come to the police interview with me. She stood behind the two-way mirror too. Would she sell my secrets?

Of course she wouldn't, I told myself, appalled that I was even considering it. *Of course of course of course not*. But the truth was . . . I couldn't know for sure. Suddenly, all that had been certain was uncertain. The trust that bound me to those I was closest to had been broken.

Bit by bit, drip by drip, more details of my case hit the national press, each article making me wince in pain. I had no legal representation – the police were still investigating, so the CPS didn't yet have my file, and I was too young and skint and scared, and too ignorant of how the world works, truthfully, to find a lawyer from whom to seek advice.

Paranoia is a curious thing. You try to ignore it, yet it winds itself around your thoughts like bindweed, strangling everything you thought was good. I began to search our house for bugs. I checked the windowsills, inside and out, front and back, running my hand along the undersides, peering into the corners.

How do they know? How do they know?

I ran taps when speaking about the case at home, to fool any listening devices I hadn't been able to find. Secretly, I checked Neil, Katie and Lizzie's mobiles for numbers I didn't recognise – numbers of journalists.

I listened out for clicking or buzzing sounds on the phone, thinking they related to reporters live-tapping the line somehow. Clicking and buzzing seemed to happen constantly. I repetitively hung up on friends and family and then called them back, joking that if anyone was listening, I wasn't going to divulge anything interesting.

Neil would at times sigh heavily and ask, 'Can we just relax?' as I checked outside before closing the living-room curtains to a bright sunny day. I did not respond. I didn't know how to relax. It felt like living under a magnifying glass, unable to see who was holding it.

A couple of articles in the Murdoch papers, the *Sun* and the *News of the World*, had a female reporter's name on the byline. The tone was almost jovial; 'true crime' aimed at titillation (the *News of the World* was at the time known as the *News of the Screws* because of its focus on exposing sex parties and sex work). Perhaps irrationally, the gender of this reporter compounded my sense of worthlessness – even the sisterhood had abandoned me.

I told myself it wasn't personal. It was business. Printing details of my allegations was just a means of making money for them. To me, it was so deeply shaming I wanted to hide my face. To them it was entertainment. Sex sells. Violence sells. It's just business.

It was late spring when the senior detective came to see me in person, to update me on the investigation. We sat in the sun in the back garden of our little house in East Dulwich, south London, as he told me that the Met had passed my file and interview to the CPS. The CPS found me to be a 'credible witness'. They were prepared to press criminal charges against The Famous Man, if that was what I wanted.

'What about the others?' I asked. *Hadn't my name been added to a list of people who had made complaints about him?*

'Others were credible, but no one else met the charging threshold. The CPS will only proceed with your case.'

I have since discovered that over forty people made allegations of sexual violence against The Famous Man at that time. Seven of the allegations were investigated by the police, yet only my case was considered winnable under the guidelines CPS lawyers were following. I didn't know there were that many potential victims as I sat in the garden that day, but I did know that if I didn't do this, none of the women he had hurt would get justice. I asked for some time to think.

A few months earlier, when The Famous Man was first questioned, it had been requested by the police I attend a line-up to see if I could identify his friend. If I could, he would be questioned too.

The line-up wasn't in person. The police had video recorded the faces of a number of men who they said looked like The Wolf and I was taken to a police station to watch them on a screen.

I had an image of him in my mind: dark hair, fat nose, heavy stubble. He was squat, weighty, he had a big watch and thick, hairy arms. But for some reason I couldn't pick him out in the line-up that day. Perhaps it was the proximity of his lawyer, a hostile presence, in the same room. I questioned whether the officer leading the line-up was sure these photos were of the right person. He assured me they were. The lawyer didn't bother to hide his delight when I failed to pick out his client. This was the moment I felt the first sting of how adversarial this process would be. It was preparation for combat. Welcome to the boys' club.

After the detectives left, I walked in loops around Dulwich Park with Katie and Lizzie, discussing my options. I already felt exposed and frightened; pressing charges would only make it worse. If I said I would prefer not to, all of this – the magnifying glass, the fear – would go away. It was Lizzie who said, 'But [The Famous Man] will not go away. What if he hurts other people? What about the others?'

Watching TV that night, I felt a familiar cocktail of panic and shame as his face filled the screen. It was an advert for the new album he was promoting.

'Cunt,' said Katie.

Enough. I dialled the detective.

Then I called Mum.

'OK,' she said, softly, down the phone. 'Wow. That is brave. Well of course I will back you whatever you want to do.' She sounded scared. I could hear it in her breathing, in the pregnant pauses between her carefully chosen questions. But she didn't tell me not to do it.

I had deliberately kept Mum at a distance thus far. It was just one year after Will's death, and I was trying to protect her. Yet Mum, who spent a good chunk of my childhood volunteering for

Women's Aid, using our campervan to drive women to safe houses late at night, had never shied away from sticking up for women. Nor from doing what she felt was morally right. She wanted to protect her little girl, but perhaps because I am her little girl, I felt I could not shy away from this. This man was dangerous. It wasn't just about me.

17

The police warned us of a media storm once The Famous Man was charged. To escape it, Katie and I packed her little black Volkswagen with veggie sausages, tea bags and sleeping bags and headed west, to Cornwall. I'd made music compilations, burned onto CDs (hello 2000s), and we set off on the six-hour drive, singing at the tops of our lungs. Lizzie was already there with some mates from uni. Mum had decided at the last minute to join, and would meet us there. Not wanting to be too far away either, Neil borrowed a car from someone in his office and turned up on day two. How I loved them. We were frying sausages in a field at the edge of the world when the tinny radio announced that The Famous Man had been charged with a serious sexual assault. We looked at one another.

'Beer?' said Neil.

The following morning, walking the cliffs, we watched seagulls surf a sky as blue-grey as our moods.

'Nice to be free,' I said.

Then Mum spotted a man standing on a rock, naked but for a red scarf and a smile. We had hit a nudist beach. 'Now that is free.' She nodded.

We swallowed our smiles as we passed, then had the first proper laugh we'd had in ages, but I thought to myself, *A lone woman could never be that free.*

18

Back in south London a few days later, an unexpected knock on the front door gave me pause. Sensing it was unwelcome, I ran upstairs as Katie opened the door to a grey-suited man. He asked if I lived there. Katie said no. From behind my bedroom curtain, I watched him walk back to his car. He saw me as he turned to get in.

I called the lead detective. He told me that my name, though unprintable, was available in court documents, so when The Famous Man had been charged, the newspapers had access to it. Shit.

Why hadn't he told me that before? Or had he, and I had forgotten? Why was it available at all?

Again, I was too timid to ask.

But I am ex-directory, I thought, *not on the electoral register, how did that man find me? Who was he? What did he want?*

From then on, whenever I left the house, I looked both ways, to check I wasn't being followed.

As the date for the criminal case approached, press coverage reduced (a relief) but interest in The Famous Man did not. He attended posh restaurant openings, fashion shows, gave interviews; the stronger his media presence, the harder it would be for me to take him down, I guess was the thinking, or the more sympathy he might gain from any future jury.

This was a power move. My anonymity protected me – or it was meant to – but it also silenced me. I could not publicly set out the best version, or any version, of myself. And I wanted to speak. It is a surreal and nauseating experience, when the question of whether you are lying about the attack that wrecked your life becomes a matter of national debate and yours is the one voice not partaking in it.

'What do you think? No smoke without fire?' the woman on the train asked of her friend, maybe her daughter.

They were sharing a copy of a glossy magazine with The Famous Man on the front.

'No, he seems too nice,' said the younger.

'Yeah, but you never know, do you?'

'I don't think he's got it in him. I read an article by one of his friends saying there is no evidence against him, and this is just a bandwagon. They're in it for the money. He said he just wants his life back.'

'And no word from the women who said he did it. What are they hiding?'

'Exactly. Poor man.'

'Poor man.'

I heard a version of this conversation play out at bus stops, in coffee shops, in the park. I was always desperate to point out that, for legal reasons, 'the women', if they had felt able to go to the police, couldn't speak out before the trial. In fact, I was 'the woman' and I was doing this to try to stop a dangerous man hurting *other women*; I wasn't in it for money. What money? There was no bandwagon to join.

But of course, I said nothing.

One afternoon, as I stumbled off a train at London Bridge, I didn't see what the other passengers were laughing at until it was too late. When I looked up the world went into slow motion. A 'stag do' of around twenty men streamed past me, all wearing masks bearing The Famous Man's face. They were drunk. One of them bumped into me, 'Sorry, love'.

What the . . .?

Does everyone think this is a joke?

This was the era of lads mags, *Zoo* and *Loaded* and *Nuts*, WAGS and Page 3: everyday sexism. Media misogyny made being a woman trying to be taken seriously as a crime victim almost impossible. How do you win a sexual assault case in a cultural landscape that so gleefully celebrates the dehumanisation of women, then gaslights them by selling it as empowerment?

I felt afraid.

19

'Wine and chips?'

Rachel rang, the actress I'd met on *Twin Town*. Once I moved to London, she and I made sure we spent regular afternoons catching up. We called these days 'Wine and chips'. She had recently been interviewed by the police, because I had called her from The Famous Man's house on the night of the assault – she had even spoken to The Wolf. So, she was now a witness in my legal case. We needed wine. And chips. As we settled into our deep leather seats at a gastro pub in the West End, Rachel pushed a small blue envelope across the table to me, and smiled excitedly. 'I've found a letter.'

I used to write to Rachel when I still lived at home with Mum, sending her my thoughts, sometimes poems, occasionally written by me (oh dear). She was charmed by it. I was so naive and innocent, desperate to impress, despite my bravado, so optimistic, so full of love for her. I grimaced as I began reading the letter, *Alright, bitch*? (A term of endearment in the '90s. Let's call it irony. There was so much I didn't question.)

'Oh God. Why are you showing me this?'

'Keep reading.'

The Letter, heartbreaking in its faux jolliness, oozed vulnerability as it disclosed the fear I felt in the wake of the violence. It mentioned that I'd tried sleeping with women, in my search for connection, because I could not relax with men. It tried to come up with reasons that I might have been targeted by male violence more than once. Perhaps I wanted Rachel, older, more experienced, to come back to me to explain how it all worked. I was so bound up in my thoughts, it took me a moment to work out why she was looking at me and grinning.

'Good evidence, no?' she prompted.

My mind began to race. *Is it good evidence?* It didn't contain detail, but it did mention The Famous Man. It proved I hadn't decided to report him to jump on the fictional 'bandwagon'; that I wasn't part of a 'witch hunt', that I wasn't a gold digger, a media-whore.

'I think it's brilliant evidence,' I said.

I called the liaison officer and told her everything. She didn't show any emotion. I thought it was weird that she said, 'Nothing must happen to that letter. Do you understand, Jenny? Do not destroy the letter.'

Why would I destroy the letter?

A feeling of unease crept into my bones. I ignored it, because I didn't understand, and I was used to not understanding.

Later, as I watched the lead detective read the letter, it became clear that his face was not lighting up. Why not? What was wrong? This was the evidence we needed to nail him, wasn't it? The man who had ambushed me with his friend, changed the course of my life. This proved that an attack happened, no?

The detective's face remained blank, like I'd passed him a menu and he couldn't decide what to order.

'Jenny, well done for bringing this to us,' he said at last. 'I'll have to discuss it with the Gold Group. I'll call you later.'

While I waited for that call, I tried to focus on writing an essay about a playwright. Mum had bought me a second-hand laptop for Christmas, and it was a very generous present, but the space bar kept sticking and the shift button had come off, and – I just couldn't take that level of frustration that day. I stood up and huffed, paced the room, sat down, tried again, huffed again.

'Please stop,' came the eventual plea from Neil, from the sofa. 'Just stop. Let's watch something.'

'It's impossible!'

'I know. So, stop.'

He went to the DVD collection. 'Bill?' *Bill Hicks: Revelations* had been a favourite of mine and Will's. I shook my head. 'Richard?' Richard Pryor's Alsatian impression had made me cry with laughter more than once, but I shook my head again. He grabbed *Pulp Fiction* and satirical TV series *Brass Eye*, shaking them enticingly.

'I don't want to watch anything. I am too stressed,' I sulked, massaging my still-frozen jaw.

'Roddy?' Now he was holding up a copy of *The Commitments*, the film adaptation of Roddy Doyle's novel about soul music and belonging. As a teenager, my mates and I had played the soundtrack endlessly. I nodded. Comfort in old friends.

Neil and I were spooning on the crappy red sofa that came with the house when the detective rang back. 'Thanks again for bringing this letter to my attention, Jenny. This is significant evidence.'

YES. I knew it!

'We need you to do another interview about it. A filmed interview. Can you come to Camberwell tomorrow? I'll pick you up.'

'No problem,' I said. Neil held up a large hand for a high five and went to make toast and tea.

Alright, we're in the interview suite at Camberwell. I'm a DS from the Special Enquiry Team at Scotland Yard. It's 11.52 now. OK, the reason for this chat, Jenny, is because a letter has come to our notice, which you brought to our attention, and we wanted to talk partly about how it came into your possession and a little bit about the contents of the letter . . .

The contents of the letter.

Oh shit.

Given that I had hinted at other sexual traumas, incidents from my teenage years, The Bar Manager, other shit stuff that had happened, it suddenly dawned on me that the police now expected me to talk about these other events. Why? I didn't want to. They weren't relevant. As I sat there, unsure, wrestling with the steel trap to recall details of these memories, the reason they were asking me to do so became suddenly clear: The Letter discredited me. One assault is bad luck, two is careless – no matter the context – three, or more, you are now an undefendable, fantasist, lunatic slut. As Baroness Helena Kennedy KC, author of *Eve Was Shamed*, observed, 'True victimhood has very demanding standards.'

The police were not high-fiving over this brilliant evidence, they were trying to work out how bad the damage was, to the case and, I now assume, to the reputation of the Met. Was either salvageable?

The detective and my liaison officer did their utmost to preserve my sense of self-worth as they prepared to dissect my credibility. I was asked why I hadn't mentioned these other 'run-ins' before. I thought about it.

'I didn't think they were relevant,' I said.

It was true. They were investigating The Famous Man. I knew something about The Famous Man. I went to a police station to tell the police what I knew about The Famous Man. Plus, and this might not be immediately obvious to those who have never experienced sexual assault multiple times, each experience has its own circumstance and context. Each holds a distinct place on a spectrum of fear. Each leaves a unique imprint on your body and soul. I began to talk about The Bar Manager, keeping him anonymous. As I was doing so, I foresaw having to do this again, in court. I imagined The Famous Man's legal team using my own letter to undermine me.

What is it about you, Ms Evans, that leads these men to assume they can take advantage of you? If that is what has happened on these occasions, as you say?

Was I going to be blamed for the violence? Was I going to be shamed for being singled out, and terrified and humiliated? I thought about the tabloid coverage and a sandstorm of panic swept through me. Black pixels began to frame my vision, as they had during The Famous Man attack. Was I going to pass out?

'Could I have a glass of water please?'

I already had one. They pointed at it. My mind was racing, my breath was shallow. I felt ambushed. *I'm not safe.* How could I make myself safe? *I need this to stop.*

In a moment of piercing clarity, I realised that part of the reason I didn't feel safe was that everything I had told the police so far had ended up in a tabloid newspaper. I already had experience of becoming some kind of national joke. It had felt like being skinned. I didn't want to risk that again and the truth was, though I hadn't been able until that moment to admit it to myself, I didn't know if I could trust the police.

'So, Jenny, incident one, as we will now refer to the sexual—'

'Sorry. But I can't speak about incident one . . .'

Incident one had happened in my mid-teens. I didn't want to talk about it. And all I needed to do, I realised in that moment, was refuse to speak and they had nowhere to go. I had done the math. It was my fastest way out of there.

The lead detective nodded. *Does he understand what I am doing?* I wondered. *Does he understand why?* I told him, truthfully, that my mum didn't know about incident one, and added that I didn't think it was relevant. I didn't want to discuss it in court, and then – I refused to say any more. I felt the breath leave my body. It was over. I wouldn't get my day in court with The Famous Man, but in that moment, I didn't feel angry or frustrated or sad. My overwhelming sensation was of intense relief; I could no longer be hunted. I was no longer prey.

As I had anticipated, the CPS had no option but to 'offer no evidence' against The Famous Man. If your key witness refuses to speak about material evidence, in this case The Letter, I guess the case cannot be pursued, though whether my personal history should have been considered relevant to this case is another matter. Let's be categorical about it: It. Was. Not. Perhaps if I had taken legal advice, I might have been advised not to disclose The Letter at all.

A few days after this interview, a statement was released by the CPS that the charges against The Famous Man would be dropped. I had never even met the solicitor representing the Crown. It is still uncommon for a sexual assault survivor to meet the CPS lawyer working their case. This is not good for the well-being of a person who has to put trust in an organisational structure they cannot clearly see. It is one of many systemic black holes in a criminal justice system that could do more to help survivors of violence feel seen and understood and, therefore, feel safe.

The statement from the CPS was released both to me and to the press at the same time. On reflection, this seems highly insensitive, but it is perhaps indicative of the function of the Gold Group and the dual focus of its remit – on criminal justice and also on the reputation of the Metropolitan Police. It also shows its power.

I thought I could return to Lizzie and Katie and our little house and get back to being normal. It didn't go down like that. Rather than tail off, now that I could, in theory, speak out, tabloid interest became intense. They began to vie for my story. Our home was besieged by reporters offering large sums of money.

And the truth was that I wanted to talk. I wanted to explain; being silenced is painful. A thousand times a day, I thought, *It's not that they think he's innocent. It's not that I can't prove it. I just can't keep talking, because I don't know who I can trust.* But, for the same reason, there was no one I could risk telling.

By now the press had got hold of Neil's phone number. His mobile seemed to ring every half-hour, with requests for him to speak to me to see if I would talk to a particular paper, or editor, or reporter. Journalists started hanging around the house I grew up in, they went to my school and the drama centre in my hometown. They sent flowers to my mum and to my very confused grandparents. Again, we keep secrets not just for ourselves, but to protect others. Reporters knocked on doors of houses I had rented in London in the past, some of which uni friends like Joe still lived at. They offered them money to talk.

'Yeah, that's her . . .' I arrived home to find a neighbour pointing at me. The female journalist spun on her heels, dazzled me with a plastic smile and spoke to me as if I were a child, 'Hellooo, Jeeeennnny.'

As I made my way towards the front door, she started offering large sums of money under her breath: 'Thirty K. Might be able to get forty . . .'

'Give it to a rape charity,' I said.

When the lead detective turned up to find out how I was, he could see I was exhausted. Now I understood what grown-ups meant when they said they were 'shattered'. I was in my early twenties. So young. It was six years since I had taken the part in *Twin Town*. It was five years since violence had rammed me off course. And then Will. *Will.* I wanted to scream his name down empty roads and at seafronts and from mountaintops. *Where are you, Will? Where is my brother?* I longed for the calm I had always felt in his presence.

The detective organised for me and Neil to be put up in a hotel for a few days until the press frenzy calmed down. He said he would drive us. As I lugged my wheelie case towards the car, he turned back, adding, 'There is one more thing.' He handed me two brown envelopes. 'I've been asked to pass these on to you.' They were letters from journalists at the *Sun* and the *Mail on Sunday*. The detective looked uncomfortable, but behaved as if this were normal procedure.

In the back of the car, I tore open the envelopes.

> *Dear Madam*
> *At the Sun we have followed your case very closely . . . We would be willing to give you a platform so that what really happened can reach a large audience. I understand as well from speaking with the Police that you're still standing by your story . . .*

> *Dear Ms Evans,*
> *This must be a terribly difficult and testing time for you . . .*

> *The Mail on Sunday has followed the court proceedings involving you and [The Famous Man] very closely indeed. As you may be aware, he has accepted a substantial sum of money to give an interview designed to establish his blamelessness. But we believe strongly that there is another side to this story . . .*

Both offered me a monetary fee to speak exclusively to them. I felt sick. The tabloids were ruthless, yet they were powerful. They had such reach. Being in proximity to their operation was both frightening and thrilling.

What would happen if I broke my silence? How would it feel to finally get to speak?

I caught the detective's eye in the rear-view mirror. 'What do you think I should do?'

'I think you have been through enough. I think the best thing to do is say nothing. If you talk to one newspaper, the others will take you down to punish you. Keep your anonymity. Walk away.'

'I could talk to them, but make it known that payment was going to a rape charity,' I mused.

The detective shrugged. 'I can't tell you what to do. You have to do what you think is right.'

As he drove Neil and me to our hideout hotel on the coast, he suspected we were being followed by the press. He put a blue light on the top of his unmarked car, fired up the siren and we lost whoever was tailing us. This, too, was thrilling. This, too, was power. But there was something uncomfortable about the letters – the proximity between the press and the police, *I understand as well from speaking with the Police that you're still standing by your story.* What was the true relationship between these two such powerful factions? Cops and robbers? One chases the other . . . then back again?

20

The following morning, Neil set out for the papers. I was hiding. Our hotel room was art deco, green and gold, and furnished in shiny mahogany. It overlooked the sea. While I waited for him to return, I wrapped myself in the duvet and sat on the floor, positioning myself just inside the open balcony window, in case someone tried to get a photograph on a long lens. *Who knows I am here?* When Neil came back, with takeaway coffee and almond croissants, we climbed back into bed. The *Mail on Sunday* had informed me, in its letter, that its coverage of The Famous Man this weekend would be critical in tone. Why?

Did they know his reputation and were taking a punt that he was guilty? Or – did they somehow know there was more to the case being dropped than there appeared to be?

How?

Neil and I had discussed many times what we would spend the money on if I had decided to sell my story. We were sick of being skint – that unrelenting, mood-suppressing negotiation between you and every little thing in the world you want or need. I had many times chosen food over tampons, tampons over train fare, slunk through Tube barriers behind a commuter with a ticket, head down and heart racing. Take-away coffee and croissants were a luxury. We had envisioned a life free of bank charges for being overdrawn, monthly travelcards for Zones 1–6, bread you cut yourself and the posh peanut butter. I thought I might get a new laptop, driving lessons, *go on holiday*.

It was idle chatter; the decision I had made – silence, anonymity, protection for my family – was the right one. So, when I opened the *News of the World* that sunny Sunday morning to a double-page spread that contained pretty much every detail of my case, and much of my private life, some information even my friends didn't know, it was not just exposing, it felt like being robbed. It felt like being stripped. I was violated.

'She kept secrets', the tabloid screamed, 'she was molested before', 'there were other attacks', 'she claims they happened before and after [The Famous Man]'.[*]

The words were taunting. Bullying. I felt mocked.

Thank goodness I hadn't said more, either to the police or in my house or on the phone, to anyone. Thank goodness I hadn't risked the exposure that comes with fully trusting. Thank goodness the most tender parts of myself were still locked inside my chest. I had kept some of my secrets. Thank goodness. For I was discovering in the most brutally public of ways that neither the criminal justice system nor the tabloid media – or any media? – is interested in the complexities of human life. Of women's lived experience. Of revictimisation, which is particularly psychologically and intellectually complex. Of trauma. A fact that is astounding when you consider that women make up half of us (and, of course, are not the only

---

[*] These are approximations of the quotes, which cannot be quoted for legal reasons.

victims of sexual assault) and that trauma is almost all the criminal justice system and the media deal in at all.

Neil and I looked at one another in disbelief. 'Holy fuck,' I whispered.

The article said I'd kept secrets from the police, *which was not true*. It painted me as a fantasist, *which was so unfair*. It implied I had accused The Famous Man of assault because he was famous, nothing more. Some details were accurate. Some misinformed. Some taken out of context. I was quoted, almost accurately, *an anonymous police source was quoted*. The tone of the article was one of breezy dismissal, of my allegations and of any feelings I might have in relation to this case being dropped. It did mention that the police did not consider that I had acted with any malice, but the gloating tone hit hard; it felt like tacit support for The Famous Man.

How is this happening? What the fuck is going on here?

As if The Famous Man had once more covered my mouth, I couldn't breathe. Grasping at furniture, I made it onto the hotel balcony, crouched down in an effort, still, to hide, and tried to find air. Tried to find calm. The deep gasping sound I was making was primal and frightening. Neil was shouting my name somewhere behind me. I shrugged his hand from my shoulder, thinking only, *Air. Air. Breathe. Breathe.*

The worst of it over, still dizzy with shock, I accepted a glass of water from Neil. 'Fuck them, Jen. Fuck them. Forget about it.' I looked up at him. How could he say that?

'I turned down all that money. I chose to keep my secrets. I felt it was dignified. And *yet again*, my dignity has been stolen. *Yet again*, I am humiliated.' I felt shame and, in its wake, self-disgust. I was the loser in the great power game playing out around me. But of course I was. It was never a level playing field.

'I'm going for a walk.' Unable to comfort me, Neil left again. We had been trying to ignore that our relationship was in trouble for months, but I could not seem to stop it unravelling; there was no time to be normal any more. After the first few arguments, he would put Coldplay on and dance me around the kitchen, singing, 'Let's go back to the start', brown eyes smiling down at me.

I had let him hold me, twirl me, kiss me. I loved his carefree spirit. I loved the smell of him, the warmth of his skin beneath his T-shirt. I wished we *could* go back, to who I was when I was just enjoying being a student, before I walked into that police station and said those no-going-back words. But I had changed, and he could no longer reach me. I had risked everything and lost. Somehow, I had said too much and yet not enough.

Alone once more in the hotel room, I reread the article. Deep in my gut, a knot of anger formed.

How did they know? How did they get details of my case? How did they learn this stuff? How did they know? How did they know?

I began to pace the room.

How do tabloid reporters get information? Who do they pay? What for them is legal? And what is not? Is that different for what is legal for me? And – why?

It made no sense that tabloids would be allowed to work to a different legal system. That they would be above the law.

'Something illegal must have happened,' I said aloud to myself. *It must have*, I thought. I didn't know enough about how – everything – worked. But this was surely wrong.

Round and round I paced. Then I set my laptop on the little hotel desk and searched 'journalism courses'. I was about to graduate from Central. Why couldn't I just do an MA? In journalism? OK, I knew nothing about journalism – and I was terrified of it – but I wanted to claw back for myself a little of the power that journalists held. They controlled the information.

As we were packing to leave the following morning, the lead detective phoned. 'Jenny. I meant to tell you. You might be entitled to something called Criminal Injury Compensation. It is money paid to survivors of violent crime.'

He wanted me to know that despite the charges having been dropped, he – they, 'my team' – believed I had been hurt and was entitled to compensation for the damage that had been done to my body. It didn't matter that there was no conviction. 'That doesn't mean the violence didn't happen. We believe you, so does the CPS. Still. You are entitled to it. Take it.'

He added, 'It's not much. A couple of thousand pounds. But I can apply for it for you if you want.'

'No thanks,' I said. The idea of receiving money, however it was packaged and for whatever reason it was awarded, smarted. I had turned down the offers from the tabloids because this had been about stopping a man I had experienced as violent from being violent again. Nothing else. It could never be about anything else.

Irritated, I turned back to my laptop to pack it away and spotted the email confirming my application for a journalism course at London's City University. I checked out the fees – £5,000 – and, with a sigh, climbed down from my high horse and called the detective back.

'I'll take it,' I said.

When I got back to London, Joe came with me to Tottenham Court Road to help me choose a better second-hand laptop.

21

'Can a journalist ever go too far in reporting what she knows to be the truth?'

The lecture hall was full; an arc of tiered seats, packed with trainee reporters and aspiring TV and radio producers. Who would be brave enough to speak first? Ethics tutor Roy Greenslade, a Fleet Street veteran in yellow cords and red braces, asked the question again. A student from the broadcast course raised her hand. 'No. The truth *is* the story . . .'

Roy rocked on his heels, anticipating the coming debate. 'How many agree?' A smattering of hands – most students were hedging their bets, not wanting to look stupid.

'What if that truth amounts merely to gossip?'

'Gossip sells papers' – a newspaper trainee – 'gossip gets clicks. Let's be grown-ups about it. If you don't attract advertising, your publication fails, and you don't get to investigate anything at all.'

'What about the gossiped-about's right to privacy?' Roy pushed. 'Doesn't that count for anything?'

Anyone with an interest in press ethics knows this debate well. The question comes down to public interest versus interesting to the public, an individual's right to privacy versus the public's right to know. Though the debate is an old one, we were new to it, and some fought like their lives depended on it. I felt like mine did.

But I didn't speak.

There was some discussion about what constitutes public interest: 'hypocrisy', 'corruption', 'anything that impacts on the well-being of the public'.

Roy posed more questions. 'Is every aspect of MPs' lives fair game, then, as their job impacts the well-being of the public?' He waited for response.

'What about a senior cop?' He surveyed the room.

'How about a sanctimonious footballer, or actor or musician? Who *deserves* to be exposed for hypocrisy?'

Pause.

'What if they are *un*sanctimonious?'

Pause.

'Do any of them have a right to privacy? Or does their aspiration to lead, or their reliance on the press to further their careers, preclude that?'

The newspaper trainee again – braver than any of us. 'Yes. It does. Oh, come on. Celebrities can't turn press interest in their behaviour off and on when they feel like it. They need the press, the press needs them. We are interdependent for survival.'

Roy scanned the rest of us. 'Who agrees?'

Not me. I took the point – how do newspapers stay relevant? How do they retain power? By trading in information. The information has to be of high quality, hopefully exclusive, definitely interesting. And they need more of it every day.

But I knew I didn't agree; some stuff is private. It just is. And newspaper owners should not line their pockets with the secrets of the people the public are interested in. Not unless there is hypocrisy, or illegality, or deceit. And *only then*, if that in some way impacts the well-being of the public. Sorry, but otherwise they need to get their clicks some other way.

I wanted to raise my hand to say some of this. I wanted to ask whether those who bought the 'anything for clicks' logic thought crime victims should be sacrificed to the gods of journalism too. We didn't use the media for self-promotion, but we certainly did sell papers.

But I didn't want everyone to look at me.

And anyway – I was here for one reason. I wanted to pick the brains of former tabloid editor and professor of ethics Roy Greenslade about how newspapers get news. I had about an hour before I was due to meet Lizzie to start work at the bar we worked in. She would cover for me if I was late, but I'd miss the free staff food, and that was pretty much all I could afford to eat.

As everyone else made to file out of the lecture hall, I headed straight to the front, smiled my broadest smile and asked Roy Greenslade, 'Do you have time for a cup of tea?'

It has become the question I have asked, professionally, more than any other. I have got everywhere by enquiring if people have time for a cup of tea. Tea is softer than coffee. It is friendlier. Kinder. Journalists don't have to be hard-nosed, in my opinion. They have to be focused, and they have to be compassionate. Tea has a soft nose.

In a café near the university (or, I think it may have been a pub. I seem to remember Roy had a Guinness – fuck the tea) I got straight to the point. Did Roy, as a former tabloid editor, know how reporters on those papers got their information?

'Now what do you mean exactly?' he asked.

'I mean, is it possible to bug people's houses, listen to their phone calls, pay, in some way, for private information? Is there ever a public interest in that? Or would a newspaper editor stop her journalists from doing that? Because it's all illegal. I assume.'

Roy studied my face. He asked why I wanted to know.

'Just that, on the train here, I overheard a young woman talking about trying to take [The Famous Man] to court . . .'

'I see,' said Roy.

The case had been running for about a year, and the accuser (me) had never spoken out, so of course he was interested. I told Roy I had followed the woman off the train and persuaded her to talk to me. I'd like to say – I am still totally ashamed of that lie. It was so self-aggrandising, aside from anything else. I was nowhere near approach-strangers-on-the-train-to-ask-journalistic-questions brave at this point. But neither did I want Roy to know the truth. I didn't want anyone to know my secrets any more, and I certainly wasn't ready to show anyone any trust.

'She told me she stopped talking to the police because everything she said aloud about her case ended up printed in a tabloid newspaper and she didn't know how it could have happened.'

Roy was clearly impressed with my journalistic instinct. Cringe. What a fucking liar. He said he would look into my question about news-gathering techniques and come back to me.

One week later, at the end of our next lecture, he gestured for me to stay behind.

Over very nice fish in a very nice fish restaurant (on him), he explained that he had dug out his notes about The Famous Man case from when the story broke. He had looked into it a little bit at the time because he had a media column in the *Guardian*, and because the media lawyer The Famous Man had used happened to be a friend.

Oh right. Shit.

Roy fixed me with a kind but no-bullshit-please sort of a stare and explained, 'It was like a kick to the solar plexus to see that the person who made the accusations had the same name as you.'

TIP: try not to lie to veteran Fleet Street reporters, if you can help it – to any reporters – they are really good at finding stuff out.

I blushed the sort of blush you feel when you wish you were dead and croaked a meagre apology. Roy smiled. 'I understand perfectly well why you lied.' I asked him if he thought I would ever find out how the tabloids knew so much about what had happened to me. I expected him to say, 'No, you will probably never know'; journalists protect their sources above all else, as they should. We had discussed this many times in his class.

'Maybe,' he said.

Three weeks later, on a grey Saturday morning, I found myself at the back of an investigative journalism masterclass taught by Roy's friend and *Guardian* colleague Nick Davies.

Roy had discovered that Nick was about to start an investigation into the state of journalism in the UK. As soon as I heard that I had laser focus; Nick Davies must employ me. Only if I was working with Nick Davies could he teach me how to 'do journalism'. Only if I was being paid to do journalism could I finally jack in the bar job and do the research I needed to do. Only if I did the research would I find out what the fuck happened with my case.

Nick was talking a spellbound class through the means by which public interest information can legitimately be gathered, 'Happy to take questions'. Of *course* everyone else had at least one interesting question. Of *course* I couldn't speak.

When we broke for lunch, I waited in the classroom until the others had left, pretending to look for something in my bag, thinking, *Say something to Nick. Say something. JennyEvanssaysomethingrightnowyouabsolutefuckingcoward.*

I realised some floppy-haired dickhead was also hanging around with some apparently important question. I needed him to leave. *Stop talking to Nick. Stop talking. Floppyhaireddickheadgetoutofhererightnowyouabsolutebastard.* It seemed like they might go out to lunch together when Nick doubled back to grab something, and the boy miraculously vanished. I looked over. 'Do you have time for a cup of tea?'

Nick smiled at me politely. I waited for a no. 'Where do you suggest?' he said, gathering up his papers.

At a pavement café in Islington, Nick, like Roy, a kind-faced, kind-eyed, no-bullshit kind of a person, waited for me to disclose why I'd offered him a hot drink. I was building up to it, I just didn't quite have the guts. He knew this. There is something brilliantly instinctive about Nick's approach to journalism – and, to people. He sees that everyone has a story, or something interesting to say, or something they want to say, and he teases it out of them, with enquiring glances, comfortable silences, perfectly timed questions.

And when he absorbs and then disseminates that information, repeating it back to ensure he understands, it's kind of mind-blowing. He seems to see things from all angles at once and be able to feed his insight back to you more clearly than you understood it yourself. And a minute ago, this was information that *you* were telling *him*.

So, there we were – Nick, in his fifties, greying hair, red scarf, leather jacket. Me, in my twenties, blonde bob, Topshop parka – sharing a pot of tea, trying not to burn our mouths on stringy cheese paninis, chatting about the state of journalism. Nick waited patiently to find out what I really wanted to know. I was stalling. 'Do you know much about Andy Coulson?' is what I went for, in my state of mild panic. 'He's the editor of the *News of the World*.'

In retrospect, it's amazing that I chose Coulson's name. I could not at this point have known just how much this man would come to dominate our lives – especially Nick's – over the coming years. But I had done a small amount of research already into how the tabloids worked and had retained Coulson's name, and the name of the editor who preceded him, Rebekah Brooks (née Wade) – I had a ring binder labelled *Tabloid Editors*, containing scraps of information about them, in my bedroom (I appreciate how weird that is). There were also *Tabloids General* and *MPS* (Metropolitan Police Service) ring binders. I would clip relevant articles out of newspapers, print off any research I had found that suggested wrongdoing or illegality at tabloids, or by the police, and file them. Sometimes I reread what I had before bed, as if I might suddenly find a clue I had missed as to how, or why, details of my police case were leaked.

Of course, I didn't really want to know what Nick thought of Andy Coulson at this point, and I can't actually remember what his answer was. I was building up to the question I really wanted to ask. Deep breath. 'Do you ever take on researchers? Not work experience, but – a proper job?'

Now Nick understood. He took a sip of tea and said that, as it happens, he did.

'Do they have to be very experienced?'

Nick said that they did not.

'Is there somewhere I can apply?'

Nick said a pavement café in Islington was the perfect place. He needed to go and speak to Alan Rusbridger, his editor at the *Guardian*. We agreed to meet again in town the following week. I remember noticing that he seemed charmed by how happy he had made me. I couldn't hide it from my face. This was it. I was in.

22

My first assignment was working on what would become Nick's book *Flat Earth News*. As prescient as it is alarming, it predicts the proliferation and normalisation of fake news in our media. The message is a stark warning as to what happens when we allow money to distort and influence journalism. What do we do when we can no longer trust what we read, or even what we see? The evolution of social media, deep fakes and AI has raised these stakes, but no government has yet provided an answer.

Nick would email me with someone to interview, or something to follow up, and I would head out from the little flat I shared with my mate Bob to do his bidding. It was a small role to play in a very big story, but it felt like a first step towards finding out the truth about how newspapers sought out what they considered to be news.

A sidenote about Bob, 'Bobba'. He and I – during the wilderness years, before I went back to uni – managed a divey nightclub together opposite the Ritz in Central London. He is tall and athletic; big hands, big feet, charmingly prominent front teeth. He had trained as a ballet dancer before an ankle injury derailed him, so he found himself running bars and nightclubs and working out what to do next.

When Will died, Bob heard the news, got on a train from London and turned up at my mum's front door. He still says, laughing and rubbing his hands together in the way he always has, 'I honestly don't know why I did that.'

He just . . . came. He stayed for a week, unafraid of the big emotions around him, making bacon and eggs for anyone who needed it. Available for riverside walks, in silence or in the dark gallows humour we love in each other. An easy companion. A friend. And for a while, after I split with Neil and as I embarked on my journalism career, my flatmate, in a tiny first-floor two-bed in East Dulwich, which we loved.

My City University training was in *TV Current Affairs Journalism*, so when not investigating with Nick, I was learning documentary filmmaking. City had at first seemed incredibly daunting; I had never been in so many rooms full of so many public-school kids in my life. They seemed so blithely relaxed about everything – though I soon learned that that's a facade. They're not; they're hugely competitive. They're also usually very well connected, by a cobweb of alliances the rest of us don't realise exist. Many of the others had family or school or university connections to the journalism industry, for example, plus they all seemed to have several languages and to play several instruments, and to ask questions like, 'Where do you ski?'

I was impressed and intimidated. They answered questions fast and seemed very at home with the thought of existing in the world of journalism, a job that hadn't occurred to me until recently. My bar mates, though never discouraging, thought it was hilarious that I had made such a huge about-turn from thinking I might possibly teach. Mum and Deb were a little surprised too – asking where my ambition to write or direct theatre had gone and checking if I was certain that I no longer wanted to work in a primary school (my sister still asks this sometimes, and the truth is – I am not. I think that would have been a very good life for me).

Mum came to London to test me with current affairs questions prior to the interview to get onto the City course, basing them on that day's paper. 'Make sure you know the president of Sudan – Omar al-Bashir. How will you remember it?', 'Can you tell them the difference between Sunni and Shia Islam?', 'Definitely have all the British prime ministers and chancellors.' She was nervous. 'Are you sure you want to do this? YOU CAN DO THIS.'

I had to do it. I had to find out how my secrets had ended up in the tabloid press. And then I had to expose it.

If I had a free afternoon at City, I'd head to a computer room to research *Tabloid Editors, Tabloids General* and the *MPS,* making the most of the free printing. I was learning names not just of editors and deputy editors, but of other executives and desk 'heads' at tabloids. That a news desk was different to a features desk. That each had senior and junior reporters. That often they were set against one another, despite working for the same paper, because it was felt that all competition was healthy.

I educated myself in other ways at this time, too. At Foyles on Tottenham Court Road or Waterstones on Piccadilly, both near my bar job, I bought books on politics, law and philosophy, absorbing everything I could about the state and the systems that run it; how they are meant to operate compared with how they really work, and who pulls the levers. I've always loved the hushed promise of a book shop and in those days spent any spare hour I could reading in them. I was fully engaged; learning, questioning, occasionally going out dancing with Bobba, Lizzie and Joe. This was not an unhappy time. And the study paid off – I managed to stop having to work in the bar . . . eventually.

On graduation, I talked my way into some unpaid work at a TV production company. Based in a four-storey office on the corner of Soho Square, its walls were orange, its desks crammed at right angles into open-plan spaces. There was a tiny lift (in which I once travelled with the legendary Barry Humphries), a reception with a desk and a person behind it. '*A reception*,' I told Lotte, another mate from the bar days, when she came to meet me for lunch. I loved everything about this TV company, even though my first project was on a factual entertainment programme called *Diet Doctors*, and they only paid me £150 a week.

A 'company meeting' was held on Thursday mornings in the corner room downstairs, which had windows onto the square. Here, all commissions currently in production were discussed and the company updated on problems, pitfalls, progress. I went to every one of these meetings. The people running the shows appeared to be happy and fulfilled in their work. To me, they all seemed incredibly interesting and clever and kind. I made a couple of very close friends.

What these meetings gave me – aside from free food – was access to the list of 'upcoming productions' the company had secured commission for. I scoured it every week for anything that looked remotely political or journalistic, so that it dovetailed with my training. Four weeks in – bingo – there was a BBC Two series already in production titled *Boris Johnson and the Dream of Rome*. Charismatic young MP 'Boris' (real name Alex) had been given his own series, in which he was to compare the working of the modern-day European Union with that almost-as-successful European project of the past . . . the Roman Empire. Most of the filming had taken place in Europe over the previous few weeks, so none of the crew had been around. Now the team was back and there were some shoots to organise in London. The series producer, a lovely man with grey hair and glasses, came to the weekly meeting. Poor man. I stuck to him like glue.

Perhaps he was charmed, perhaps he was exhausted, I don't know, but eventually, he agreed that *yes, OK, there's some research that might need doing*. If I wanted, I could join his team. Also, and this really was amazing, he told me he didn't believe in using free labour. He offered me a wage of £450 a week. That Sunday, at 'the Dog' in Dulwich Village, I paid for Lizzie's roast. Then I cried.

The producer knew an executive on the foreign affairs series *Unreported World*, so he got me an interview to be a researcher on that show when my contract with him ran out – this is how TV works. I had claimed for myself a sticky little string of the cobweb and I clung on for dear life.

I was still doing my tabloid research, and worked for Nick in-between filmmaking jobs, but otherwise I was growing into my role as a TV producer. I learned how to develop and then make both observational and 'narrative' documentaries – the former, fly-on-the-wall in style, follow ordinary humans in extraordinary circumstances. The latter, often told retrospectively, interweave first-person testimony with dramatic elements and archive footage.

I worked on presenter-led series, as well as more hard-hitting current affairs investigations, which are what I found most meaningful. I flew to Brazil, India and Vietnam for the BBC. I travelled across the US, producing documentary-dramas about crazy characters and insane prison escapes, always flying alone into a strange place, renting a car and setting out to hunt down access. I have knocked on the front door of a sheriff who was ghosting me in Mississippi, searched for the home of an ex-drug dealer in a vast trailer park in Indiana, filmed a gang member in a Super Max prison in New Mexico.

Travelling for work, I discovered, is singularly thrilling; the closest you get in adulthood to having a proper adventure. You have a clear objective but no real idea of how you will achieve it, you must solve your immediate problems alone, you must find a way to push to get what you need in an entirely foreign place, sometimes in a new language, always with new rules.

Working abroad forced me to find within myself a confidence to problem-solve and to remain calm under pressure. I was changing and growing. Finding my feet. What City and working in television were teaching me was that though others are better educated than me, occasionally more articulate (almost always less likely to dissociate and totally mind-blank – God), I was, in the end, just as good as them. I was just as good at understanding what needed to be understood and getting stuff done. And these skills – particularly the ability to remain composed when under stress – are skills I would soon be very glad to have learned.

23

July 2009.

Newly returned from shooting abroad, I was packed into a London commuter train, reading someone else's newspaper over their shoulder, when a *Guardian* headline brought me crashing back into my story.

Murdoch papers paid £1m to gag phone-hacking victims.

The article had Nick Davies's byline. I hadn't spoken to him in a while, because I'd been away so much.

The Murdoch papers in question were the *Sun* and the *News of the World*, the tabloids that had most accurately printed details of the violent experiences I could barely think about. I felt dizzy.

Phone hacking. What is phone hacking?

Of course. *Clever Nick.* Phone hacking was how the tabloids stole secrets.

Before WhatsApp, when friends used text messaging, voicemail was still the primary source of communication between an individual and anyone official. And if you wanted to convey to your mate a message any longer than a couple of sentences, you left long rambling voicemails in the way we use voice notes now. You'd tell them about recent experiences, about plans, about thoughts and feelings. Being able to access a person's voicemail, in those days, was like being able to read their diary.

Nick's article stated that only public figures were targeted by the tabloids. I was reminded of the debates in Roy's ethics lectures. What about crime victims? Were we targets too? My first instinct was to call Nick, tell him everything about my background, ask him if I could help him investigate. But I realised my legs were shaking.

I got off the train and sat on a bench. As the crowds thinned, I retrieved my phone from my handbag, found Nick's name and . . . did not press 'Call'.

I had only told the police the most minimal and surface-level facts about my experience with The Famous Man and his friend, and that had been excruciating. I had been overwhelmed with fear at having spoken. My jaw had frozen. When I had told The Crew Member immediately after it had happened, and when I told my boss at the bar, months later, I had both times very much wished I hadn't. It did not lead either to compassion or to help. Roy had been kind, but that, too, had been an exercise in enduring please-world-swallow-me-whole embarrassment. What would Nick's reaction be? How could I know? As ever, I wasn't sure I would even be able to get the words out of my mouth.

The day was humid. I fidgeted with the neck of my dress and attempted to fan my face with a hand (why do we ever do that?). Commuters streamed past, towards the Tube or nearby offices; trainers, blouses, midi-skirts, suits. I was jealous. Not for the first time, I was gripped by a deep desire to be *one of them*. Someone else. Anyone else, with anyone else's life. The attack had recently begun to flash back more readily in moments of stress. It reminded me of its power with zaps of fright, slivers of colour, a millisecond of a memory of the intensity of the scuffle. It made me want to hide, not turn to face it. Certainly not to call up my mentor one morning when I had come so far in my recovery and risk telling him how vulnerable I had once been. Suddenly desperate for air, I put my phone back in my bag and walked the rest of the way to work.

I strode at pace across London Bridge – no easy feat in heeled ankle boots, but a talent I developed in the noughties – looked out at the ancient flow of the Thames and took deep breaths. Not as good as the mountain air of home, but grounding. *You still have a TV producing contract to finish*, I told myself. *There is no point in calling Nick now.* As I made my way through the City, past Pudding Lane, which sparked London's great fire, this thought became, *Nick's just published a front-page article! He's today's entire news agenda! He will be too busy to speak to you, you dickhead.* My fear had grown ankle boots of its own to stride in. On I went, repeating with every anxious step, *Just wait. Just wait. Just wait.*

It was terror, of course. I was afraid. So, I held my secrets to my chest, and when I got home that night – struggling through the door with a brand-new printer – I dusted off the ring binders labelled *Tabloid Editors*, *Tabloids General* and *MPS*, and resumed my status as a scrapbook warrior.

Taking to bed with tea, toast and cut-up apple – some habits die hard – my laptop and I discovered that a lot had happened. Clive Goodman, the royal reporter for the *News of the World*, and Glenn Mulcaire, a footballer turned private investigator (PI) who hacked phones for him, had been *imprisoned* while I was away, for breaking into the voicemails of royal aides. Holy shit.

I sipped tea and thought about this. *The* News of the World *used PIs. How surprised am I, really?* If anything, I felt ashamed I hadn't worked that out myself. Of course they did. *And clearly, some of what the PIs did was not legal.* Of course. *Of course.* I reflected that none of my friends or family had told me about these headlines while I had been travelling. Either this wasn't top of the news agenda, so they didn't know, or — could it be that they knew but they didn't really care? *Shouldn't we all be a little outraged that this newspaper was making money out of stealing people's secrets, and publishing them?* I thought, *Even if we aren't surprised? Why should we just accept that they do this?* Perhaps, unless it is your secrets that are stolen, it's hard to appreciate the toll of that, both on individuals and on the ecosystem of the state — giving newspaper barons and their executives unfettered power is not a route to social equilibrium.

But — arrests had been made. Time had been served. It appeared there had been some consequences, at least for the reporter who commissioned the hacking, and for the hacker himself. The *News of the World* editor at the time, Andy Coulson, had fallen on his sword, denying knowledge of unlawful information gathering, but accepting it happened on his watch.

The line from Murdoch HQ was that no one else at the paper knew about Goodman's rogue news-gathering practices. As he and Mulcaire had been caught and punished, News International (now News UK), the Murdoch company that published the paper, had declared that the matter was now closed.

No one else at the paper knew? That sounded dubious. *Why would you hack a royal aide on Monday and not a senior politician on Tuesday, if you knew you could?*

Coulson had been one of the editors when the articles were written about me. The other had been Rebekah Brooks. I remember this moment of research so clearly because I became aware, as I was flipping through the relevant ring binder, that I had raised my hand to my jaw. It had clenched at the sight of their names, as it had when I reported to the police, as if my body remembered the stress of that time. Then, my hand was at my throat, a flash of the panic of not being able to breathe during the assault bringing me to tears. *The fear is still inside my body*, I realised. The physicality of it was frightening. It was the first time there had been a clear correlation in my mind – in my body – between the violation of the assault and the violation of my privacy. I was of so little worth to both sets of perpetrators. *Don't cry. Drink tea. Find out what they stole. Expose the shit out of them.*

I drank tea. Since resigning, the BBC website told me, Coulson had been elevated to a new and far more respectable job. I nearly choked – head of communications for the Conservative Party. The political party widely tipped to be the next party of government.

'Fucking hell.'

I texted Mum: *Have you seen the paper?* I meant Nick's article: phone hacking.

I saw it and I thought of you, came back an instant reply. She called: 'How does it make you feel?'

I thought about that. 'Scared.'

'Because . . . ?' (Therapists always ask 'because?' instead of 'why?'; it apparently encourages us to explore our feelings rather than try to explain them. I use it in journalism, and in friendships, all the time. It works.)

'Because if this is how they knew so much about me, I'm going to have to confront it. And I want to. I have always wanted to. But I don't know exactly how. And I don't know how it will end. But I know I have to try.'

'I understand,' was all Mum said, but she sounded sad. This was another huge risk. She didn't want me to take any more risks. She wanted me to be safe, and happy, and not someone who instinctively clutches her throat when she senses danger, in case someone stops her being able to breathe. I wanted that too, but I had to know what happened. Not just to expose them, but in the hope that, in understanding, the fear might stop.

We small-talked as I watched night fall outside the window and signed off with love.

24

Nick's article explained that huge settlements had been paid to victims of phone hacking beyond royal aides. This had been revealed at the Goodman and Mulcaire trial, though it had not been widely reported and had certainly not been questioned by anyone in the press or in the broadcast media. The former is unsurprising, the latter somewhat disappointing, for beyond the royal scandal sat five names that showed that hacking could not have been solely down to Clive Goodman, as News International had stressed. Why a royal reporter would be interested in the chief executive of the Professional Footballers' Association, Gordon Taylor, Liberal Democrat MP Simon Hughes, celebrity PR guru Max Clifford, model Elle Macpherson or football agent Sky Andrew had not been explained.

Gordon Taylor's lawyers had pushed for a higher settlement, presumably banking on the fact that News International would be keen to cover up unlawful information gathering related to him – he was not, after all, a royal aide. The amount had become so high – £700,000 in costs and damages – that it had had to be signed off by James Murdoch, Rupert's son, CEO in Europe and Asia of News International. Paperwork associated with the settlement named one senior reporter – not royal reporter Clive Goodman – and one junior reporter at the *News of the World* in reference to a transcript of a stolen voicemail.

Nick did not name the reporters, presumably because one of them was junior. His language was vague enough that I assumed he got access to the paperwork off the record. Which is to say, he had seen it, but could not divulge enough detail to reveal its provenance. He was protecting his source.

Non-Disclosure Agreements (NDAs) were signed as part of the legal settlement, so Gordon Taylor has never spoken about it. The question Nick's article posed was: Why would this settlement have been so high if it wasn't an attempt to hush up the extent of phone hacking? Surely this was proof that *News of the World* and News International executives knew that illegality went far beyond the royal reporter alone.

A second article, published the same day, stated that paperwork seized by the Metropolitan Police when PI Glenn Mulcaire was arrested contained the names and contact details of 'several thousand' potential victims of phone hacking. *Were mine in there? It would explain so much.* This pointed towards industrial-scale theft of private information, yet the Met had taken the decision not to inform all victims.

In response to Nick's articles, the force put out a statement that it would review the material and take advice on whether to re-open a phone-hacking investigation. *Wow,* I thought, when I heard that on the radio the following morning, *the power of journalism.* I assumed Nick would be thrilled.

I was at work in a glossy TV production company in east London, preparing for a trip to the US, when the lunchtime news informed me that this was not going to happen. I nearly choked on my noodles as I watched the Met's second in command, Assistant Commissioner John Yates, announce that he had reviewed all the relevant information (*all of Glenn Mulcaire's notebooks?*), that 'no additional evidence has come to light', despite Nick's revelations, and therefore that no new investigation would be launched.

What could he mean? I went cold – had Nick somehow got this wrong? Murdoch's lieutenants would crucify him if he had. It would be career ending.

How is this happening? What the fuck is going on here?

Shortly after that, the Press Complaints Commission (PCC), which regulated the press, released a report supporting the same view: phone hacking was a storm in a teacup. Nothing to see here.

Rebekah Brooks, who had been promoted to CEO of News International in June 2009, a month before Nick's article, and prior to that had edited both the *Sun* and the *News of the World*, released a statement:

> *The* Guardian *coverage, we believe, has substantially and likely deliberately misled the British public . . . We believe it is essential to defend the reputation of the* News of the World *and News International as independent media that make a major contribution to life in Britain.*

Oh God. Again, I took out my phone, scrolled to Nick's name and . . . just looked at it. *This is why you trained, Jenny. This is what you are doing here.* The fighting part of me always had a voice. *Other crime victims might have been targeted. Find out. Expose it.* But the fear part was stronger in that moment, perhaps influenced by my perception of Mum's reticence. I was happy working at a prestigious production company. I was travelling a lot in the States. The senior staff liked me, they thought I was good. I *was* good. I didn't have to make myself vulnerable, I didn't have to tell Nick – or anyone – any of my secrets. I put my phone away.

By the time I had got home, my resolve had flipped back the other way. Or halfway; I thought I had found a compromise. I would offer to work with Nick on his investigation, but I wouldn't reveal to him my secrets. He didn't need to know everything. I could openly find stuff out for him and secretly find stuff out for me. It wasn't lying, it just wasn't telling the whole truth. *I'll contact him as soon as this TV contract ends.*

Plus, I had other stuff to sort out. Starting with a new place to live. The problem with making all your friends in London is that most people tend to leave again. The original bar friends had all coupled up and left: Katie and Evan to Australia, Charlie to Suffolk, Lu to somewhere in Zone 6. Lizzie had gone to Cambodia. Bob went to live in Exeter for a bit. Joe returned to Bristol. I was thirty and most of my mates were basically married, but I had clung on far too long to a doomed relationship that had smashed my heart into little bits. The man I had given it to, and who had dropped it, had been confusing to me, because his words said he loved me, but his actions did not. Perhaps there was some love there, we definitely had some brilliant times, but clearly there wasn't enough. We had been due to move in together, but he bottled it a week before and backed out, not just of the flat, but of the relationship.

With all my belongings in storage, crying into the dim sum the friends I was staying with in east London were feeding me, I took a call from my big sister, Deb. She and I spoke at least once a fortnight. 'I've been thinking about it,' she said. 'No man should ever be able to make you homeless again.'

Deb was fifty and CEO of a Primary Care Trust, which was how the NHS was funded at that time. She offered to help me buy a flat, something Mum would not be able to afford to do (this was in 2010. Obviously, the same thing could never happen in London now unless you were a millionaire). I chose to return to Stoke Newington, the part of London in which I had lived with the 'True Colors', and where I still had a community of friends, old and new. Deb and I found a small two-bed in the eaves of an old house. I fell deeply in love with it, feeling for that first time that true liberation really is to be able to close out the world, in a room of one's own.

It was in that flat, five months after I had resolved to recontact Nick Davies – beneath a little Christmas tree and before *It's a Wonderful Life* – that I downed a glass of red and opened my laptop.

> *From: Jenny Evans*
> *Sent: 10 December 2009, 14:57*
> *To: Nick Davies*
> *Subject:*
>
> *Hey Nick,*
>
> *How are things?*
>
> *What are you up to? My contract finished on Friday so I'm free til Xmas, and just after if you need any help with anything. I hate having nothing to do!*

I talked up a few stories I was pitching, said they hadn't been picked up by those bastards who commission TV, and waited.

Half an hour later.

Ping.

From: Nick Davies
Sent: 10 December 2009, 15:23
To: Jenny Evans
Subject: re:

Bastards indeed. They're everywhere.

I've just started doing my Christmas shopping. This means I am a saintly person.

xx

Oh. A blow-out. I hadn't anticipated that. I said I hoped he had a good holiday, closed my computer and poured another glass. *Fuck it.*

That Christmas, I spent a fortnight with Mum in her miner's cottage on the side of a mountain in Wales. She had sold the family home a couple of years after Will died, unable to live, any more, with the prospect that it was never him walking through the back door. It snowed heavily that year. We had to leave the car at the bottom of a steep hill and walk my luggage and all the presents the half-mile to the front door. Mum had already done the same with the Christmas tree. Then we had to negotiate wide, white fields to deliver presents to Granny and Grandpa in a village across the valley. We picked ivy as we went and made wreaths for our heads. We sang Christmas carols and Victoria Wood songs, relived *French and Saunders* sketches – 'Tan tights!' – we always do that. Mum could sense my heartbreak, so she did what she always does and tried to love me better. 'He did love you, Jen. He *does*...' she said, picking at holly with bright red berries still attached. 'He just doesn't love himself. He can't do it. But *you* – he knows how lucky he was to have you.' I listened hard, trying to believe her.

My experience with The Man Who Didn't Love Me Enough had brought back feelings I struggled to find words for: *He didn't love you because you're ugly. He didn't love you because you're replaceable. He didn't love you because you are of no worth.*

Mum linked arms with me and started 'The Holly and the Ivy' in the wrong key. I joined in, our footprints the only disturbance in miles of snow. It is lucky to have a good mum. Maybe the luckiest thing you can have in the world. She would do anything for me. I would do anything for her, but she would do it for me first.

When the door of the little Welsh cottage was once again closed, we spent two weeks in our pyjamas in front of an open fire eating chocolate.

Some bereaved people can't bear Christmas. I do understand. For those of us who celebrate, and who have happy Christmas memories, our losses are made greater. Our favourite people are missing. We *miss* them. The pain can be physical. For most of the year, we are forced to disconnect, just a little, in order to survive. But at Christmas, we watch all the same films, listen to all the same music, do all the same things we did with them. It is a form of re-connection, and though it makes their loss more real, I have taught myself to welcome the ache.

Mum and I have watched *The Muppet Christmas Carol* every Christmas Eve since the first year I saw it – with Will, at the cinema. The film was the first made by the Henson company after Jim's sudden death aged fifty-three. His son Brian directed it. It is a love letter to a lost father, recognition of the importance of connection in the face of life-blitzing loss. It is a message of hope for happiness despite life's cruelties, and it came into my life just after Dad died, at exactly the moment I needed it. Well done, Brian. Thank you, Charles.

'Thank you, Mum.' The hug was a long one. She cried. Then I lugged my suitcase and an extra bag, full of the presents she had given me, on to the train for London. When I looked up, she was waving. She always waved until she couldn't see me any more.

I turned to the book she had bought me, *Olive Kitteridge*, a novel also about the importance of connection and about how little we see or value it, and indulged in some fiction. A hot chocolate and some time with the deliciously curmudgeonly Olive was welcome escapism from the real world. A world in which I was single, unemployed and no closer to getting answers to how the tabloids knew so much. I had begun wishing I lived in Olive's New England town. Anyone else's life would do.

Then, on a bright day in the first week of January . . .

Ping – an email from Nick Davies.

From: Nick Davies
Sent: 09 January 2010, 09:20
To: Jenny Evans
Subject: Re: RE:

Hi Jen,

You still free to do some research? I need somebody to help me for a couple of weeks.

Needs to be somebody who's good at calling up strangers and persuading them to talk. If they happen to have a sledge and a team of huskies, I guess that might be useful.

I hope you're well.

Nick

x

I called him. As we spoke, I realised my legs were shaking again. This was it. Not only was he still investigating phone hacking, but he had also amassed information from multiple sources about other forms of unlawful information gathering.

He said he felt he could not let the story go for two reasons. Firstly, because every time he tried, the tabloids, the police, someone in parliament either minimised or denied his findings. Secondly, because there was a general election on the horizon, and Andy Coulson, head of communications for the Conservative Party, might soon be Andy Coulson, head of communications for the government. If he was dishonest, if some kind of cover-up had happened, if that cover-up involved corruption of some sort, then at this point, it massively fucking mattered. *And if phone hacking happened as far back as when I reported my crime, it might explain what happened to me*, is what I didn't say. Nick sent me a memo to get me up to speed.

> *I'm not advertising the fact that I'm writing this book, just because the* News of the World *are quite unpleasant and I don't want to provoke them into any bad behaviour in which they are not already indulging.*

He told me anything explosive we discovered would not be saved for the book but printed in the *Guardian*. Regardless, he was looking for information of two kinds:

> *First, raw facts which can be given to us deeply off the record in conversations which, we can all agree, have never happened.*
> *Second, any kind of concrete evidence which we can put into the public domain to prove that what we are saying is true, whether that takes the form of documents, photos, videos*

or witnesses who are willing to be quoted on the record. Both kinds of info are useful.

He wanted me to speak to current and former *News of the World* employees about use of PIs at the paper and any other 'dark arts':

'blagging' information from confidential databases (bank statements, credit card statements, itemised phone bills, ex-directory numbers, DVLA records, tax records, social security records, medical records);

tapping live phone calls by inserting bugs into BT junction boxes or by using microwave scanners;

inserting listening devices in rooms and cars, sometimes by breaking and entering;

using tracker devices to follow cars;

using hidden miniature cameras to follow movements of targets;

using 'trojan horse' attachments to obtain the contents of a target's computer hard disk;

installing 'mirror walls' in a target's computer to obtain copies of all email traffic;

stealing the contents of dustbins;

paying bribes.

Some of these activities are illegal.

Listening devices, cameras. *I knew it.* I thought back to those moments that I had closed the curtains to the sunshine, searched the windowsills for bugs, argued with Neil about his answering his phone to strange numbers. Neil's frustration, 'I'm a fucking freelancer. I have to take calls!' The distance that grew between us as I withdrew. I remembered how floored I was to read the article in the *News of the World* about the case falling apart.

Nick had information that Glenn Mulcaire, the PI who had been jailed, was not the only PI who worked for the *News of the World*. He had a list of names and what each of their specialisms were. The period of time he was interested in was from 2000 to 2007, the years Rebekah Brooks and Andy Coulson had been editors, because they had denied any knowledge of unlawful information gathering, and Nick already had information that cast doubt over that.

Other names to look out for:

There followed a list of key *News of the World* editors, executives and lawyers during the Coulson years. He moved on to former reporters.

> *Here are the people I'd like you to approach. None of them will be easy . . . It's a question of trying (and of using your mighty powers of persuasion). It's worth being a tiny bit paranoid just in case somebody tries to trap you into saying something compromising on tape . . . Don't worry about this, it's just a question of not saying anything odd which could be twisted into some kind of smear.*

He listed the reporters I should approach.

> There are some others, but that should be enough to take over your life for a while . . .

Little did Nick know how much it already had. This thought – *Nick doesn't know* – buzzed at my head like a fly. If, as I began this research, I asked the odd surreptitious question about my own case, as I hoped to, might one of the reporters, or parliamentary aides, or lawyers, do what Roy Greenslade had done – look into the case, recognise my name and find out I had an ulterior motive? Would it be seen as an agenda? It *was* an agenda. Could it be used to discredit the investigation? '. . . *it's just a question of not saying anything odd which could be twisted into some kind of smear.*'

I made a cup of tea, curled into a spot on the battered green Chesterfield I had bought from Bob for five hundred quid – I don't know where he got it – and stared at the treetops outside my living-room window. This was it. I felt excitement. And I was scared. I had carefully cocooned myself in a good job, authentic friendships, the safety of my flat – my castle. I had the kind of social status I felt shielded me from the scorn and violence of people like The Famous Man. This was a fallacy, of course, but a psychological backstop we can probably forgive. Now, I had decided to lower the drawbridge a little. To allow myself to overcome the fear that I could not stop running towards, and then away from, and back again. To fight.

Part Three:
The Reckoning

25

I began to contact the list of reporters, feeling more Joan Didion than I wanted to admit to myself,

> *I do not like to make telephone calls, and would not like to count the mornings I have sat on some Best Western motel bed somewhere and tried to force myself to put through the call to the assistant district attorney.*
> Slouching Towards Bethlehem.

Cold-calling people, particularly those who are potentially hostile towards you, never gets easier for me. Perhaps some people become used to it. I never have. Not only could my potential sources on this story be assumed to be unreceptive, at best, but they were also journalists of far longer standing and many more wiles than me.

The trick I developed was to write out a kind of 'introductory patter' I could use: 'Hello, my name is Jenny Evans; I am doing some research for Nick Davies at the *Guardian*.' If I got that far and they hadn't hung up, I would continue, 'We are interested in understanding how tabloid newsrooms operate – how they get their news and the dynamics in the room. Do you have time for a cup of tea?'

Some of the reporters were cold, as expected. Some politely but firmly told me to piss off. Some agreed to meet, and when that happened, I gave them a code name, bought them that tea and asked them about their time at the paper. I then wrote up notes for Nick and followed whatever leads they gave.

Nick would sometimes chip in with pointers (teaching me how to 'do journalism', you could say):

From: Nick Davies
Sent: 13 January 2010, 17:35
To: Jenny Evans
Subject:

One thing to keep an eye out for when you're talking to News of the World people is that there is a suggestion that the paper (possibly through Greg Miskiw) had got somebody working inside at least one of the mobile phone companies, either somebody they had placed there as a spy or somebody who worked there who they had persuaded to spy for them. Such a person could provide PIN numbers to help with hacking as well as passing on name and home address and itemised bill of any customer.

The legendarily cunning Greg Miskiw. Miskiw knew everything – all the secrets. He recruited and 'handled' Glenn Mulcaire and other PIs and was unafraid of the 'dark arts'. He was assistant editor for news at this time, having worked at the *News of the World* for many years, and his famous quote about his work is, 'That is what we do – we go out and destroy other people's lives.' Admirable in its honesty? We were desperate to speak to him and, tantalisingly, he did sometimes pick up the phone . . . but then said nothing.

'Hello, Greg? . . . Hello?'

I could hear him breathing, but he would just wait until I gave up. Why was he answering at all? I have since confirmed from experience what I suspected back then – those who pick up the phone, those who agree to meet, have something they want to say, whether they can admit it to themselves or not.

When another former *News of the World* executive gave me the brush-off, Nick had advice about how to go back to him (to anonymise the man in question, I'll just call him John).

> *From: Nick Davies*
> *Sent: 20 January 2010, 21:08*
> *To: Jenny Evans*
> *Subject: Re: Response from [John]*
>
> *Jen,*
>
> *If you haven't already replied to [John]'s brush-off, can you send him a message to indicate that you're having no luck in persuading people to talk? It is highly likely, as we discussed, that he will tell the bad guys of our approach, and I think it would be helpful if they felt unthreatened. If you don't mind doing it, it might help to come on a bit naive and helpless and say that you're not terribly surprised that he said no because that's what everybody seems to be saying and ask if he has any ideas of anybody who might be willing to talk. You could also say that you're coming to the end of a very short period of time working on this and you feel a bit embarrassed because you haven't really come up with anything for me.*

Doing journalism could be fun. He was teaching me some of the tricks, and I was learning where I drew my own red lines in terms of cunning and subterfuge. But I was still capable of being shocked. 'Blagging' I found the most jaw-dropping. A reporter or specialist PI would call up someone's bank, or their doctor, or a psychiatric hospital, if rumour had it a public figure was staying there. They would pretend to be an accountant, say, or a psychiatrist, and request the individual's most private information. Very often, they were able to be so convincing, and had already stolen enough private information to answer security questions, that they would be sent it.

Burned into my brain is the image, as described by a veteran *News of the World* reporter, of the medical records of a venerated British actress arriving line by line in the newsroom, via fax.

26

We met in a cinema lobby.*

'Plausible deniability,' he said. 'If anyone I know comes along, they won't guess you're anything to do with Nick-fucking-Davies.'

'Can I take notes?'

'Write it down *after*.'

We shared weak tea and expensive popcorn on a bright blue, hexagon-shaped bench, surrounded by posters for *The King's Speech*, where I learned that the features department at the *News of the World* stole a woman's medical records and used them to shame and blackmail her. She was an actress. Very famous – a 'national treasure'. Her career had dipped for a couple of decades, but she'd had a comeback. She must have been delighted and incredibly relieved to be earning money and professional accolades, despite an advancing age. So, it was decided at the *News of the World* to 'blag' her medical records.

'But why?' I asked, trying to sound like a seasoned journalist and not someone totally baffled by the world she was uncovering.

---

* All sources have been anonymised and identifying details such as location or gender changed, obscured or swapped. Some interviews have been amalgamated for the same purpose and timelines skewed.

The reporter looked at me like I was a moron.

'Probably just for fun. But also . . . to control her. Woooo.' He waved his hand in the way people do when they are pretending to be spooky, attempting to undermine how seriously he knew I was going to take it.

My mouth must have hung open, because he laughed and nodded, urging me to believe what I was hearing. It got worse.

'You should have seen them dancing with glee,' he said, 'when they found out she'd had *two* abortions . . .'

My eyes filled with tears. *Shit*. I would have hidden that if I could have. 'Because then she was ours.' The way he said this was neither sarcastic nor mocking. It was matter of fact. But then came a deep sigh, the first sign of conscience.

I was trying to remember a story about a famous actress who had had two abortions. I couldn't think of one. As if reading my mind, the source continued, 'Oh, we didn't publish.'

'Why not?'

This is how it worked; the juiciest or potentially most humiliating of secrets that were stolen were not immediately printed in the newspaper. They were passed to the editor, who called the public figure in question, or his or her representatives, to inform them of what the paper 'knew'. They would then offer up a deal along the lines of, 'There's no need for this nasty business to go to print. Perhaps, in exchange for the paper's silence, your client would give an exclusive interview.'

It's textbook mafia intimidation, just as that fool who makes deals with Tony Soprano finds out – once that Faustian pact is sealed, you're trapped. They'll rinse you until your entire sports shop goes bust.

It also didn't help the reporters, who were under pressure to keep their byline count up. 'If your count was lacking you could be in serious trouble, [but the editors] would let reporters or PIs find out some juicy information about someone high-profile and, rather than splash it, which would have furthered the reporter's career, they'd take the nugget to the high-profile person's publicist and negotiate a deal whereby the paper got an exclusive and the story was squashed.'

It occurred to me on the bus home that what this source had described was a protection racket. The tabloids stole your secrets then claimed to be the only people able to keep them, and you, safe. Power by private information. But there was a price – whenever the paper needed extra clicks, or greater sales, *for the rest of a target's life*, they could be called into action. They might be asked to divulge titbits of personal information, or gossip about high-profile figures they were working with. They could be phoned by an editor or executive if they dared to allow a rival tabloid preferential access. 'We had an agreement . . .'

The agreement didn't go both ways, of course, because neither did the power dynamic. Once the high-profile person's fame and associated wealth and influence waned, as fame and its associated wealth and influence almost always does, those secrets were no longer safe. Suddenly the terms of the bargain shifted and the high-profile person who had jumped through all the hoops could find their character carelessly wrecked. *That is what we do – we go out and destroy other people's lives.*

I was learning that tabloids had no qualms about breaking promises, despite making a lot of money from exposing hypocrisy themselves.

It was remorse at breaking a particular promise, however, to a source of his own, that gave me my first glimpse of an apparently 'hard-nosed' *News of the World* reporter's red line. It was related to how he was made to treat a rape victim.

27

I'd met this source a few times. Usually in a greasy spoon in north London, near where he worked. He preferred coffee to tea. I heard from others he would refer to me as 'that *Guardian* bitch', but let's pretend that was just to cover up that he was speaking to me.

He agreed to talk on the same terms as everyone else I had spoken to so far – some information was off the record, so could not be shared. Most was 'unattributable': I could use it, but I had to anonymise the source.

This reporter had a lot of bravado. He told me he generally enjoyed the testosterone-fuelled nature of the *News of the World*. Like many of those who opened up in the early days of this investigation, he did so because he didn't see what they were meant to have done wrong. 'We used any trick in the book to get a story. Was it illegal? Probably. In reality it was what we did.'

He had written for most of the tabloids, across a long career, and all the papers worked in the same way: getting the story by any means was the only important thing. 'We did anything and everything we could.' To succeed, you had to be robust. 'If you can't stand the heat get out of the newsroom.'

For this reason, it was surprising to me that when he began to recall the treatment of a young woman by the *News of the World* – a source of his, a survivor of violence – his fingers began to drum on the table, and his feet to tap with shame.

'The message was: story at any cost. *Make it work* was the phrase thrown at reporters.' He looked up at me. I nodded – I'd heard it before.

'It was all about being as wily as possible. So, we'd promise these girls the earth, you know. All the support. Money. Large sums of money.'

Oh, I knew.

'We'd persuade them to give up their anonymity, and tell their side of the story for money, and we'd say we'd pay them on publication . . .' Here, he lowered his voice along with his gaze. 'Then, once the story was out in the paper, when they asked for the cash, we'd say, "Sorry, love – Clause Eleven."'

'Clause Eleven of . . .?'

'Under Clause Eleven of the Editors' Code, "to the best of your knowledge, this story must be true" – and we don't believe you.'

We don't believe you.

The words struck like hammer blows. I could have curled up into a ball at the horror of them, but I couldn't risk showing my shock in that moment. The source clearly held shame, and I wanted him to keep talking. I allowed my pen a momentary pause, as I made certain I could retain my composure, then carried on scribbling.

The source picked at the skin around his fingernails as he told me, 'We did it to a lass who accused a footballer of rape once. Offered her £100k. Got the story. Didn't pay her.'

Again, he struggled to meet my eye, adding, 'Yeah, hacking really is the tip of the iceberg. The *News of the World* was a horrible place. A diabolical place.'

I asked if there was any police involvement with those kinds of stories. Otherwise, how would the paper get the access? How would they even know about the case, without a tipster – assault and rape victims are anonymous. The cinema source had told me he had seen editors pay police for stories and that this had once led to the suicide of someone accused. 'Did you see the same thing?' The source shook his head. 'But the editors knew everything that went on. Everything. Coulson's such a liar – he was in it up to his earlobes.' (Somehow, one my favourite quotes.)

'All payments were signed off by senior staff. And if they wanted to know how a story was sourced, they got answers.'

Rebekah Brooks, former editor of the *News of the World* and the *Sun*, and in charge when some of my stories were printed, once admitted to a committee of MPs that the papers paid police for stories.* Labour MP Chris Bryant had asked the question and once Rebekah had answered, Andy Coulson interjected with, 'We operate within the [Editors' Code of Practice] and within the law'. He mentioned public interest and aligned possible payments to cops with general use of subterfuge in journalism to uncover a story.

The MPs did not push, perhaps because Coulson seemed so assured in his response, but the truth is it is never within the law to pay police for stories. Sometimes, police and other public servants need to whistle-blow, in the public interest, but accepting money for giving out private information – that's just illegal.

---

* The footage can be found on YouTube.

Brooks did issue a correction:

> *Thank you for... giving me the opportunity to clarify comments I made towards the end of my appearance before the culture, media and sports select committee in March 2003.*
>
> *As can be seen from the transcript, I was responding to a specific line of questioning on how newspapers get information. My intention was simply to comment generally on the widely held belief that payments had been made in the past to police officers.*
>
> *If, in doing so, I gave the impression that I had knowledge of any specific cases, I can assure you that this was not my intention.*

Chris Bryant, the MP who had asked the question, was reportedly threatened directly after asking it. In 2011, he told the *Independent* newspaper that he was approached in Parliament's lobby shortly after the interaction, 'by a senior editorial figure of a popular tabloid' who told him, 'We will have killed you by Christmas.'

There is no suggestion that that person was Rebekah Brooks, or that she knew such a threat was being carried out, but when I asked a different source about this alleged intimidation, she was unsurprised. 'If [tabloid executives] could charm you [they'd] do that first. But [they'd] threaten anybody.'

I was also warned to be very careful. One reporter, who would only talk on the phone – would not meet – told me that a senior journalist at the *News of the World* used a 'PI and villain' in the Midlands to get stories, who had 'done time for beating someone up with a cricket bat'. He described the reporter, his colleague, as 'Thoroughly unpleasant. Corrupt. Disgusting. A decrepit character.'

'What are you saying? Are you warning me? Do you think he would hurt me?'

The source paused to think. Yet again, I realised I had raised my hand to my throat.

'He is powerful, and he is dangerous. He is a scary man, and he will do what he has to do to stop you.'

28

It was an overcast London morning the day I had what Nick calls a 'Hang on a minute' moment investigating this story. He had published work proving that, contrary to what was claimed by News International, it was well known that reporters beyond the disgraced royal reporter knew about PIs and phone hacking.

I was sitting on the top deck of a bus, listening to the *Today* programme on headphones and monitoring news sites, in case the Murdoch camp or the Met made any further moves.

The source I was heading towards had agreed to meet me at the Imperial War Museum, which I had picked at random because it was near his office. It soon became my new favourite meeting spot; walking and talking in public places eradicated the Nick-fucking-Davies factor, as expressed by the cinema lobby source – none of them wanted to risk anyone they knew seeing us talking. Plus, the high ceilings and hushed tones allow for privacy.

The symbolism of the museum, monument to the basest and most ruthless aspects of humanity, was not lost on those I met there. Most raised an eyebrow as I made my way towards them. This man was the first. I laughed. 'This is a battle. It's a battle for the soul of Britain,' I told him.

'OK, Winston Churchill, let's go in.'

'I'd rather be Attlee.'

We made our way around tanks, planes, ghostly uniforms I couldn't think too much about, and discussed the source's time in the *News of the World* newsroom. He had experienced it as an unhappy workplace.

'Can I ask why you agreed to meet me?' I asked.

'Because they're cunts.'

'OK. They are cunts because . . .'

'They tell lies as a matter of course. They screw people over. They treat the staff like shit. The *News of the World* newsroom is a fucking nasty, horrible place. Insidious. Back-stabbing . . .'

I was reminded, as I listened to the detail, of some of my own experiences in TV. One, in particular, had seen me bullied by the presenter – someone with tabloid connections – despite my risking my safety to land the story abroad. 'I used to go in to work every day with a knot in my stomach,' the source told me. 'You were always being judged, every single day. It made decent people behave in very strange ways. No one trusted anyone else.'

A different source explained that reporters who were out of favour at the *News of the World* were publicly humiliated, berated in front of the newsroom: 'Loud bollockings for not very much.'

She described rookie reporters being punished by being sent to cover outlandish stories, sometimes entirely invented by an editor or desk editor. 'Andy insisted one guy jump into the Thames to look for that whale that got stranded that time . . . and they made a reporter who was five months pregnant get in a dinghy and go to the North Sea to look for the whale's family . . .' Getting pregnant was frowned upon, I was told. 'If you had the temerity to do that, they'd try to make your life so unpleasant you'd resign.'

'Did that happen to you?'

'No, but the girl who was pregnant who they told to get in the dinghy was a friend of mine. She pushed back against the desk editor, and he said, "Are you calling to say, I can't do my job? Say it then. Say, 'I can't do my job.'" She got in the dinghy.'

That's when it happened.

Hang on a minute...

Where are the humiliated people? I wondered to myself. *Where are the reporters who were mocked and mistreated and lied to? Where are those who were punished? Where are the bullied? The pissed off? Pissed-off people like to talk.*

Typing up my notes at home, it occurred to me that the reasons most reporters had given for talking could be categorised into:

1) they felt that fellow reporters were being 'thrown under the bus' by cowardly executives keen to save their own skins, and

2) they had been bullied. Tabloid newsrooms were as ruthless as the executives and editors who ran them. They were powered by hierarchy and run on fear.

I had been told that almost every time, but I hadn't seen it, until that moment, as my way in. I called back the cinema source, who had told me about the actress, and asked if he could give me examples of reporters being bullied. 'Is it possible, even, to identify the journalists by the types of stories they were made to write? Can I spot them by their byline?'

He laughed and said something like, 'Look for this: stories when reporters have been sent undercover in shithole sink estates. Punishment. Stories when reporters have been made to dress up. Punishment. Stories when reporters have been made to do stunts. Punishment. Start there.'

That is where I started.

29

The newspaper library in Colindale, in suburban north London, contained a copy of every paper ever published. It was updated each day. The following morning, and many mornings after that, I made myself a cheese and pickle sandwich and a flask of tea, trundled up the Northern Line, handed over a pink slip requesting copies of the *News of the World* from particular dates, and settled in.

At lunchtime, I sat on a bench outside and tried to track down the reporters who had bylines seemingly connected to punishment.

When they agreed to talk, I met them for a tea, gave them a code name and asked for their story. Before we parted, I asked each if they knew of anyone who had been treated any worse than them. Slowly, the mistreated, marginalised and ignored showed up.

'When my mate was pregnant, they sent her to France on a fake story.'

It was as a punishment for something, but the source couldn't remember what. 'Possibly just for being pregnant.'

'It was a five-hour drive. She started bleeding and called the desk editor who had sent her, in tears . . .'

I asked for his name. It was the same guy who had requested the woman who was five months pregnant get into the dinghy in the North Sea.

'He told her she had to keep going. If she did not, she would receive a verbal warning. When she got there, he told her it was the wrong location. She had to drive for another seven hours. She did it, although she just needed to be in hospital. When she finally got to the second location, she called the desk editor and he said, "Oh no sorry, there's no one for you to meet in France after all."'

It was just a power trip. Bullying. That desk editor in particular was singled out by multiple sources. 'We all know they're bastards, but there's no bigger bastard than [him].'

This man was described to me as an intellectual and journalistic 'lightweight', who got so far in his career because, 'he did what the bosses told him'. He had a particular mentor in Neil Wallis, I was told. Coulson's deputy.

Often, between themselves, the reporters laughed at the desk editors, who lorded so much power over them. The name of one in particular came up a lot. 'He tried to give himself the nickname "Love Rat" even though no one else wanted to call him that. He used to tell new people that was what he was known as, when it wasn't. He even changed his own pigeon-hole name to that.'

Another said, 'He was an absolute bloody liar. He couldn't stop himself... He told me he had trialled for Blackburn Rovers youth team *and* Ipswich Town youth and that both times he had scored the winning goal, in the closing minutes of the game, with an overhead kick.'

But many also said that these editors were genuinely scary; if they compulsively lied, you never knew where you were with them. If they shouted or humiliated you, you never felt safe. One in particular knew some very scary people, 'Mates with [south London gangsters] Dave Courtney and Kenny Noye. He hero-worshipped gangsters. He would use them to get stories. He fell out with Reggie Kray, who he used to visit regularly, because the *Screws* [an old nickname for the *News of the World*] printed something he had been told in confidence. It was just before Ronnie's funeral. Reggie refused to speak to him after that.'

Working from home, another source who would only speak to me on the phone told me a different story about this man. About his publicly berating a reporter of far longer standing than him, older, who had far more respect within the newsroom.

'This reporter requested time off to care for his kids. His wife had been diagnosed with terminal cancer and he needed to be with his family. The desk editor told him, "No. *You're* not ill. No time off."'

The source's voice filled with emotion as he remembered the scene. 'Did the reporter stay?' I asked.

'Yes. But he sat at his desk, with his head in his hands, and he just sobbed.'

The source paused and sighed. 'It was so unusual for any of us to dare to show any real emotion, let alone a long-standing, seasoned old hack like that guy. No one knew what to do.'

I found that I increasingly needed a little time, and fresh air, to process these conversations. Travel to and from meetings was very useful to gather my thoughts. If I was at home, I'd head out at dusk and get as close to nature as I could, often jogging round a nearby cemetery. When I ran out of steam, I'd wander the gravestones, reading the names of those whose time is spent, musing on all the different ways to live a good life. The sensation that had gripped me when Will died – that I was living for both of us and could not waste time, because time is a luxury – still held power.

Do we all think we are leading good lives, even when we are not? I pondered as I wandered the graveyard after the conversation about the reporter who had cried. I picked ivy and split it down the centre with my thumbnail, something I have been attempting to do perfectly since I was a child. *Even when we are cruel, or vindictive, or corrupt, do we find a way to tell ourselves we are good?*

One source, commenting on morality at the *News of the World*, had recently described a senior reporter's approach as 'the box method'. This man had apparently told him, 'If I have any problems, I put them in a box in my head and I bury the box.' Denial. It can be very useful.

It was getting dark. *But do we always know the truth underneath?* I wondered, as I started to run again, towards home *Or . . . do some people really just not care?*

30

10 a.m. Battersea Park.

I had suggested it because I discovered when I first spoke to the source that we both loved dogs but that neither of us was in a position to own one. 'Good for dog watching,' I told her, as we met at the gates.

She nodded, in a muted way – rightly wary of me. We hadn't been able to talk for long before, because she was on deadline, but she had told me, 'I was so badly treated at the *News of the World* it nearly drove me to a breakdown.'

I wasn't sure whether to relax her by self-disclosing a little, so that it wasn't only her who was showing vulnerability, or simply to wait. She had surely met me with an idea of what she wanted to say.

'I realise this is difficult,' I said in the end. The source looked at me. It was as if she was trying to work out if I could possibly know. To my surprise, she said, 'It will be hugely unfair if they dump all this on Greg [Miskiw].'

I nodded. 'You liked Greg?'

'Yes. He wasn't as bad as the rest of them.'

'Can you tell me what you mean by "as bad"?'

'The *News of the World*'s public interest threshold is very low . . . Illegal, immoral, hypocritical.'

'Do you mind if we sit down, so I can take notes?'

The reporter had worked for both news and features. 'What kind of stories did you cover?'

'Posing as a hooker, buying drugs, getting in with people who commit crimes. We were kind of vigilantes. Almost doing police work.' She seemed proud of this.

'I used to have a letter with me with *News of the World* headed paper, dated and signed by a lawyer, in case I got in trouble.' She laughed, but it was clear there was some disbelief that she took such risks at that time. She had only been young.

'Were you safe?' I asked.

A wan smile – again, partly amused, partly incredulous. 'I got left on the side of a road at midnight once, so the senior reporter could go back to the sex party we had secretly filmed, to have more sex without the camera there. Pitch-black night. Essentially dressed like a hooker. That happened to a friend of mine too, more than once.'

We sat on a bench, the smell of autumn in the air, wet leaves beneath our boots. The source picked at the paint flaking from the wood. 'The police said I got really lucky once . . .' She cleared her throat. 'They actually said I had been a very silly girl.'

'I'm so sorry,' I replied, sensing the sadness in her and feeling a little anger rising in myself. 'Because that is so fucking patronising, and because it sounds like you were maybe put in danger . . .?'

'We turned over a pimp. I needed to get the escort agency bods on tape, and I did it and then the paper involved the police, and they nicked [the main guy] on his street that Sunday as the story came out . . .'

'So, the police knew what you were doing?'

'It was a case of you scratch my back, I'll scratch yours. We'd pursue the story and then at the eleventh hour, for extra kudos and drama, we'd involve the police and take photos of the arrest.'

I made a mental note to come back to that. It hadn't landed for me before that the *News of the World* and the police actively worked together. There is a strong argument for public servants whistle-blowing to, or even working with journalists, but only in the public interest.

'Why were you so lucky with the pimp?'

The source had posed as a potential sex worker looking for a job to get this man on tape.

'The police said, "He's just had a heart bypass. Before that, he used to ask [new workers] for a blow job." The police thought it was too risky to send a policewoman in for that reason.'

'So, you did vigilante police work, in effect, because the police had more stringent rules than the newspaper around safety? Or – women's safety?'

It seemed like it was her turn to properly hear something for the first time. The paper had allowed her to be unsafe. Her face dropped and I resisted the urge to find a positive spin, choosing instead to sit with her in her sorrow. I felt it too. The fact was, the more senior reporters, the male reporters, had never been in as much danger as they had let my source and her female colleagues be in.

'Why do you think they did that?' I asked eventually.

She looked at me, raised an eyebrow, then raised one hand, rubbing her fingers together to show she meant money – newspaper sales.

'Money is power,' I said.

'I remember once, a chief inspector called the paper because he wanted help IDing a rapist. Out of courtesy we did a double-page spread. Three people identified him by name, and he was arrested. The police were very grateful. Good for us, good for them.'

'You really did work together. Did you ever see anyone pay the police?'

She shook her head. 'It wasn't as crass as that, from what I saw. It was favour for favour. Although ultimately that does put money in the newspaper's pocket, of course.'

She went on, 'There were certain policemen at the top level who were very good friends with the *News of the World*.'

'Can you give me any names?'

She shook her head. We sipped our tea. Rain clouds threatened. 'Do you know about the Posh and Becks kidnap?'

I did know. In 2002, the *News of the World* had splashed on the Met arresting a group of men alleged to have planned to kidnap Victoria Beckham and her children. They had been caught on tape discussing it, and this tape had been shared with the police. The story sold a lot of papers and was considered a career high for Mazher 'Maz' Mahmood, otherwise known as 'the Fake Sheikh', the *News of the World's* chief undercover reporter.

Legal action by the men accused would later reveal that the entire thing was set up by Maz. Entirely invented to sell papers. He reportedly paid an agent provocateur £10,000 to encourage some young men he knew to start talking about the kidnap as a means of making money. He tape recorded it, as requested by Maz. That was the basis of the 'investigation'. So intent was Maz on making money from his fabrication, he was prepared to send to prison the innocent men he had set up. *That is what we do – we go out and destroy other people's lives.*

The trial collapsed, inevitably, and when many years later I spoke to the barrister who represented one of the accused, a man who also represented a separate cohort of innocent men Maz framed, his opening line to me was, 'Mazher Mahmood is a cunt.' That word lands so well when it's unexpected.

In the end, Maz's lies caught up with him. He was jailed himself, for tampering with witness evidence in a drugs entrapment scam involving popstar Tulisa Contostavlos. Another 'story' he had entirely set up to destroy her, to sell papers, and it nearly worked.

Roy Greenslade, my ethics tutor at City, had made it a mission to expose Maz's entrapment practice. The articles he wrote made up a chunk of my *Tabloids General* ring binder.

Most of the time, Maz set people up, used his team to put pressure on them to do illegal things, recorded it, then exposed them. It was frightening in its ruthlessness; it was not journalism. But the *News of the World*, the press regulator, the Press Complaints Commission (PCC) – which was largely run by the tabloids as well – and the rest of Fleet Street pretended it was. A rotten media landscape passed off as some kind of Turner classic.

Why didn't the police investigate any of this? I had marvelled when I first read Roy's exposé of Maz. My work with Nick was giving me some insight into that. Two words: Vested interests. When I reflected on how little I understood of the closeness of the Met and the tabloids' relationship before I reported my crime, I winced. Two more: Lamb. Slaughter.

31

One of the bullied who was prepared to talk early on was former *News of the World* showbiz reporter Sean Hoare. More than one person told me the story of part of his nose falling off onto his desk one day at the office, because he'd taken so much coke.

Sean was infamous, even for Fleet Street, for overindulging in the celebrity lifestyle he was meant to be reporting. In another of the many hypocrisies I was uncovering, reporters often took coke at the same time as ruining other people's lives for doing the exact same thing.

When Sean became addicted and could no more be of use, the paper dropped him, though one source told me Andy Coulson tried for a while to help him. I guess, if a person isn't functioning due to drug and alcohol addiction, it is fair enough that they should be asked not to come into work.

Whether they should first be made to stand in a Perspex box, in a nappy, for the same length of time as David Blaine attempted his famous stunt over the Thames, is questionable, however.*

So marginalised had Sean become, and so hurt by his alienation from the newspaper he had given so much of himself to, he was

---

* Sean reportedly broke out of the box to buy himself 'refreshments' and the stunt had to be abandoned, so hopefully he felt he had the last laugh.

one of the first to agree to speak on the record. First, to *the New York Times*, when it published a phone-hacking investigation in late 2010, then to Nick. Before he could detail the illegal practices he had witnessed at Murdoch newspapers for Nick, however, he unexpectedly died, sparking a raft of conspiracy theories.

'Did you know Sean Hoare?' I asked the next reporter who agreed to speak. 'A bit.' He told me the nose falling off story. 'Do you think he was bullied?' I asked. The reporter pulled a face that said he didn't know or didn't care.

'The *News of the World* was a horrible place. A diabolical place. The [desk heads] were all slippery. Slimy. You only get to that position by being a cunt.'

'That's what I'm hearing.'

'The biggest bully was [a particular desk head]. But they loved him.'

'Because . . .?'

'Because he knew dark arts.'

'Which ones?'

'Well, he was greeted with a hero's welcome [in the newsroom] for getting hold of [a prominent TV presenter]'s "friends and family" numbers.' These were mobile numbers of people most regularly called from a landline, which British Telecom (BT) gave a discounted rate to for a while in the noughties. 'That was how they knew she was having an affair.'

'Did you question it? *How* he got the numbers? Whether he *should* have?'

The source looked at me like I was stupid. 'I thought it was amazing. He had paid someone at British Telecom for the information and everyone thought it was genius. It didn't cross my mind how illegal it was.'

I met this man in Canary Wharf, a smoothly concrete part of London's financial district. It is so manmade as to look unreal, somehow, like a film set. Like architects' drawings breathed straight into life.

We walked as we talked, looking out over the tumbling grey of the river. With men, it can be easier to get them to open up when they don't have to make eye contact.

'Did you know about other dark arts?'

'I was a desk bod, so I never really got involved with the actual mechanics of these things.' Most sources, understandably, admitted to seeing but not doing. As one memorably said, 'No [reporter] can risk sticking their head above the parapet. They risk going to jail.'

'So, I never dealt directly with PIs,' he continued, 'but I knew about them. We all did. Hacking was the tip of the iceberg. The newsroom was, for many years, able to get criminal records checks done via the police national computer. That stopped after Neville Thurlbeck [the chief news reporter] was charged with corruption and stood trial at St Albans. He was acquitted. Draw your own conclusions.'

We paused to watch a couple of pigeons scrat about for food before us, pink feet expertly picking the best bits out from the cracks in the paving.

'I knew nothing about phone hacking until the Clive Goodman case and by that time I had left the *News of the World*,' he continued. 'I think every journalist knows that it is possible to access mobile voicemail by using the default security setting used by the phone manufacturers, but I never did it and was not specifically aware of anyone else doing so.

'As far as I was aware, the PIs were blagging information, or using contacts to get ex-directory numbers, car details from DVLA, addresses from utility companies, etc. Nothing too sinister.'

Nothing too sinister. Unless you're a supposedly anonymous victim of sexual crime.

'There was a woman [deputy head of news] Greg [Miskiw] used for blagging. She is a former journalist but I can't recall her name. She was a very good blagger. I recall asking Greg how on earth he managed to get hold of medical records. He whispered something about this particular woman. Black arts and so on.'

'Do you have any proof for any of this? Did you keep tapes or logs, receipts for payments to people who shouldn't have been paid?'

The source shook his head. 'I didn't keep any logs, sorry. The only other thing I can tell you about is the corrupt officials that the *News of the World* had on side.'

'From where?'

'Well. There was a civil servant who would root around in the records at the passport office, a tax official who would do the same thing at the Inland Revenue, someone at the office in Holborn where divorce records and wills are kept. These people tended to be paid in cash, with all the payments signed off by Stuart Kuttner . . . he was ruthless, a good journalist, I liked him.' Kuttner worked at the *News of the World* from 1980 until 2009, first as deputy editor, then as managing editor. A post he held for twenty-two years. Many sources mentioned his tight control of, and forensic focus on, the paper's finances, asking reporters to account for every snack, every cup of tea.*

'[JS] was the name of the person you called if you wanted to find an address. For a couple of hundred quid, she'd find you someone fast. All the tabloids used her.' The source gave me her number. 'There was also a guy in Essex – ex-cop. He could credit check

---

* Kuttner also signed off hundreds of thousands of pounds in payments to private investigators. He has always denied knowing the true nature of all the payments he approved.

people for us. There were definitely others, but talk of dark arts was mostly kept between the top people.'

'I see what you mean about tip of the iceberg.'

He laughed. 'We did everything. We even did Rebekah's phone.'

'Why?'

'Why not?'

It made logical sense, if you trust nobody, to watch everybody, I guess.

'Did you like Rebekah?'

The source sighed. 'Yes. She was ambitious and clever and I liked that. But you would put nothing past that girl. She was really, really good at her job, nothing slipped by her. She didn't claw her way up by being dumb, by not checking her sources. If you pitched her something at conference, she would definitely have asked how the story was got.'

The *News of the World* was a Sunday tabloid, so Monday was quiet in the office and 'conference', where ideas were discussed for next week's issue, was held on Tuesdays. It would be attended by the editor, the lawyers, the PR team, the heads of departments and all reporters, though not everyone was in the room all of the time. Most people were in and out of the meeting, according to what was being discussed.

'We sat round a table and one by one had to pitch stories.' I had returned to my Battersea Park contact to double source this information. I trusted her. We met on another misty morning. Hug. Tea. Walk. Bench. Smile at the dog walkers (smile at the dogs).

'Conference was more difficult for the non-phone hackers than the others, because we didn't have access to the same volume of celebrity gossip. [Love Rat] would be taking notes, and often his response to an idea would just be, "Shit." Regardless of what was pitched, we would usually receive an email from him a few minutes after the meeting saying they were the worst ideas he had ever heard and that he wanted another three ideas from everyone.'

'He sounds like a bully,' I commented, hoping I was adequately reflecting what she wanted me to hear.

'I honestly think he was deeply affected by being bald.' She laughed. Then, she was serious. 'There were so many bullies. The company cultivated an aura of fear. It's actually good to talk about it.'

'Do you wish you hadn't worked there?'

'Honestly, sometimes it felt like being the Queen. There was a time when the *News of the World* gave all their young, female reporters swanky cars and thousands of pounds in cash to buy up stories. The "girls" used to swoop down in convoy, all high heels, glossy hair, designer handbags and big smiles, and nobody else – no other tabloids – stood a chance.'

'Is there a but . . .?'

'Well. There was my friend who once or twice refused to go on jobs, which is something you just didn't do, and it meant [Love Rat] hated her. Once, she called in sick, so he took the opportunity to go to her house and knock on her front door. When she answered, he told her she didn't look ill and sacked her.

'Another mate was having problems with her pregnancy and told someone on the news desk she had been advised not to drive. He said, "OK, but you do have to drive to Brighton. Now." And when she got there, same old story, he told her the job had been cancelled and she had to drive back.'

'I'm so sorry.'

She shrugged this time. 'Sometimes I think, OK there is a bullying culture, but you sign up for it. It's not that bad and the expenses are good.'

'OK.' I could understand that, when seeing it through her eyes. Others had also presented me with the counter narrative for working for these very powerful newspapers. Literally, sex, drugs and rock 'n' roll. I got it – life is complicated, people and workplaces can be both good and bad, enjoyable and stressful.

I was nodding, but the same fog of sorrow settled over the source. 'In retrospect, there was a lot of immoral things that we did. I have got morals, but . . .'

'We all have elements of our past we wish we could change,' I offered. 'There are so many times I wish I had asked more questions.'

She seemed to listen to this intently. We sat in silence for a short while, before she almost whispered, 'We were made to make up quotes. Manipulate stories.'

I knew this, of course, from Roy's reporting of Maz, and other sources had told me it was commonplace, but I hadn't seen anyone else show this level of remorse.

'One executive used to stand behind us and dictate copy. He thought, if he had paid for a story, it gave you carte blanche to put any words in [the source's] mouths. And [a deputy editor on the *News of the World*] would hear what a source really said and then ask, "Can we say . . .?" to try to change it to fit the story he wanted.'

God.

'And you'd protest and they'd say, "Make it work."'

'My boss once rang me at five a.m. screaming that my copy was "shit" because I had taken out the made-up bits he had dictated. He told me the story wasn't worth the sum we had promised the source and I had to renegotiate. It was highly embarrassing. It had taken me a long time to get the source to trust me and I had come to like her.'

'What did you do?'

'I tricked him into paying what we owed by saying the source had more information to give us and spreading the original information over two weeks.'

'Clever.'

'Yeah. But I got a verbal warning.'

She decided this was so unfair she would complain to the editor, Coulson. He knew what she wanted, so he left her sitting outside his office for nearly five hours, to let her know whose side he was on. She watched others come and go, and saw Coulson himself spinning in his chair, seemingly making a point of doing nothing other than not inviting her in.

A verbal warning, punishment and bullying for not agreeing to fake content and trying to report being made to do so.

32

My conversations with these sources stayed with me. The knot of anger remained in my gut, but fear was ever-present too. At night, certain words, specific sentences from interviews, ran through my head as I tried to process the scale of misogyny, the level of vindictiveness I was hearing. I was particularly distracted by the complex and long-standing nature of the Murdoch press's relationship with the Metropolitan Police. It was mutually beneficial for both brands to keep the truth of this out of the public domain. If only a fraction of what I was hearing about the extent of their collaboration could be proved to be true, long careers on each side stood to be wrecked. Was the corruption already so well hidden that it would be impossible to substantiate? Were the people who perpetrated it so powerful they could not be touched?

Like lifting a log to reveal a nest of woodlice, these kinds of details give us a glimpse of the hidden power connections in the UK. I knew that exposing this stuff – talking about it – was why this story mattered. I was rediscovering with every meeting the reasons that transparency matters, accountability matters, public interest matters. But it didn't help me sleep.

I would throw off my duvet. Grab it back again. Turn my pillow over for the cold side. Put on some music. Turn it off. Then, find myself sitting up and typing madly into my laptop things like,

> *If we allow ruthless people unfettered power, which they have acquired through stealing private information and generating fear and have used that to make money, which gives them more power – we lose independence. Not just of the institutions of state, but also of our democracy. This is oligarchy.* <u>*Who runs this country, really?*</u>

Once these streams of consciousness were out of my system, I might finally drift off. But the next night, the thoughts would return and I'd have to do it again – my hair in bird's nests from the tossing and turning, my face hot with the adrenaline of fear.

Historian David Olusoga put the sentiments I was processing far more eloquently in a 2023 *Observer* article about Meghan and Harry:

> *Tabloid rule is rule by intimidation. It has long rested on the presumption that no one – not even the royals – would dare to stand up to the papers.*

How brave Prince Harry is.

Rereading my slightly crazy 'night notes' is what gave me the courage to go out the next day to try to get more, despite the fear and the increasing exhaustion. The fact I was still keeping my own agenda a secret did not help. With every new link I made, every reporter to whom I gave my name, the threat of exposure increased.

What if someone discovers my history? Will they expose me? Will they use me to discredit Nick?

And yet – though I was finding out a lot of useful information, I hadn't found out who stole *my* secrets, or how. And the truth is, I partly kept going because I still wanted to know.

33

'Nice.' The source nodded, sarcastically, as we entered the War Museum.

He had worked at the *News of the World* for a long time and I was amazed he had agreed to the meeting.

'Was working at the *News of the World* frightening?' I asked.

'As frightening as this place?'

I gave an apologetic shrug.

'Yes. Greg Miskiw, the news desk editor, was ruthless. But the man above him, Alex Marunchak, could be fucking terrifying. He wouldn't shout at you, if he thought you'd in some way humiliated him in front of the editor or something, but he'd sidle over and whisper threats to you through gritted teeth. He seemed very well connected in the police.

'Can you give me any names?'

'Sid Fillery. Once Catford CID, left the police to become a PI.'

Not an uncommon career move. I asked the source the usual questions about his time in the newsroom: the characters he met, the stories he worked on, use of the dark arts. As with almost every other, he gave me very useful insights and more names and details to follow. Typing up my notes, I googled cop-turned-PI Sid Fillery, saw a photo of him and went cold. *The grey-suited man.* The man who knocked on my door, when The Famous Man was charged, when my details were ex-directory. I was sure. The man who looked up as I tried to hide behind a curtain, but saw my face.

What the fuck is going on here?

I knew I'd heard Fillery's name before, I just hadn't ever seen his picture. Keyword searching my computer revealed nothing, so I made tea and searched my old notebooks: a library of identical black Moleskines I keep stored in a cupboard in an old apple crate.

I finally found Fillery's name next to that of a solicitor contact of mine, Glyn Maddocks. Glyn is from the same part of Wales as me. Alongside his work across a range of disciplines in the small firm in which he worked for thirty years, he spent much of his spare time exposing and challenging miscarriages of justice. Acting pro bono for those fighting to clear their name. It is a passion that has seen him awarded an honorary KC.

The date scrawled on the front page of the notebook told me that about a year before, Glyn and I had been discussing the prospect of a documentary about the UK's most investigated unsolved murder – that of private investigator Daniel Morgan, who was found with an axe in the back of his head in a south London car park in 1987.

Morgan's mother was from Hay-on-Wye. When he was murdered, it was Glyn, as a prominent local solicitor, who represented their interests at his inquest. It was the family's belief that the Met Police was implicated in Daniel's murder and that the force had managed an immediate cover-up of such dexterity that it was already impossible to seek justice for Daniel.

The story is long, complicated and well documented, but in short – Daniel had run a PI firm called Southern Investigations with a man named Jonathan Rees. No one knows why he was murdered after meeting Rees one evening, but one of the many theories is that he had threatened to expose corruptions including drug dealing run from a police station in south London.

Despite extensive journalistic investigation and an independent inquiry that concluded that the Met Police were 'institutionally corrupt', we still do not know who killed Daniel Morgan, nor why. Sid Fillery was, at one point, part of the murder investigation team and was later charged with perverting the course of justice, but the prosecution was dropped and he received substantial compensation. A trial involving other defendants had to be abandoned.

Fillery retired from the police shortly after Morgan's murder and took his place at Southern Investigations, alongside Rees. Theirs was one of the PI firms favoured by the *News of the World*.

In 2000, Rees was jailed for planting cocaine on a woman, employed by her ex-husband, as part of an acrimonious divorce. He was sentenced to six years, but was nevertheless put on a retainer by Andy Coulson at the *News of the World* as soon as he was released.

In 2003, Fillery was arrested for making indecent images of children. He pleaded guilty and was handed a community rehabilitation order.

Again, my sleep became disturbed as I wrestled with anxiety around the depths of the *News of the World*'s criminal links. Was it the paper's greatest hypocrisy to have made its name exposing criminality, when, according to my sources, it was so embedded, not just with gangsters – *just* – but with the seediest of police corruption and, by extension, even murder? No wonder the reporters Nick and I were speaking to, who had had a glimpse of the reality of this operation, were too frightened to speak on the record. For the second time in my life, I became aware of my phone seeming to make strange noises, to echo and click. It cut out a lot.

My mobile was stolen from my hand as I walked out of the Tube towards home one evening. The green shoots of paranoia returned. *News International surely know about me by now.*

Most of what I was getting was good information – each source corroborated the next – but if no one would talk openly, the investigation risked being dismissed as insubstantial. This is what John Yates had already done, when announcing his decision not to re-open an inquiry after Nick's July 2009 article. And his statement had led to Rebekah Brooks's open letter accusing the *Guardian* of attempting to deliberately misinform the British public.

One reporter warned that a systematic deletion of emails was in operation across the *Sun* and the *News of the World*. Everything was being erased, even as Murdoch HQ announced it was investigating Nick's allegations: it had appointed a law firm to go in to search for evidence of criminality. News Group Newspapers has always maintained that the timing of the deletions was coincidental and that it was merely tidying up its archives.

Whatever the truth behind the deletions, if we were going to unearth evidential proof, we had to find another way in.

34

From: Nick Davies
Sent: 13 January 2010, 16:30:35 +0000
To: Jenny Evans
Subject: Victims

Jen,

I know you're busy and have plenty to do already, but, if and when some time opens up, I'd like you to have a look at another route into this story, by contacting people who we believe may have been victims of phone hacking or other forms of illegal surveillance by Glenn Mulcaire or any other investigator working for the News of the World.

The pitch is to ask them if they have been approached by Scotland Yard to be warned that they were victims of Glenn Mulcaire's hacking. If so, very interesting. If not, you can tell them that, although they have given this absolutely no publicity at all, Scotland Yard, in the wake of my stuff in the Guardian in July, have gone through all the paperwork and computer records and tape recordings which they seized from Mulcaire and have created a database on which they have listed all of the masses *of names of people whose names show up in Mulcaire's material, together with a summary of the material which he held on each of them. So it might say 'Prince Harry. Mobile number. PIN code. One recording of a message.' And the point is that if they are asked formally in writing by a public figure or somebody acting on their behalf, the Yard will hand over the summary in relation to them, without the need for a court order and without any publicity. A lot of people who I've contacted had not realised that they could do this and have now written off and will, I hope, come back to me if they do discover that they are in there. Those who do find that there is evidence in Mulcaire's material that he may have been hacking them can then choose to sue the News of the World and Mulcaire, but that's an optional extra.*

From our point of view, the importance of gathering evidence of further victims is two-fold, a) every extra victim is further evidence that the original official version of this story was not true; and b) the more victims there are, the less credible it is that Mulcaire could have been operating without the knowledge and consent of senior execs at the News of the World.

I've done quite a lot of work contacting lawyers who act for public figures, and that may yield some info. But there are a few names I have not chased down – generally people who we know have been the victims of aggressive stories in the News of the World. I'm not expecting you to be able to go to them direct, but if you can get to a PR person or lawyer, that'd be marvie.

There followed a list of famous names, including former England football manager Sven-Göran Eriksson, TV executives, celebrity chefs, sportspeople, actors, criminals and musicians.

At the bottom were three names I knew; 'X', a young woman I had discovered via my own investigation may have been a victim of phone hacking. She, too, had accused a high-profile man of sexual violence. There was also an actor who had been in *Coronation Street* and who happened to be a friend, and, making my cheeks flush and my head swim, the name of The Famous Man. There was no way I was contacting his lawyer, but once I had calmed down a bit, I saw my opportunity – if he was hacked, surely I'd been hacked too.

I used my connections with my *Corrie* friend and 'X' as cover when I replied to Nick,

> On 13 Jan 2010, at 18:45, Jenny Evans wrote:
> Do you know who they should write to at Scotland Yard?
>
> From: Nick Davies
> Sent: 13 January 2010, 18:47:01 +0000
> To: Jenny Evans
> Subject: Re: Scot Yard
>
> To [redacted], director of legal affairs at New Scotland Yard

OK. Deep breath.

> From: Jenny Evans
> Sent: 14 January 2010, 14:51
> To: [Redacted]
> Subject: Glenn Mulcaire phone hacking
> FAO: Legal Affairs Dept, New Scotland Yard.
>
> I have reason to believe that my phone may have been hacked by someone in the employ of tabloid newspapers, possibly by Glenn Mulcaire.

I was involved in a high-profile court case and the tabloid media became such a hindrance that I was moved from my home and to a hotel where they weren't supposed to be able to find me, but they did. Certain other information alluding to my identity was also printed in the press, despite the CPS granting me the protection of life-long anonymity. This information can only have either been leaked by a police officer or picked up via some form of bugging or surveillance technique.

I understand you have created a database listing all the people whose names show up on Mulcaire's material, together with a summary of the material which he held on each person.

I would like to request all information you have recovered from his, or any PI's files, about me.

I can be contacted at this email address or on my mobile at any time – [number redacted].

Many thanks for your time

All best wishes,

Jenny

I pressed 'Send' and stood up in shock. What had I done? What had I started? Trying to talk myself down, I told myself I hadn't started anything much. Yet. I hadn't lost control of any information. I only needed to make another move if my name was in those notebooks. And maybe I wouldn't need to make another move at all. But – yet again – I was scared.

When you have been sexually assaulted, the thing that stays with you the longest is the fear. A shard of fear lodges in your heart like shrapnel when you realise what is about to happen to you (or when you understand what has happened to you, without you knowing). It is a visceral fear, an I-might-die (or might have been killed) fear and somehow, regardless of how much you move on, a sliver of it stays.

Perhaps it is associated with the shock – when someone is unexpectedly violent towards you, it isn't the physical pain you feel first, it is a cold shower of shock. Perhaps it is associated with confusion – you didn't realise you were unsafe, so you can't know how to ensure you are ever fully safe again. Perhaps it is associated with justice – to feel that justice has been done is to feel protected.

I began to feel I needed protection, but I didn't know where to turn. Nick had asked me, in the course of the investigation, to try to speak to a female lawyer who had a couple of clients who might have been hacked. Her name was Tamsin Allen and her specialism combined media law with human rights.

I wanted to meet her, hopeful that I would be able to get the words out more easily over a cup of tea and, worried about a paper trail, I didn't want to email. Of course, if you contact a lawyer to ask advice as a potential client, rather than as a journalist, it makes the exchange privileged – entirely confidential – but I was rookie enough at this stage not to understand that.

Tamsin wasn't in the office when I tried to call. I didn't want to leave a message. I tried a few times over the next few days, but each time was passed to an assistant who said she was busy – in court, maybe? I can't remember. So, in the end, I stopped trying to get hold of her for advice and carried on with my work.

35

The Met took three months to respond to my email.

From: [Redacted]@metpolice.uk
Sent: Mon, 22 Mar 2010 13:17:17
To: Jenny Evans
Subject: Your request for disclosure

Dear Ms Evans,
We have now completed a search of all the material that was seized as part of our investigation into the intercept activity. There is some documentation in our possession to suggest that you may have been a person of interest to Glenn Mulcaire During the investigation, 2 pieces of paper were found which contained your name Jenny Evans, with mobile telephones 07768 [redacted] and [redacted] written underneath. It appears that these details were attributed to you by Mr Mulcaire. However, there is no documentation in our possession to indicate that these numbers' voicemail messages were unlawfully intercepted.

Should you remain concerned as to whether your communications may have been unlawfully intercepted, may we suggest you contact your phone service provider(s) who may be able to assist further.

Yours sincerely

[Redacted]
Lawyer
Directorate of Legal Services
Metropolitan Police Service

Holy shitting fuck. I looked at the phone numbers attributed to me. The one beginning 07768 looked familiar, but I couldn't remember what my number had been back then – I had swapped a few times to escape the press.

Back came the buzz of the fly – should I tell Nick? I didn't want to. Instead, I asked him what victims should do if they found out they were in the notebooks.

> *The simple answer to your question is that they should contact a very nice and very clever lawyer, called Charlotte Harris, who has been handling a lot of these cases and who will give them good advice...*

Our phone call went something like this:

> *Hi, my name's Jenny and I'm helping Nick Davies with his research into phone hacking. He gave me your number because someone I am in touch with has had a positive response from Scotland Yard – her name appears in a notebook. She is the person who was sexually assaulted a few years ago by [The Famous Man]. What Nick doesn't know is... she is actually me.*

Charlotte said she would meet me at a pub that afternoon. 'You bring the courage, I'll bring the Marlboro Lights.'

Over Diet Cokes and cigarettes, Charlotte – petite, doe-eyed, absolute firebrand – and I hatched a plan to find out exactly what the *News of the World* had stolen from me. The first step was to write a 'Letter Before Claim' to News International, to let them know we knew I had been spied on. We would tell them I intended to start civil proceedings – that is, to make a monetary claim to compensate me for the damage I had been caused. This is how civil justice is administered.

Of course, I didn't want just to make a monetary claim. I wanted also to get some answers. None of the reporter sources could go on the record, but if we could force the executives into a courtroom, they might have to own up. Then, reporters need no longer fear personal recrimination.

Here, Charlotte cautioned me: 'You have to be aware that the civil justice system is not necessarily set up for people to find out the truth.' It is designed to encourage litigants to settle out of court. This removes the prospect of the potential trauma of the court experience, as well as reducing court waiting lists and substantial costs. Indeed, it is considered by the judiciary a waste of court time if a case that might have 'settled' instead comes before them, and this is punishable. If either side, for example, turns down a monetary offer the judge deems to have been fair, that side can be ordered to pay the legal costs of both, which can amount to hundreds of thousands of pounds.

Charlotte stubbed out her cigarette. 'In short, if a good offer is made, you basically have to take it.' She saw my face fall. 'Let me think about this,' she said.

A couple of days later, we made our way through the airport-like security in New Scotland Yard on our way to view my 'Mulcaire papers'. I was nervous but we were both excited. Barely anyone had seen what was in these notebooks before; the Met was still in the process of cataloguing them. My knowledge of Nick's investigation, and the secret investigation I was running of my own, meant I had got in early.

As we waited for our escort, Charlotte told me that if I needed a moment, or some air, anything at all, just to let her know. 'Wave at me, if you can't speak.'

'Why wouldn't I be able to speak?'

'I am with you. Let me know.'

Two plain-clothes officers arrived and invited us into a small room, thinly carpeted, corporately furnished. I was reminded of the rooms I had filmed my police interviews in seven or eight years before. On top of the coffee table were spread A4-sized photocopies of Glenn Mulcaire's notebooks: a mêlée of scribbles, names, email addresses, phone numbers in black biro. Certain details had been redacted.

It took a moment to decipher, then I saw it. There, in black and white, was not just my name but Rachel's: *Twin Town* actress, 'Wine and Chips', recipient of The Letter that led to the collapse of my case against The Famous Man – or, the collapse of my trust in any protection from the criminal justice system. The reason I stopped talking to the police.

Rachel's address and her date of birth had also been scribbled down by Mulcaire. He got my date of birth wrong. Next to my name he had written 'fragile'. Who had told him that? *Or had he heard it in my voice?*

How is this happening? What the fuck is going on here? I began to feel dizzy. *Focusfocusfocus. Think.* I was aware of the policemen looking at me.

Mulcaire could have got my details from court documents, the lead detective told me that, but how did he get Rachel's? *It must have been from my voicemail.*

I grabbed my phone to make copies of the documents, but a policeman stopped me. No duplicates until the investigation had concluded. I didn't understand. Hadn't John Yates already said it had?

I didn't need to wave at Charlotte. We locked eyes, she nodded, thanked the officers for their time and steered me towards the door.

I don't remember leaving Scotland Yard that day, nor saying goodbye to her, nor how I got home. I do recall a bodily urge to be somewhere safe, unobserved, inside. The spying felt like violence.

In behaviour reminiscent of my teenage breakdown, I closed my curtains, turned off my phone and curled up powerless on the bed. What did I think I was doing? I could not take on these men, they would just crush me and move on. They already had.

I had had no notion of the extent of the spying. My central question evolved from *How do they know?* to *How much did they know?* Yet again, shame seeped tar-like from the centre of my body and covered me whole. I was immobilised. I couldn't work.

Journalism requires a certain breezy audacity. Much of the job involves manoeuvring your way, as gently and politely as possible, into the centre of someone's life and asking incredibly sensitive and intrusive questions (questions you hope they don't notice are sensitive or intrusive. Or that they like you so much they don't mind you asking). It is a skill you learn 'doing journalism'.

Generally, in the work I have done, I like my sources. More often than not they have been mistreated in some way. Mostly, the experience of being seen and heard is validating and rewarding for them. Always, I feel deeply privileged to be trusted with the soft underbelly of their personal story. I treat it, and them, with great care. This involves communication beyond words; instinctively, your source needs to know that whatever he or she has to tell you, you can hold, and you have to be able to sense that they are robust enough and ready to tell it. This is the essence of journalism, in my experience. This and a) double-sourcing or seeking evidence and b) asking every question you have three different ways. Try it. You get an answer.

Needless to say, if you are drenched in that slick of shame, you can't connect to people in the same way. None of that is possible.

I couldn't call Mum or Deb. I had been doing so well. I didn't want to worry them. When I managed to get out of bed, I'd lie on the Chesterfield in my pyjamas, eating fish fingers dipped in ketchup. I'd watch old movies, or read the tattered poetry books I'd lugged a hundred times around London since I was a kid.

This might have lasted indefinitely. Seeing my name in the Mulcaire notebooks meant I teetered once more on the edge of The Well. I could feel it and I was frightened by how far I might fall, and how fast. We might now understand this as 'triggered', but I didn't realise then that the shrapnel of fear I felt lodged in my body was unresolved trauma from the assault.

36

It was one of Maya Angelou's works that began to shift the fear in me. I re-found her poem 'Life Doesn't Frighten Me', and one morning, after about two weeks of living, if not inside The Well, then Well-adjacent, and after reading this poem for the hundredth time, I put on my running gear and left the house. As I ran, I listened to the only hymn that Will ever loved, 'When a Knight Won His Spurs'. I had been listening to it every day, desperate to find courage in connection with my brother, my person, always on my side. It is a song about valour, and it seemed now to describe him,

> *When a knight won his spurs, in the stories of old,*
> *He was gentle and brave, he was gallant and bold.*

This is the final verse,

> *Let faith be my shield and let joy be my steed*
> *'Gainst the dragons of anger, the ogres of greed*
> *And let me set free with the sword of my youth*
> *From the castle of darkness the power of truth*

When I got home from my run, two things happened:

1. I sat at my desk. Typing up notes from meeting sources, I stumbled across a story about *News of the World* news editor Greg Miskiw that I had forgotten I had been told, and that pissed me off.

   Greg was once dubbed 'the Prince of Darkness' by the newspaper industry, for his enthusiasm for the 'dark arts' (illegal acts) of newsgathering. It was not pejorative. His ruthlessness was both feared and admired across Fleet Street.

   The infamous quote attributed to him is the *That is what we do – we go out and destroy other people's lives* retort.

   The story that turned my head that day concerned a *News of the World* exposé of a paedophile. The man in question, I had been told, had lived on a council estate in the North East of England. When he was released from prison, a senior reporter was dispatched to knock on doors and ask neighbours how they felt about 'living next to a kiddie-fiddler'. By the time he had got the train back to London to file copy, news had come in that the house had been firebombed. But the paedophile hadn't been released to his old home – his ex-wife lived there with her new husband and he, an entirely innocent man, had died in the fire.

   The reporter, senior at the paper and apparently not someone prone to attacks of conscience, approached Miskiw to express remorse at this death and was heard to be told, 'You know what the moral of that story is, don't you? Don't marry the ex-wife of a fucking paedo.'

2. Nick got pissed off too – *with me*.

That, I couldn't bear. I had to invoice him, because he was my only source of income – I wasn't in a robust enough psychological state to pitch for, or carry out, documentary work – but it was clear that since I had last invoiced, I hadn't delivered information on anyone new.

Perhaps I sent the invoice as a means of starting a conversation I was too afraid and ashamed to approach, I don't know, but it did elicit a response. A lot of very powerful people were out to get Nick at this point. He needed me to keep doing my thing, he needed me not to crumble. But he had no idea how personally invested in this investigation I was and how frightened I was becoming.

When his phone call came, I nearly didn't take it. At the very last second, a surge of either fear or courage, or a weird admixture of the two, led to an almost whispered, 'Hi . . .'

'Jenny. I've received your invoice. I haven't received any work. Can you tell me what you have been doing?'

I said I would send through a contacts list showing all the calls I'd made. I meant later, but Nick said he'd wait. Barely breathing, I emailed him my list. Nick was familiar with the format, I always keep an immaculate contacts list: sub-headed, alphabetised, dated notes against each name, reminding me of every conversation I have had. That day, this worked against me.

Nick scanned it. 'I don't think this adds up to the amount of hours you have invoiced for.'

God, it wasn't fun being in the shadow of his sun. I climbed out of bed and put the kettle on. Then, shaking so much my teeth chattered, I told Nick everything.

He listened very carefully and attentively. I waited for a bollocking. Instead, I heard a deeply sad sigh. Nick disclosed that he had experienced violence as a child, at the hands of someone who should have protected him. It had resulted in his lifelong hatred of bullies. A hatred he had harnessed and used in all of his work. 'We must stand up to the bullies, if we can, Jen. We can stand up to them together. If you still feel you can.'

A shiver of relief swept through me. When I lay down on my bed after this call, I lay on top of the cover. Progress.

37

On 6 May 2010, the Conservative Party won the general election, as expected, and Andy Coulson was catapulted into Number Ten as head of communications for the government. Rupert Murdoch was the first person to meet new prime minister David Cameron. He reportedly entered Downing Street via the back door, so as not to be seen.

I had been meeting sources throughout the election campaign. The chatter was that Murdoch was hopeful of increasing his share of BSkyB, the company that owned Sky, giving him yet more control of the UK's cultural landscape. This was proven to be true within a few weeks. It was something his detractors feared would allow him a monopoly of the British media.

This was not Rupert Murdoch's first tango with accusations of monopolisation. On 4 January 1981, as reported by legendary editor of *The Times*, Harry Evans, Margaret Thatcher invited him for lunch at Chequers, the prime minister's country retreat. Thatcher was vulnerable – lagging in the polls and struggling beneath the weight of a recession. She needed some good PR. Murdoch was hungry – he did not feel he owned sufficient of the British press to wield the influence he craved. Nor to make enough profit. Both parties wanted a tighter grip on power.

Over roast beast with all the trimmings, a deal was struck that enabled Rupert Murdoch to gain control of nearly 40 per cent of our press industry, by buying up *The Times* and *The Sunday Times* to add to his ownership of the *Sun* and the *News of the World*.

In return, according to Evans, he agreed to use the might of his newspapers to champion Margaret Thatcher.

> *The fact that they met at all . . . was vehemently denied for 30 years. Since their lie was revealed, it has been possible to uncover how the greatest extension of monopoly power in modern press history was planned and executed with such furtive brilliance.**

It certainly was brilliance on the part of Murdoch. The moment the deal was done, he became more powerful than any politician. The prime minister still needed him; he no longer needed her. Murdoch 'owned' Thatcher in the same way he has owned every prime minister since.

It had not gone unnoticed by any of the reporters I was speaking to that Murdoch having Coulson in an influential place in government might be very helpful in terms of helping that BSkyB deal along. It had not gone unnoticed by Nick and the cohort of activists and lawyers concerned about British democracy either.

A message from Charlotte. Could I meet her in town at Payne Hicks Beach? A law firm that was not her own. 'I've been thinking about your push to find answers via your breach of privacy case,

---

* *Guardian,* 28 April 2015

rather than having to settle. I may have found you a benefactor. I'll tell you more when we meet.' I was googling 'benefactor', 'law' as the front door closed behind me.

When I got to the firm in question, I began to feel somewhat underdressed. Marble and glass and monogrammed water bottles gleamed intimidatingly from every surface. After a short wait, I was shown into a meeting room by a very charismatic, very polite, very posh man I now know to be top media lawyer Dominic Crossley.

This was the first time in my life I had encountered 'top' lawyers, and the core of steel I could sense in each of them was equally impressive and terrifying. Their job is not simply to support and protect their clients, as journalists do, it is also literally to fight for them. Warriors in well-cut suits. Dominic emanates these qualities in abundance and at this point, I probably would have followed him anywhere.

Charlotte stood as I entered, as did the diminutive figure she had been sat beside. He had white hair and wore black trousers and a black polo neck and immediately apologised for keeping me waiting because he'd been on the slopes.

This was Max Mosley: former boss of Formula 1, son of fascist aristocrat Oswald Mosley and socialite Diana Mitford. This was also the first time in my life I had encountered properly rich people; it took me a moment to realise he meant he had literally *just* come back from skiing. Like, on a private jet or something. Every other time I met Max, he wore a suit.

Max explained to me that he had heard that I potentially had a breach of privacy claim against News International. 'You're in the Mulcaire notebooks, as I understand.' I nodded. 'I'm sorry you've had to experience that. As you might know, I have had my own battle with the *News of the World*.'

Of *course*. Max had been secretly filmed inside his bedroom. Because he was rich enough to attempt to pursue justice, the paper had had to come up with a public interest argument for the filming. It had tried to say that as some of the sex party they filmed involved uniforms and speaking German, it was 'Nazi-themed', which the head of Formula 1 should not be indulging in, even in his own bedroom. As Formula 1 is not a public body, and this encounter was clearly of the most private nature, the argument is flimsy. Max's father was a fascist and Max supported his father's racist views when he was a young man, so perhaps an interrogation of his current views would be legitimate. But publishing, as they did, a photograph of his naked bottom on their front page, from a still image of a film taken in his own bedroom, is not that . . . *We go out and destroy other people's lives.*

Shortly after publication, one of Max's son's, who had long struggled with mental health problems and addiction, died via drug overdose. Max always believed there to have been a connection.

Charlotte explained that she had told Max of my frustration at the possibility of having to settle my case out of court. I had imagined being able to use it to force executives to tell the truth about what they knew about illegality at their newspapers. It would mean they could no longer blame their reporters, the foot soldiers, for taking part in a system they created.

But if I forced it to court, and was ordered to pay any of the costs, I would lose everything. 'I've just bought my first flat with loads of help from my family. I can't lose it.'

Max countered with, 'I have put a quarter of a million pounds aside, in a bank account, just for you. I can increase that amount. If you are willing to force the executives into court, I will pay the legal fees.'

I remember he laughed at how wide my eyes went. I remember too that Dominic and Charlotte were watching me very intently.

'OK,' was all I could muster. Reality bit. Memories of being the sole individual up against a more powerful foe flooded my body and I froze. Again, Charlotte read my mind. She asked for the room, whispering to me, 'Take your time. They don't need an answer now.'

I shook hands with Dominic and Max and expressed my genuine gratitude before sitting at the glossy table with my head in my hands. *How is this happening? What should I do?*

I decided to go to New York.

38

A friend from journalism school, Kris, worked for Reuters and lived near Wall Street. She had invited me to stay with her hundreds of times, but I usually opted to holiday in Europe with Mum. We had a rhythm that couldn't be beaten – reading during the days; eating on a lovely square or terrace somewhere, getting lightly pissed, in the evenings. It was easy and calming. We laughed a lot. We talked philosophy and politics and psychology and literature in the kind of way that's only possible when you don't feel judged. Our hearts were replenished by the family time, but we always missed Will – we talked about him a lot and we needed that, too. This year, however, with my biological clock ticking, feeling like all my mates were coupled up and there was something wrong with me, I decided not to go on holiday with my mum. Holidaying with your mum felt like the saddest holiday in the world right then. Whereas Manhattan seemed like the kind of place you could visit alone and not really notice your loneliness. *I'm not lonely*, I told myself as I boarded the plane, *I just need some thinking time*. Half of this was true.

As soon as I got into the yellow cab at JFK, I knew I had made a good decision. The city air, soft and lived-in, warm and pretzel scented, was intoxicating in its unfamiliarity. Each morning, I planned a route across the city, south to north, west to east, back again. Every street thrummed. I could feel the history vibrating beneath my feet. I took deep breaths, which in New York City might not be the best idea, and I walked. I walked and walked and walked and walked, and I thought, my steps a drumbeat untangling my mind.

You. Can. Do It. You. Can. Do. It.
You. Don't. Have. To. You. Don't. Have. To.
But. Who. Else. Will? But. Who. Else. Will?
Max. Will. Help. You. Max. Will. Help. You.
They. Might. Hurt. You. They. Might. Hurt. You.
They. Might. Hurt. Mum. They. Might. Hurt. Mum.
Find. The. Truth. Out. Find. The. Truth. Out.
You. Don't. Have. To. You. Don't. Have. To.
Is. That. A. Burger? Is. That. A. Burger?
I could do with a burger . . .

I drank the world's most incredible blueberry milkshake. I ate the sweetest sweetcorn at Café Habana. I sunbathed on the roof of Kris's building, as we talked about love and life and journalism, and what to do about Max. Finally, I reached for my phone.

'Charlotte? I'll do it.'

I heard the smile spread across her face. 'OK. Let's talk when you're back.'

Kris looked emotional when I turned back to her. She hugged me and whispered, 'Brave.'

It didn't feel brave. It felt scary, but it also felt, as it had when I brought the case against The Famous Man, as it had when I trained in journalism, as it had when I told Nick the truth, like in the end it was the only path I could take.

Kris and I bought beers from a 7-Eleven and took them in brown paper bags to an outdoor Monty Python screening in one of the parks. 'This is the most English thing we could possibly be doing.' She laughed. 'Why are we doing it?' Kris is half German and half Welsh. 'This isn't English,' I commented, nodding at the paper bag hiding the booze. She agreed. 'Terry Jones is Welsh,' I added. She gave my bottle a chink, looked hard into my face, squeezed my hand.

The following morning, as I made my way out of a tenement museum on the Lower East Side, clutching a book about immigration and feeling disgustingly privileged, my phone rang.

'Jenny Evans! How are you? Are you abroad?'

It was Kevin Sutcliffe, head of Channel 4's investigative strand, *Dispatches*. I'd worked with him on a few documentaries, and on *Unreported World*, a foreign affairs series. He said something like, 'I hear you have been working on this phone-hacking story with Nick Davies. Could you come into the channel? Prash and I would like to have a word.'

Prash Naik was head of legal affairs at Channel 4. He had all those core-of-steel qualities I have described in top lawyers, as well as a very gentle and humane demeanour. We agreed to meet when I got back.

My favourite thing about Kevin was that he was a Blackpool lad, so he had none of the snobbery I encounter so often in TV journalism. It is well documented that most of journalism and documentary-making is headed by white, middle-class (upper-middle-class?) people and that those people are mostly men. It is assumed that their schooling and university education is what puts them ahead. I don't think that's entirely true. By my observation, it is self-confidence that does that. When they speak, they believe what they say is important and that they will be listened to. Then, they tend to employ others like themselves, because they communicate in the same way; they are all guided by the same levels of confidence in one another. It means that Oxbridge, Russell Group, public-school kids are employed for their potential, while everyone else is employed for their achievements. And the opportunity to achieve is hard fought. When I run the world there will be schemes to support the development of good ideas, wherever they come from.

I don't know about Kevin's education, but he instinctively rejected the hierarchy of self-belief. He recognised that great storytellers come from any background and that allowing them to tell their stories is to the benefit of us all. His tenure at *Dispatches* was the better for it.

In yet another glass-panelled meeting room, this time at Channel 4, I sat before him and Prash and discovered that Nick's boss at the *Guardian*, Alan Rusbridger, had taken Kevin out for dinner to confront him about why TV wasn't investigating phone hacking yet.

'It's a good point,' Kevin said to me. 'We should be. Are you in?'

He wanted to make a 'fast-turnaround' – to broadcast in three weeks' time. A well-established director would base himself in an edit suite in Soho with an editor. A team of producers, of which I would be one, would act as satellites creating the content. We'd meet sources, interview those who could go on camera, send the footage back to the edit suite. It was going to be tight, there would be sleepless nights, but it would bring this story to a whole new audience.

I excused myself and called Nick. 'Is it all right if I take a three-week hiatus? Another one?' (I had just been to New York.)

'Jen, I gave them your name. We are fully behind this. If you're telling the story of phone hacking from the start, I am your first interviewee. How did it go with Max?'

I told him that I had agreed to bring a claim against News Group Newspapers for hacking my phone and to resist all offers to settle. 'Well done. Are you going to tell the *Dispatches* people that?'

Oh, bloody hell. I rejoined Prash and Kevin, let them know I'd be delighted to help with the documentary and added that I thought I had better explain the extent of my involvement in the story, in case they considered it a conflict.

'So, when I was nineteen, I was sexually assaulted and quite badly hurt by [The Famous Man] . . .'

From somewhere deep inside me, a well of sadness began to fill. Oh God, please not now. I had barely ever cried about this experience, unable to connect to it, thanks to the steel trap. To do so at this moment was highly inconvenient . . . It was also, apparently, uncontrollable; I apologised as fat, syrupy tears rolled unstoppably down my face. Kevin looked like he wanted to climb down a well himself – he left the room to get some tissues. Prash sat with me, calmly and sympathetically, entirely unfazed.

When I could speak, I told him everything. It was terrifying to once more spill my secrets. Burned by my experience with the police, I felt very unsafe whenever I had to talk about it, which I did the absolute minimum that I had to. It was another reason it took so long for me to be open with Nick. That conversation had been on the phone, so he hadn't been able to see that I was hiding my face. Prash was well aware that my instinct was to hide in that moment – he let me cover my eyes with my hands for as long as I needed.

'I don't think there's a conflict,' he eventually said, quietly and matter-of-factly. 'But it's right that I'm fully in the picture. Because then I can protect you.'

I looked up from my hands, but the tears did not stop. Prash nodded, kindly. Warrior. I was beginning to love lawyers.

39

As planned, the satellite producers based ourselves in a neighbouring edit suite to the director. Every morning we'd have a production meeting – to discuss who and what our targets were that day, who would do research, who would be dispatched to get footage. When we returned, we'd eat take-away, complete any more research, follow up our leads.

As I had the best links with tabloid reporters, my main focus was trying to find someone willing to go on the record to say that News International executives *knew everything*. I had been told this so many times. Surely, someone, somewhere could speak out, even anonymously.

I re-contacted all my sources to ask who they knew who might talk. It had to be someone senior enough to have been invited to stay behind at conference, to listen to the evidence that proved a story could be run. That meant heads of departments, lawyers or senior reporters. Some of these might be considered the bullies rather than the bullied, so my regular way in was less effective. But slowly, one source led to another and to another. I began to meet new people. I talked guardedly, they responded cautiously. I asked who else they knew who might talk, contacted them, organised to meet.

When you are interviewing a source on a job like this, your brain naturally tries to walk around the information they are giving you, to look at it from all angles. Or, perhaps I learned this from Nick. You need to make assumptions and to test out theories because you don't want to miss asking a crucial question – this person may never pick up the phone to you again. Ordinarily, it's safe to muse openly about what you are thinking. You can use the source as something of a sounding board, think out loud a little. With these meetings, I had to be much more careful than that. I could never be sure if these sources were meeting me to give me information or to pump me for what *Dispatches* had. I had to assume they were recording everything; I never knew if they were actually on my side.

It was brave of the channel to commission something before we had any on-the-record sources. They hoped we might find someone, with so many producers on the case, but the reasoning was that even if we didn't, the extent of the lawlessness at newspapers was still a story that hadn't quite made it into the public consciousness yet. This fact was unsurprising; it wasn't in the best interests of the press to cover the extent of their lawlessness, so, predictably, they hardly did so at all. But that, as Kevin said, is where TV came in.

We interviewed Nick, we interviewed Charlotte and others. It was a reporter source I often met on the South Bank who really came up with the goods – quite unexpectedly. I'm not sure she even realised the gold she was handing me at the time.

She introduced me to a former colleague at Embankment Tube and then left us to talk. It was a warm evening, so we bought drinks and sat on the grass on a little green just outside the station. Other people lounged in deckchairs; office workers with their ties off and trousers rolled up, tourists clutching iced coffees and camera phones.

'Am I OK to take notes?' I asked, removing my pad from my bag.

'Take notes, use the information, but this is strictly unattributable, OK? I still freelance for the Murdoch press.' This was the standard response.

'OK.'

'OK. What do you want to know?'

'How did you find working at the *News of the World*?'

'It was horrible. I hated it.' I already knew the source had been bullied by a particular desk head. I had been informed it was the reason he was talking to me.

He picked at the grass, either wrestling with his conscience or unable to choose where to start. Eventually, quietly, he asked, 'Are you interested in the fact that we stole medical records, DVLA records, that we had someone who could turn round number plates?'

I sensed guilt and sought to reassure him. 'I've heard those things before. It's always useful to corroborate. As you know.'

The source nodded. 'We did it all.'

'Did everybody know? The senior team?'

'That [senior] people didn't know is laughable. Laughable.'

'So far I have no proof of that. It was only the most senior who stayed behind after conference to see and hear the evidence. No one I have spoken to was one of the chosen few.'

'It was desk heads.' He meant: the head or deputy head of news, of features, of the foreign desk, for example.

'Yes.'

'I was a desk head.' He stopped picking at the grass. He looked up to meet my eye. We both understood the significance.

'You were a desk head?' I attempted to sound casual.

'Sometimes I was a desk head, yeah. Whenever the head of [my desk] was away, I would deputise.'

We both knew what my next question would be – falling down the rabbit hole together, not breaking eye contact: 'Were you asked to stay after conference? When reporters revealed their sourcing or their evidence?'

'I was.'

'Can you tell me who else was there?'

'Editor . . .' He ran through a list of job titles, summing up with, 'Senior team, you could say.'

'Senior team,' I repeated. He nodded.

'The editor. Was Andy Coulson editor when you were at the *News of the World*?'

'Yes, he was.'

'He was.' I bit my lip. Deep breath, keep it steady. 'Were you party to any references to, or evidence of, for example, phone hacking?'

'I was in meetings where phone hacking was openly discussed, and tape recordings of voicemails were played to Andy Coulson.'

If I hadn't been sitting on the floor, my legs would have begun to shake. I could feel them trying.

'Did you hack voicemails?'

'Not me,' he replied (they always said that). But he had seen it. And he would say that.

I thanked the source for his time and asked him if I could call him later, 'In case I have any follow-up questions'. He nodded and smiled – he knew what was coming. I was going to ask him to do an anonymous interview. I just had to find out from my own senior team what the terms of that could be.

I closed my notebook, waited until the source had got back on the Tube, then ran as fast as I could past Charing Cross, up St Martin's Lane, through Leicester Square, round the edge of

Chinatown, across Shaftesbury Avenue, up Dean Street, where I had waitressed so many years before, and into the edit suite where the director was holding the afternoon meeting.

So as not to get anything wrong, I read to the team from my notebook. 'I was in meetings where phone hacking was openly discussed, and tape recordings of voicemails were played to Andy Coulson.'

The director, who had been considering ten different things he needed to do at once, paused and held up his hand. 'Wait. This is what we've been waiting for.'

'I know,' I told him, breathless and almost disbelieving that it had happened. *How brave you are*, I found myself thinking, as I reflected on what the source had told me, and what he was offering. *What kind of a person takes this kind of a risk to get out the truth?* A whistle-blower. A truly good, a truly brave person.

'Will they go on the record?' the director naturally asked.

'No. But they might speak anonymously. My instinct is they will. I just wanted to check with you what you thought we could offer in terms of anonymity.'

It was decided that, if the source could tolerate it, the director, rather than me, would record an audio interview and an actor would portray him in the documentary. It was a leap of faith to trust someone other than me, but it is the director's job to get the content he needs and when I explained that, the source agreed. A couple of hours later, the director was dispatched to his house – only he and I ever knowing his identity – and an explosive interview was recorded.

Dispatches: Tabloids, Tories and Telephone Hacking aired in October 2010.

This is what the source said about phone hacking:

> *It wasn't regarded as illegal as such. It was regarded as something slightly dodgy . . . It was fairly common. Not so common that everybody was doing it. That wasn't the case at all. But the people who did know how to do it would do it regularly.*

This is what he said about the police:

> *The reaction in the newsroom [to royal reporter Clive Goodman's arrest] was huge shock. People couldn't believe that he may actually be facing prison for what he did on a day-to-day basis, and what lots of people did day-to-day . . . There were huge rumours swirling every day of who they were coming for next and who was, you know, going to come and cart away, this person, that person and the other. And then I think the feeling in the newsroom turned to surprise that nobody else was affected.*

This is what he said about Andy Coulson:

> *Andy was a very good editor, he was very conscientious, and he wouldn't let stories pass unless he was sure that they were correct . . . So, if the evidence that a reporter had was a recorded phone message that would be what Andy would know about. So, you'd have to say, yes, there's a recorded message. You go and either play it to him or show him a transcript of it, in order to satisfy him that you weren't going to get sued, that it wasn't made up.*

When the documentary was broadcast, viewing figures were high and other TV news outlets began to cover the story more readily, exactly as we had hoped. Pressure was building.

The crew watched the film air together, from the edit suite we had lived in for the past three weeks. We were tired. I had one of those eye twitches you get when you're so sleep deprived you can barely say your own name, and a mouth full of ulcers.

Nevertheless, I deliberately got off the bus a couple of stops early. I had had the idea when I ran past the bar I used to work in in Soho, trying to get to the *Dispatches* edit to tell them about the source. I wanted to walk past the road I had lived on with the 'True Colors'. Twelve years had passed since we had lived there, dancing into the early morning in a Spanish place, Bar Lorca, on the corner of Church Street. They were brilliant times, but I had been so low. So lost. I was beginning to notice quite how far I had travelled.

I looked at the exterior of the red-brick basement flat and I thought, *I still don't know how this ends.* I was still scared. *Maybe the worst is yet to come.* But I was no longer such a stranger to the systems that had so confused and betrayed me, neither the criminal justice system, though I had a lot more to learn, nor the invisible cobweb that bonded the power elite: politicians, police, press, all scratching each other's backs, as my Battersea Park source had put it.

I understood a little more of how things work. I hoped it meant I was harder to fob off. As I made my way back towards my flat, I realised that the lightness I was feeling, like a cloud inside my chest, was hope.

40

Two months later, with television executive Jay Hunt incoming as chief creative officer to Channel 4, someone senior decided it would impress her if we made a follow-up phone-hacking film. They gave us eleven days to turn it around. We decided the most interesting element that might be considered 'new' was profiling the tabloids' dark arts, the detail of which the general public were mostly ignorant of. The problem once more was – who would talk?

News International still denied any knowledge of wrongdoing, despite lawyers for Hollywood A-lister Sienna Miller having sent a Letter Before Claim to its owner, News Group Newspapers, in respect of unlawful information gathering. Miller is another victim of the Murdoch papers' blagging skills. In 2005, her medical records were obtained as her relationship with fellow actor Jude Law was ending. Their pregnancy was revealed by the *Sun*. In a state of paranoia and overwhelm with which I can entirely relate, she terminated the pregnancy, later commenting,

> *[The* Sun*'s] actions, their words, their 'tittle tattle' compelled me into making decisions about my future and ultimately about my own body that I have to live with every single day.*

When the first *Dispatches* aired, Coulson's press team had put out a statement attempting to undermine the revelations, because the source was anonymous. How would I find anyone to go on camera, when the stakes were so high?

Nick solved this one for us.

'Can you talk?'

'Always.'

'I've found a reporter who's willing to go on the record.' My heart practically stopped. 'I can't give him to you, I'm afraid. I'm going to do an interview with him today and publish as soon as I can after that – tomorrow, latest – but I think he'll talk to you after he speaks to me. I'll give you more information when I'm done.'

YES, NICK. I phoned the news into my bosses. They didn't want to wait and asked me to call Nick back and push him to release the source to us. Even his name. I knew there was no point, and it didn't feel fair. Not my source. I would wait my turn. I wasn't going to jeopardise my relationship with Nick for TV.

When we were making the first phone-hacking film, the *New York Times* had released its own investigation into the story. I knew it was happening because I had given them an anonymous interview. That was the first occasion that my TV bosses pushed me to call the journalists involved and ask them to tell us what was in the piece before it ran, and then who their sources were. It makes me cringe now to think that I actually agreed to do that. Of course they were never going to tell me. All it did was make me look – and feel – like an amateur who didn't understand the rules of journalism. And hadn't I spent a *lot* of time and money learning the rules exactly so I didn't have to ever feel like that again? I wasn't going to make the same mistake with Nick.

It was around this time that it occurred to me that all my sources said they had taped pretty much every conversation they had had at the *News of the World*. 'Oh, we taped things as a matter of course,' one had mentioned, over flapjacks and Earl Grey – an unusual choice for a *News of the World* reporter, I have to say – in a small north London café covered in mosaics. I had been asking for evidence to back up his claims of bullying. 'As a matter of course, I taped the news desk,' he repeated. 'Had to have a fall-back.'

'A fall-back?'

'In case they tried to force me out of my job.' He met my eye. 'I saw a reporter sacked for having to stay in and look after his kids *on his night off*. The news desk called at eleven p.m. and demanded he got to a restaurant because Enrique Iglesias and Anna Kournikova were eating at it. He couldn't go because his wife had just given birth, and he was looking after his toddler and the newborn whilst she slept. They sacked him.'

'Wow.'

'I didn't want them to squeeze me out of my job somehow.'

'Did they do that because they didn't like him? Was it bullying?' The source shrugged. Not for the first time, imagining the stress those reporters were under, despite the perks, made me wince. Now, the million-dollar question: 'I don't suppose you kept the tapes?'

I had been phone bashing sources for days asking this question. All had been evasive. I suspected that as ever there was very sensible caution around self-incrimination.

This source looked at me long enough for me to decide that he almost certainly had kept the tapes, clearly calculating the most sensible response. 'They were at my mum's somewhere, I think. In her attic. But – I think I threw them out.'

'That's kind of what everyone says,' I told him.

He laughed and added, 'The truth is, most tapes and notebooks and everything got junked in the big clear-out.'

'Which was . . .?'

'When we got the tip-off that Clive Goodman was about to be arrested for phone hacking, everyone started to clear out their desks, because they thought we were about to be raided by the Met Police.'

'A fucking tip-off?'

He laughed again. 'That's what I heard. The news desk was alerted to the police raid the night before it happened, so people stayed late deleting and shredding stuff.' He gave me a name of someone he had heard had definitely been there.

'Only him?'

'Well, I wasn't there, but I have heard from loads of people that senior reporters on news and features were sneaking bin bags of documents out.'

'And?'

'And the Met only searched one fucking desk. Clive's. They never *investigated* us at all.' He whooped with laughter at this, 'And do you know who the officer in charge was?'

I did. His name was Andy Hayman, I had been told many times that he had good links with tabloid reporters. Hayman rose to be deputy commissioner of the Met before retiring and taking up a newspaper column . . . at Rupert Murdoch's *The Times*.

As is standard with any information offered in this context – an off-the-record or unattributable meeting – while I carried on looking for tapes, I asked others if they had heard or, better, seen, this tip-off happen, followed by destruction of evidence.

One told me he was there. He saw it. He also said he destroyed all his own tapes that day. 'Everything I had worked for. It felt like destroying gold.'

It was nice to catch up with these sources again. Mostly we spoke on the phone, though some made time for a cup of tea. Rumours were rife that individual reporters might soon start taking the flak for the executives again, as Love Rat had been sacked, though he was senior. People thought Rupert was losing his rag.

A source recounted Rupert Murdoch joining conference and ordering senior staff to hand over 'all the paperwork we've hidden to the police'.

'"But [Love Rat] will go to prison," someone said, to which Murdoch replied, "I don't care, this stops now."'

Rupert Murdoch has always denied knowledge of unlawful information gathering at his papers. Multiple sources told me he spoke to his editors once a week, but these were always private conversations.

The fear of being scapegoated meant some sources were more determined to help, hoping the truth would finally land, while others notably pulled away. They couldn't decide if talking was assisting their comrades, as they had originally hoped, or making everything ten times worse. Might the executives continue to sell them out to save themselves? Based on the evidence it didn't feel congruent to try to persuade them otherwise. If I had been working solely for Nick, I would have left a longer break between contacts, but TV can be demanding.

I was about to give up asking for tapes when one of my sources finally called back to say he had found a couple he had kept from the Coulson era. 'I've listened back. I basically complain about getting less money and more bollockings. And then I get another one [bollocking].'

'I'll take it.' I met him in Central London, and I don't know why I was shocked that he handed me a brown envelope containing a mini disc. But – of course. This was recorded in the early 2000s. How was I going to listen to a mini disc?

I was halfway home when it came to me – *Luke*.

Eleri, a hometown friend from the drama centre days, now lived in south London. Her husband, Luke, was a musician with a lot of tech. I picked up my phone.

'Jen, Jen! How are you? Do you want Lel [our nickname for Eleri]?'

'It's you I want this time, in fact. I think I might need your brain. Can you play a mini disc? And then, can you transfer what's on it onto, say, my computer? And can that be of broadcast quality, do you think?'

A pause.

'Dude, have you met me?'

I raced round to Luke and Eleri's – kiss, hug, NDAs – then together we listened to the reporter's tape play out onto my computer.

Coulson didn't incriminate himself in any way. As I had been told many times, he is very far from stupid. But he did imply to the reporter that if his byline count fell because he was unable to 'self-generate' stories, he would have to be let go.

> *I need more stories. I need more exclusives, and I need it to be self-generated stuff . . . being a* News of the World *reporter is no longer about . . . going out and covering a story . . . it's about self-generating.*

It was chilling to hear someone's job so casually dangled before them by this man in exactly the way so many reporters had described.

The source did also attempt to complain about bullying by Love Rat, telling Coulson he was expected to stand a story up in a day and wasn't able to do enough checks. This was dismissed as untrue. He was told,

> *I have got total faith in my news desk. I've got total confidence in [Love Rat]. I think he's a great operator and I think he's doing a brilliant job.*

'Well, that closed him down,' Eleri commented. It was true – we were listening to live-action bullying of a junior staff member.

Elsewhere on the tape, the source calls into the newsroom and requests to invite his union rep to the next meeting, but is told by the news desk, 'He's not invited.'

Another call into the office sees him mention a female reporter who is being treated comparably badly. 'She hasn't exactly committed a cardinal sin,' he comments, to a thankfully friendlier member of the desk. 'Yes, she has . . .' comes the reply, 'she got pregnant.'

I called the source. 'I'm so sorry you had to go through this. It's weird to hear it – bullying, exactly as I have heard described so many times. Can I ask, just for clarity's sake, what is your understanding of what Coulson meant by self-generating stories?'

'What else could he mean? He knew I wasn't phone hacking. He meant that I should make better use of dark arts.'

'He was encouraging you to break the law?'

'He was encouraging me to self-generate stories.'

I called what I had found into the *Dispatches* team and went back to the edit suite to continue to work. It was 11 p.m.

41

'Can you talk?'

A call from Nick woke me the following morning. The ache in my eyes told me I'd barely managed six hours, again.

'This source I told you about.' The one who was willing to go on the record.

I knew his name from my investigation so far, but I wrote it down carefully anyway, as if, if I didn't, he might disappear. My legs started doing their tremor thing. *I wonder if he worked there when they covered my story. If he's brave enough to speak out, can he help me?*

The source's name was Paul McMullan. Once a deputy features editor at the *News of the World*, he was prepared to admit to regularly phone hacking for the paper (as long as we did the interview from the pub he now ran on the south coast, so he could plug it). He said he was talking because he took umbrage at senior staff and executives allowing reporters like Clive Goodman to take the flak for doing what was expected of them. 'They colluded to let Clive go down. It's appalling.'

If you were going to make an unsophisticated comedy about tabloid newspapers, you would cast Paul as your deputy features editor. He is perfect: weaselly of face, nasal of voice, unabashedly sexist. He says things like, 'Privacy is for paedos.' Last time I saw him he asked me if I'd changed my hair. 'Maybe,' I replied, self-consciously touching a newly cropped bob. 'Right, because I used to want to shag you, but now I don't.'

He's a twat. He is also without doubt the bravest of the reporters I spoke to. Because aside from Sean Hoare, who died before he could have his full say, McMullan was the first to go on the record: 'I've commissioned hundreds of illegal acts.'

He was very proud of the work he had done on the *Screws*, producing folders containing all his cuttings. I noticed that one of his articles was about him being sent undercover in a run-down housing estate – a 'punishment', I had been told several times, for reporters who had fallen out of favour.

I had the surreal experience of interviewing McMullan as he explained something called 'double screwing' to the camera. This is the practice of using one phone to reach a target and another to hack their voicemail and delete any messages, once listened to, to prevent a rival paper hearing them. McMullan said,

> *To do this you need two mobile phones. One you call up your, the celebrity's number, who's a girl. And she will answer that phone, so as not to arouse suspicion you will say something fairly vacuous like – 'Hello this is Vodafone; we'd like to offer you a new Vodafone package.' At the same time, I'm calling the celebrity on another phone and on this first phone call I'll be saying, 'You could halve your phone bill and it will only cost you £3.99' – right, hang up that one, and I'm in. Press nine – (please enter your security code). In the olden days people never changed their code. So it was normally just four*

> zeros and that would get you to listen to all of their messages. It was just as simple as that four zeros, four nines and there it was, Robbie Williams's messages.

The exact same thing happened to my boyfriend Neil in the middle of my legal case. I remember sitting with him outside a pub when someone ostensibly from Vodafone called out of the blue to offer him a new package. I had told him off at the time for giving out our address, believing that was how he was being conned by a tabloid. But, of course, I had no notion of phone hacking.

I didn't ask McMullan, in the end, about my own case. It didn't feel safe.

Dispatches: Tabloids' Dirty Secrets aired on 7 February 2011. On 21 January, just after our 'Right of Reply' letter had been sent to Andy Coulson, he resigned. It has since emerged that Rebekah Brooks had suggested to him that this might be the best course of action. I suspect he didn't want to give us the satisfaction of claiming that our reporting had played a part in his decision.

Making a statement outside Downing Street, Coulson said, 'When the spokesman needs a spokesman, it is time to move on.' As the adage goes, 'Never become the story'. Now Mr Coulson understood a little of the trauma of the magnifying glass.

It was an extraordinary moment. Journalism appeared to have made a real impact. To genuinely have effected change. Nick and I and others he worked with, as well as other news and current affairs journalists, and the lawyers, had worked for such a long time and hit nothing but denials. It was almost unbelievable that finally, begrudgingly, someone from the Murdoch camp was admitting that there was heat and it was time to get out of the newsroom.

Quietly, the Met Police, the Crown Prosecution Service and the Press Complaints Commission all re-opened investigations into the extent of criminality at Murdoch newspapers. Nick was looking into the detail. It was as if it were the first time they had realised that the 'one rogue reporter' line parroted for so long might actually be wrong.

And it gave me an excuse to try to talk to each of those organisations again.

42

The Met and the CPS – then headed by Keir Starmer – told me to piss off. By which I mean, they told me they wouldn't comment on an active investigation, or something similar, I can't remember. The Press Complaints Commission (PCC), however, was far more interesting.

I met a very senior member of the PCC in the coffee shop of the National Gallery on Trafalgar Square. It was not lost on me, as I climbed the front steps, that its imposing columns overlook the fountains on which Katie and I had perched to sip hot chocolate the day I gave my first filmed interview to the police. The day those symbolically convenient lion statues had allowed me to hope I would somehow be safe . . . *four* days before the *Sun* newspaper printed the secrets I had prised from my chest that morning. For the police. Once again, I had come full circle.

The source was agitated. As soon as we sat down with our tea, he stage-whispered, 'The Press Complaints Commission was lied to in a calculated way by the police,' and watched me take down his words.

'Wow.' I smiled at him in disbelief. Quite the opener.

'Lied to in a calculated way?' I clarified. (This is another therapy trick my mum taught me. Again – don't ask, 'Why?', summarise or reflect; repeat back their words to them. They will feel heard and understood and may feel compelled to elaborate. Elaborate this man did . . .)

'It was a systematic campaign designed to cover up [the Met's] links with News International.'

I widened my eyes to let him know I was taking him seriously, as I scribbled down what he had to say. 'To cover up?' I prompted.

He nodded, frantically. 'To cover up the Met's close relationship with News International and to protect the company from further scandal.'

'The police were *protecting* the *News of the World*? Protecting the business interests of Rupert Murdoch? Do you have proof?'

'No. But I will swear a witness statement to the fact that a senior Met officer approached me, unsolicited, at a social function, introduced himself and informed me that there were only nine people in Mulcaire's notebooks and there was nothing else to come out.'

I had come across this policeman's name before. A photographer source who spoke to me about faking stories with *News of the World* journalists had linked him to a crime reporter at the paper. A female crime reporter. The female crime reporter who wrote several articles about me. 'Best friends with [the officer] that one,' the snapper had told me, 'and Coulson. They used to go to dinner together.'

'All three?' I checked. He had nodded, 'Why do you think that was?' I suffered another withering look and an overly polite, 'Well, I heard [the cop] was feeding them stories.'

Otherwise, why have a reporter there at all, I guess.

'In the public interest?' I had asked. The photographer had laughed.

Understanding the closeness of those ties – understanding that I hadn't understood the closeness of those ties when I naively reported a crime to the Met police – landed like kicks. I felt the knot in my gut once more. *Why is this allowed to happen?*

'I'd love to know who at the Met decided, "Let's mislead the PCC",' the senior Commission member continued. 'There must have been a meeting at which a "line" was decided upon: *Let's lie to the PCC. Let's lie to [him].*'

I watched him as he said this, his cheeks reddening, narrowed eyes fixed on a spot on the table. I became aware of a vein in his neck, visible just above the collar of a very expensive shirt. That's when I understood. This man felt humiliated, that's why he was so angry. It wasn't righteous anger on behalf of a public let down by a toothless press regulator. It was personal. This was shame.

Shame. Such a powerful force, so hard to recover from. Potent enough to ruin lives with its ability to make us want to run, or hide, or lie, if we perceive we have been cast as weak. It is a life-threatening and visceral fear of being ousted, degraded, made to feel we do not belong. In one way, it is our brain trying to keep us safe, urging us to flee if we have even a sniff of this kind of threat; a bid to stay alive, when we are in danger of being the one the rest of the pack might rip to shreds. I know it well.

Shame, I reflected, in that moment, as I watched him, *is the fuel on which tabloids' engines run*. The *News of the World* ruined people's lives by stealing their secrets, or setting them up, *and shaming them*. Other tabloids did the same, and still do. Shame is why information is power. Shame can be why good people make bad decisions. Shame could have been the title of this book – it is at the very core of every aspect of this story.

Is it perhaps also what drives perpetrators to be violent to those weaker than them? It is also what drives bullies to bully?

Maybe the question that should be asked of Rupert Murdoch and his executives is not, *Why would you do this?* But, *What is it about yourself you are so desperate to run from, or to hide?*

'What was the function?' I asked the PCC man. He looked bemused, so lost had he been in the awful sensation of shame he was feeling.

'The function?' I asked again. 'The party at which [the senior officer] approached you.'

The source looked shamefaced. 'It was Neil Wallis's leaving do.'

Ah, Neil Wallis. Andy Coulson's deputy at the *News of the World*. Other sources had mentioned him, describing him as Coulson's 'Rottweiler'. Wallis left the *News of the World* shortly after Coulson to work in PR, landing himself a lucrative deal to do publicity . . . for the Met Police.

Wallis was also publicist for Champneys luxury spa. The commissioner of the Met, Sir Paul Stephenson, the highest-ranking officer, accepted a complimentary five-week stay at Champneys when recuperating from a knee operation around this time. He denied knowledge of the link to Wallis, despite admitting dining with him eight times between 2006 and 2010, more than any other senior journalist or executive at any other newspaper.

Wallis was apparently closest, however, not to Sir Paul, but to John Yates. The two deputies – of the *News of the World* and of the Met Police – attended football matches together and regularly dined out, having been friends since the late '90s. Their children even ended up doing work experience at each other's offices, when Wallis was still at the paper.

'I'm amazed someone didn't take Yates aside and tell him how dangerous it was to have Neil as a friend,' one source who had worked with Wallis at several tabloids said.

And who was John Yates? What was he like, as a person? I had no one to tell me, but I knew his name. John Yates. The cop who made the announcement outside Scotland Yard that Nick's revelations about the extent of phone hacking were not substantive. John Yates, the head of the Special Enquiry squad at the Met. John Yates, the man who was ultimately in charge of my criminal case.

'So, the PCC felt it was reasonable to attend the leaving do of Neil Wallis from the *News of the World*, despite this being partly related to accusations of illegality at the paper? And also being the regulator charged with holding tabloids to account? Was the PCC actively investigating Neil Wallis's actions at the paper at the time?'

I smiled and blew into my tea to cool it. I was perfecting a kind of veneer of innocence that was handy for asking difficult questions. Or, not so much innocence as – polite straightforwardness: *It is my job to ask you this question. I'm assuming you have an entirely credible answer.*

The source looked crestfallen, so I filled in the answer for him. He could correct me if I was wrong. 'You work closely with the tabloids. The press self-regulates, so you knew him well.' He nodded.

'It was more appropriate for you to be at his do than for [the senior officer]?' The source made a face as if to say that that was not an unfair statement.

'And the reason the PCC backed up tabloid claims that phone hacking was not widescale, when its investigation was released, was because of what [the senior officer] told you at this party? You believed he represented the Met.'

'Emphatically, yes,' the source told me, adding, 'I didn't personally make any of these decisions, of course. I set out options, the Commission decided which to choose.'

'The self-regulating commission made up largely of tabloid executives?' I checked. The source sighed. It is the way the system works. It wasn't his fault.

It wasn't his fault, I thought, as I made my way back out to Trafalgar Square, *But whose fault was it?* I bought a hot chocolate, in honour of Will and Katie and the lions and . . . me, and sipped it at the edge of the fountain. I could just see in the distance the tower that holds Big Ben and, beyond that, the Palace of Westminster. The UK's political heartland. *If I were looking for someone to blame* . . . I thought.

Despite the knot, I was aware of how content I was in this moment, in this investigation. I was exactly where I had once wanted to be. I wasn't unafraid, but I wasn't cowed. I knew my job and I was becoming skilled at it. It felt good to be fighting back. It felt good to finally get close to some answers, with the help of Charlotte and Max. It felt good to finally be talking about my experiences, both to Nick and in the anonymous interview I had given to the *New York Times*. Among the fury and the fear, I knew I also detected happiness within me. I was getting somewhere.

43

It was around this time I met a man with kind eyes. After the emotional wasteland of the relationship with The Man Who Didn't Love Me Enough, meeting Jasper was like stepping into a warm bath. It was the leaving do of a friend of mine, Becky, who I'd met on the first phone-hacking *Dispatches*. She had been Kevin's assistant, based at Channel 4, but seconded to our team to help us meet the deadline. After one late night at work, she made me laugh so hard wine came out of my nose.

The bar was busy when I arrived at eightish, already decorated for Christmas, despite it being the end of November. I recognised a lot of people but didn't really know anyone other than Bec. We had hugged a lot and caught up – in that surface way you do before the wine kicks in – by eight fifteen. I was hoping it wasn't too early to leave when a very tall man with very broad shoulders walked through the door. *What kind eyes*, I thought. *They really do look very kind.* I was transfixed, and, to my astonishment, he waved at the person I happened to be talking to, before heading to get a drink.

'Who's that?' I asked.

The person, a documentary commissioner, looked round. 'That's Jasper. He's my assistant.'

Drink in hand, the enormous man smiled at us once more and made his way over. My eyes must have sparkled, because suddenly, he and I were alone. We talked a bit about work, a bit about our mutual love of Becky, about the weather, probably, I don't know. At one point, Jasper said he had to pop outside to call his dad, because they'd had a difficult day: his uncle had died, and they had been to clear out his flat. Even though I love socialising, I eventually become uncomfortable with small talk; I like it when people get real. Perhaps we all do. This man seemed so very nice and so very real. As soon as he left, I sought out Bec. 'Is he single?'

'Yes! And last time I was out drinking with him, he said he was desperate to meet his wife.'

'I am his wife.'

'OK, Jen, but he was also doing the splits in the middle of a dance floor, so . . . No, you're right, he's perfect for you.'

When he returned, we talked a bit about favourite books, and Jasper said he would send me one of his that I'd never read. We went our separate ways for a while, neither of us wanting to seem too keen, and I pushed it until about 9.30 p.m., but then I really was ready to go home. I approached Jasper at the bar, business card in hand (cool), tapped him on his giant shoulder and said, 'I'm leaving, but my email address is on here, if you'd like to send me that book.'

Jasper turned around. He was holding a wine cooler. 'You're leaving? That's a shame, because I was hoping you'd drink this bottle of champagne with me.'

It was freezing, but we sat outside, shivering, drinking bubbles and making our way through a packet of ten cigarettes I'd bought to give me 'outs' from the smallest small talk. It was eleven when I finally made my way home, waving as Jasper returned to the bar, calling my mum on the way to the Tube and telling her voicemail, 'I've just met my husband.'

It was snowing the first morning I woke in Jasper's flat, several weeks later. Roused by his gently closing the front door, I nosed round his bedroom while I waited for him to return: old paintings stacked against the wall, photos of his nephew and nieces, boxes of what looked like someone else's furniture. I had told him about Will on our first date, which had been a dinner, and he had cried. He had told me about his mum, Louise, 'Lulu', the love of his life. She had died when he was twenty-two. The boxes in his flat were hers. I cried too. That was before the steak and cocktails. Before the snogging in the pub. Before the coy decision about whether or not to share a taxi.

I jumped back into bed when I heard the door and pretended to be sleeping like an angel when he threw a newspaper onto the bed, kissed me and headed to the kitchen. He returned with bacon sandwiches, 'with ketchup and home-made pesto', tea, orange juice, SUCH kind eyes. I couldn't believe the man I had met. Big enough to protect me from any motherfucker who ever came too close. The world's gentlest giant, who cried easily and made his own pesto.

44

Charlotte called. 'Can you come to the office? We need to talk next steps.' We still had to write the Letter Before Claim. She was at Mishcon de Reya at the time, a glossy firm inside what appeared to be a palatial townhouse on one of Central London's garden squares.

In a meeting room at the front of the building, Charlotte told me, 'The Met won't release the paperwork yet – intriguingly, they say there may still be arrests.' She suggested we inform News International that we saw my name, two phone numbers, my date of birth in the Mulcaire notebooks. 'We don't specify that the numbers were yours and Neil's, because we don't know, and we just hope they don't ask. Otherwise, we'll have to wait for the police to release an un-redacted version.'

'He got my date of birth wrong, actually. But he got Rachel's name right, and her date of birth, I think. Her address. I'm not sure I saw her number . . .'

Charlotte agreed Rachel may also have a claim. 'How would he know about her, if he didn't get her name from your voicemail?'

I shrugged. 'She was a witness for my criminal case . . .'

We stared at one another. 'Paying public officials,' she said. Then something like, 'It's not enough, but it's something your civil case might be able to unearth. If payment changed hands, it would become a criminal matter.'

For now, she told me, without access to the paperwork and the phone numbers, all we could do was send the Letter Before Claim and wait for News International's response.

'Hang on a minute.' I picked up my phone. Hadn't the Met sent me those numbers when I first made my enquiry? I found the original email. There they were: the two phone numbers Glenn Mulcaire had attributed to me and to Neil, which had been redacted from the notebooks held by the Met.

'Genius!' Charlotte said. 'Well done. So, was that your number?'

I didn't know. After I had – again, unbelievably naively – called the *Sun*'s tip line to ask if there was a particular police station I should attend with allegations, the reporter had called me back so many times I had changed my phone number. That meant I had a burner for a while. Then another. Then I got a contract again, at some later date.

Charlotte pulled the landline phone that was on the desk towards her, put it on speaker and dialled the number Glenn Mulcaire had attributed to me. A woman answered, 'Hello, Jenny speaking.' Our eyes met and our jaws dropped. Charlotte gathered herself first. 'Sorry which Jenny is this?'

'It's Jenny Evans, who's this?' Charlotte said she would call her back and hung up the phone. We said it together, 'He hacked the wrong Jenny Evans.'

I needed to think. I left Charlotte's office and sat on a bench in the square. *If Glenn Mulcaire didn't hack my phone, I can't make this claim. I can't force News International executives to tell the truth, using the law. I can't force the Met to admit someone took money from the paper. I can't use Max's money to get answers – for me, or for anyone.*

If adrenaline hadn't been pumping quite so hard, I might have cried. This had been my chance at establishing the facts. This had been my chance at exposing the truth and getting it onto the record. To shed my shame and grab back some of the power and hold my head up and say, 'What happened to me was abuse. And I won't tolerate that. That is not OK.' *This had been my chance*. I had so much wanted to hold my head high. It was all I wanted.

I called Nick, realising I was slightly breathless. 'I can't do it.' My voice stuck in my throat, and I once again reached my hand to it. 'I can't force the News International executives into court. Glenn Mulcaire tried to hack me, but he hacked the wrong Jenny Evans.'

Nick seemed relaxed, or perhaps he was trying to calm me. He said something like, 'Unbelievable' and laughed. I trusted that he could see the situation from all angles and relaxed a little myself. Perhaps this wasn't as major a blow to the investigation as it felt. 'Have you told Max?' he asked. Charlotte was doing that.

Nick told me all was not lost in terms of getting some answers from executives via the courts. Maybe even the criminal courts, as the police had re-opened three investigations: *Operation Elveden*, which would look at police corruption; *Operation Tuleta*, which would look at computer hacking, and *Operation Weeting*, which would look again at allegations of phone hacking at the *News of the World*. It was *Weeting* that had control of the Mulcaire notebooks.

'They told Charlotte there may be some arrests.'

'Yes.'

All of this chimed with what my sources were hearing. Following Murdoch's instruction to give the police everything that was being hidden, documents were reportedly handed to the Met that were so revealing it meant *Operation Weeting* was opened the next day.

'Finally, they seem to be taking it seriously,' Nick concluded. He sounded tired.

He was pursuing multiple leads, some of which were related to other victims of crime as well as celebrities. 'The danger is, whatever the outcome, the executives let the reporters take the flak. But it seems they are going to do that anyway and the worms cannot be put back inside the can . . .'

He asked where I was in relation to getting answers. I didn't know. 'I need a moment. I need to gather myself,' was all I could manage. We signed off.

It was dusk. Streetlamps sputtered and buzzed into life around me. I could hear the low rumble of the buses on Holborn high road, smell the frost on the evening air. Life was life-ing all around me, as if the spin of the sixpence had not just upended everything. Again. *What now?*

I looked down at my boots, tapping the toes together in a kind of reverse Dorothy Gale. *No place like home.* How would I find a pathway now? How would I reach the end?

If Glenn Mulcaire didn't hack my phone, how did the newspapers know so much about me? If Glenn Mulcaire didn't hack my phone, how did he have Rachel's name and contact details? Who told Glenn Mulcaire that Rachel was significant at all?

How is this happening? What the fuck is going on here?

Why was it allowed?

It was obvious that the answer was: the police. From the start, sources had been telling me about the police. The Met and the Murdoch press worked together. And yet, I didn't want to believe it. Not of my police team. Not my team. Just as children would rather do anything than admit their main carer would harm them, I was so vulnerable when I made my allegations that I was still psychologically wedded to the notion that my police team would not have hurt me. But what if someone who transcribed interviews was corrupt, say? Or a civilian administrator, who filed stuff away? Or what if, at that time, someone like Sid Fillery – the man in the grey suit – had the means to access police files, as a PI? *How the hell am I going to even start trying to prove that, so many years later?* I needed to know how Mulcaire got his leads about me. *Who was his source?*

I pulled my phone out of my pocket and dialled Nia. She is another of the *Dispatches* producers, with a super-quick brain I love.

'Mulcaire hacked the wrong person with the same name,' I told her when she picked up. 'The wrong Jenny Evans.'

Nia had a similar response to Nick, 'Hilarious'. Then she did the mental arithmetic. 'So, how did he get Rachel's name?'

'Exactly. Who was his source?'

'Let's ask him.'

Nia suggested we kit me up with an undercover camera and knock on Glenn Mulcaire's front door to find out how he knew Rachel was significant to me. Yes, she and I had acted together, but why would he have picked her from an entire cast? Why pick someone from *Twin Town* at all? We made the film before The Famous Man attack, and several years before I reported it. The only reason she was significant was because she was part of the police investigation.

Nia and I needed a little time. I had to train in using an undercover kit. She needed to speak to some channel executives and write the 'Stage 1', which sets out, per the OFCOM code, the public interest defence for secret filming. Unlike the newspaper industry and streamers, television journalism is independently regulated. It's imperfect, but it has supported journalistic integrity. Crucially, the existence of OFCOM does not inhibit investigative work in any way, which is the argument always used by newspapers against a more robust form of regulation for them.

45

It was maybe a week or so after I first called Nia that she and I found ourselves sitting in a rental car, in suburban south London, watching our wing mirrors for Glenn Mulcaire. I had already wound myself up to knock on his front door once, but no one had answered.

Nia saw him first: an unremarkable middle-aged man ambling down the street carrying some shopping. She put her hand on my leg. We rehearsed again what I would say. Something like:

> *My name is Jenny Evans. I wonder if you could help me. I am the person who reported [The Famous Man] to the police. I now know my name was in your notebooks. But you didn't have just my name, you had my friend's name too. My name was available in court documents, though it was not reportable, but hers was not. I just wanted to ask you, can you remember who gave you her name?*

It wasn't exactly catchy, but it was the shortest version we could come up with.

With a nod to Nia, I opened the car door and floated down the street, hardly able to believe what I was doing. *Maybe it wasn't the police. Maybe he will say a friend talked. My house was bugged. Maybe all of it. Maybe he hacked someone from the police . . .*

Wearing the camera made me nervous. Despite the clear public interest in potentially exposing police corruption, it felt like an ambush. This feeling was made worse when Glenn opened his front door, because I liked him immediately. He was gentle and polite. He listened attentively to my question, then – of course – told me he couldn't remember how he had obtained Rachel's name. I said something like, 'Wasn't it Greg Miskiw who handled you [for the *News of the World*]? Didn't he have good links with police? Or – even just the means of getting their phone numbers for you to use . . .'

Glenn shook his head. He said he couldn't be sure. He told me lots of people 'ran' him; it could have been any one of a number of them.

'Like who? Can you give me any names? I just need to try and work out how this information about me got into the newspaper.'

Glenn was evasive. I don't know why Nia and I had hoped for anything else. He said he couldn't remember all the names. 'I'd invite you in to talk about it, but I expect you're wearing a camera.' He bent down and looked straight at the buttonhole on my chest.

I decided to get out of there. In that moment, in a state of panic, I couldn't remember what I was supposed to do in this situation. Could I get into legal trouble for denying this when he had asked me so directly?

I had to work hard not to run back to Nia waiting in the car.

'He asked me if I was wearing a camera!'

'What did you say?'

'I got out of there. I couldn't remember what I was supposed to do if he confronted me.'

'Did he give you a name?'

'No. Why did we think he would? Surely Murdoch is paying his legal fees . . .'*

Nia laughed. 'Because we're idiots. Worth a try.'

I began removing the kit. 'He did say it wasn't just Greg Miskiw that ran him. He said it could have been any number of people. That's new, right?'

'It's definitely not "one rogue reporter",' Nia agreed. 'And if reporters knew how to hack, which is what we know now, surely, they'd only need a PI for . . .'

I finished her sentence: '. . . illegal stuff that was harder to get? Do you think they could blag records from the police?'

Nia saw the pain in my eyes and put her hand on my leg. 'I'm so sorry you don't have your answers yet.'

---

* Court documents have since revealed that Clive Goodman, the *News of the World*'s royal reporter, was paid £243,000 by News Group Newspapers (NGN), when he emerged from prison having implicated no one else. Mulcaire was given £80,000 in exchange for signing an agreement not 'thereafter to make any statement or comment which might injure, damage or impugn the good name, character or reputation of NGN'. Both payments were to settle employment claims.

46

Channel 4 decided the information Nia and I had gleaned from the Mulcaire 'doorstep' was interesting enough that they would broadcast it on the news that night. There had been so many denials from News International, of any wrongdoing at all, it felt revelatory to have an admission that Mulcaire had worked for more than one executive at the *News of the World*. Jasp and I watched it play out from the cosiness of his enormous sofa. I had stood too close to Mulcaire, so the only good shot I got was when he looked down the lens.

We had exposed a chink in News International's armour, but it didn't help me. In fact, it widened the net: lots of people 'ran' Mulcaire, so any one of them could have given him Rachel's name. *But how did they get it?*

My old friend insomnia crept back into my bones. When I finally slept, if I wasn't with Jasp, I woke with those neck-clutching nightmares of old – the fear that I couldn't breathe.

I was avoiding something. One night, damp with sweat from one of these dreams, heart pounding, knackered, I was ready to admit it to myself.

I turned on the light and went to make a pot of tea. I remember that the clock on the cooker told me it was just after three. When

I returned to bed, with the usual tray – toast, apple, tea – I opened my laptop and found the Camden Library newspaper database (easier than going to Colindale). Legs shaking, head fizzing, I forced myself to read every article every tabloid had written about me.

Seeing my secrets so casually laid bare was teeth-grindingly humiliating; details of what The Famous Man and his friend did to me, details I struggled to think about, that I wanted not to have happened and I wanted no one to know, danced mockingly along column inches.

Intermittently, I allowed myself the relief of blurring the words with tears.

It was reading what the *News of the World* published when the case fell apart that made my pulse quicken. Statements made in my police interview, quoted. Verbatim. My exact reaction in an emotional moment. *No one knew that.* I was presented as having deliberately kept secrets from the police in not disclosing the other acts of sexual violence I had experienced. Two of those incidents were listed.

It was agony. I threw open the window to gulp down night air and roared in shame.

The following morning, I went for my run around the cemetery. I needed to get out of my head and into my body. How I longed for peace of mind. To be anyone else, still. I reflected, as I negotiated headstones and tree roots, cobbles and dog walkers, that at that moment in time, I understood deep in my soul what it is to yearn for a quiet life. And yet – my secrets had been stolen, and it had meant I had been publicly misrepresented. The articles contained just enough personal description that people who knew me might have recognised me: my age, where I was from, that I had been in a film.

I tried to do a good thing to stop a bad man, and I was ruined for it. And it took away my opportunity to stop him doing it again. I have to set it straight. I have to. I have to.

Until I did, my life story was no longer my own.

With a creeping sense of fear, as lines from the articles darted back through my mind, I began to wonder if the Murdoch press might have accessed The Letter via the Met. *Is that how they knew so much?*

How could I find that out?

47

I noted down the names of the journalists who wrote the articles, each sending a current of fear down my spine. I then texted them to my most trusted tabloid reporter contacts, asking a) if they knew the person, and b) if so, what they knew.

My next call needed to be to the lead detective on my case. I knew that. I just – needed a moment. We hadn't spoken in years. I had trusted this man absolutely. He had met my flatmates. He had interviewed my family. He had interviewed Rachel when she found The Letter. He had interviewed me that time, too.

He had organised the Criminal Injury Compensation for me, to let me know I was believed – that criminal injury had been caused to my body by The Famous Man and his friend – *even though* I stopped talking, *even though* that destroyed all his hard work.

This man was the reason I didn't accuse the police of leaking information when I first began to question who I could trust. I refused to talk about the full contents of The Letter, preferring to clam up and allow the CPS to drop the charges, *specifically* to avoid making this man feel I was in any way accusing him of letting me down.

Now I had to ask him some difficult questions and every way I phrased them in my mind sounded like an accusation.

I can struggle to be my most competent self with those who have seen me at my most vulnerable. My conscious mind, which I try to supress, whispers, 'Don't pretend you belong here. They know you shouldn't be in the room.' My subconscious, 'They know what happened to you. They know you are weak', which – and this is the part you feel rather than think – translates in your body into, 'They know you are not worthy of respect.' It can be very hard to shake this vulnerability, even with people I know want the best for me. I was not looking forward to this call.

I made a bullet-point list of the questions I most wanted answered, so that if I began to panic and my mind went blank, I had something to rely on. The blanking happened a lot. Dissociation is another long-term impact of trauma and hugely inconvenient at work. For many years, in any stressful situation, I could find myself mute, unable to connect with the room I was in – that I feared others could tell I didn't belong in. Of course, it is directly linked to my experience with The Famous Man, because at its core it is just about who in any room has any power, and who does not.

'Jenny?'

'I didn't think you'd pick up.'

'I would always pick up for you.' His voice was warm and engaged, exactly as I remembered it. 'What can I do for you?'

'This feels like a very awkward question to ask you, but I have to, I'm afraid. I am still trying to find out what happened with my case. How the press got hold of so much of my information.'

I heard him stand and leave whichever room he was in, to seek privacy.

'Go on.'

'Well, firstly, might you be able to help me get access to my police file? Whatever remains of it.'

'I can try. Is that it?' He was tense.

'No. Sorry. You told me there were only five cops in a Gold Group who knew all the details of my case . . .'

'Yes.'

'Could I please take their names?'

He gave me the names without hesitation, but he sounded concerned. Then he said something I have never forgotten: 'I can vouch for my team.'

My senses sharpened in the way every journalist's does when a contact says something important. 'What do you mean? These are the wrong names? Are these people your team?'

No answer.

I made my voice as gentle and as non-threatening as I could manage, almost whispering, 'Who don't you trust? These people? The people above them? Those above you?'

'I can vouch for my team. I'm going to have to go. Good luck, Jenny.'

I spent the afternoon finding out whatever the internet could tell me about the names on the list. A couple of the Gold Group had worked at police stations in south London in the 1980s, known to be corrupt at that time, and, via Catford at least, to have had links to the *News of the World*. These same cops moved to Stoke Newington police station in the 1990s, also known to have been corrupt at that time. Just working at those stations didn't mean anything, though, of course.

His words, 'I can vouch for my team', echoed around my mind. What did he mean?

Could senior people not in the Gold Group access my information? Would they hand that over to the Murdoch press? Who?

I returned to the Camden Library newspaper database and began searching for 'Special Enquiry Team'. Two articles stood out. The first told me that around about the time I reported the crime against me, the squad was under pressure for a 'win'. The tabloid press had turned its gaze on them because part of their remit was celebrity cases (a curious decision, by the Met to categorise crimes in that way, but a sign of the power of tabloids at that time). The team had even been dubbed the *Celebrity Squad*.

A high-profile case the squad had brought had collapsed at trial. The *Daily Mail* had run a headline asking if it was worth its mettle. The second article profiled the boss of the squad, John Yates. *Why didn't [my lead detective] mention him?*

I received a text. It was a tabloid source. Each name I had sent him of the journalists who wrote my articles came back with a short description. One of them read, *Engaged to a cop*. I texted back, *What is the name of the cop?* I got the name. I googled it. But I had no way of knowing anything about any of these men. I needed help. I emailed Max.

48

A few hours later, Max and I were sharing a pot of tea in the café opposite his mews office in Mayfair, all flaky pastry and tablecloths, waiters in black aprons with white shirts. Every time I brushed shoulders with Max's world, I was reminded of how many lives within a life I had lived. How was it I felt comfortable sipping this tea, seeking his advice?

Max, keeping his voice low enough that the waiting staff couldn't hear and – a matter of habit – removing the battery from his mobile phone so that it couldn't record us, offered to pay for a private investigator, 'To try to find out more about this "celebrity squad" and its affiliates. It's easy. Simply a phone call.'

With a smile dancing in his eyes, Max told me, off the record, he had recently employed Glenn Mulcaire to do some investigative work for him. This is public knowledge now, but at the time, with an agreement still in place that Murdoch would cover his legal fees, Mulcaire a) needed it to stay on the downlow and b) nevertheless needed to earn money, so was happy to take Max's dollar as well. I thought, not for the first time, that Max Mosley was very smart.

'I assume you know much more now about how News International operates than you used to then,' I said. Max raised an eyebrow, still smiling. I thought perhaps it was worth one last punt. 'Can you ask Glenn if he remembers who gave him my friend Rachel's name?' If his source was well connected to the Met, or an officer directly, or if he had hacked an officer, I would be closer to my answer.

Max nodded.

I turned down his offer of investigative assistance, even though he clarified that he of course meant via legitimate means and a highly respected security firm, adding, 'I do not need to stoop as low as Rupert Murdoch.' I could never have afforded to embark on such a thing without him and I was incredibly grateful, but it felt like a risk. 'I'm worried that anything I do might somehow discredit Nick,' I told him, 'if the other side discover it. I understand this is legit, but it's Nick Davies's researcher. With an agenda. Using a PI. It could be spun to look very bad.'

Max nodded. He paused for thought, glancing around the café as he did so – possibly checking for recording devices, possibly just enjoying the twinkling chandeliers. 'Elveden' was the word he came back with.

'Really?' *Operation Elveden* was the Met's active investigation into allegations of inappropriate payments, to its own officers and to other public officials. Would they be interested in this?

'Elveden!' Max said, slightly more loudly, warming to the idea. 'Jenny, this is exactly what they are there for.' He began to put his phone back together. 'I'll speak to Dominic.' His lawyer.

Dominic spoke to Charlotte, she called me. One week later, Max and I found ourselves face to face with two representatives of London's Metropolitan Police at Charlotte's offices.

I no longer had a copy of The Letter, so prior to the meeting, I had asked Charlotte to request they bring one with them. I intended to cross reference its contents with the *News of the World* article.

The police officers were grey, ruddy of cheek – like McMullan, straight out of central casting. They were from the Economic and Specialist Crime Unit of the Met, attached to *Operation Tuleta*, which was investigating computer hacking. Not attached to *Operation Elveden*. No one ever explained that to me. I should have pushed for someone from *Elveden* – if you aren't facing the people investigating corrupt payments, they aren't going to look for corrupt payments. But, still, I didn't understand the systems. Still, though I had come so far, I didn't feel confident enough to ask. And I assumed Charlotte and Max did understand. But Charlotte had sent apologies – she couldn't be with us that day. I very much liked Emma, her second in command, but I missed Charlotte's forensic mind and the fact that she often seemed to know exactly how I was feeling. The still traumatised part of me, that thin, small voice in my mind, wondered if maybe the truth was, I wasn't important enough.

One of the cops slid a photocopy of The Letter across the boardroom table to me. Despite the very efficient air conditioning, I felt the familiar heat of self-consciousness rush my face. The silt at my core stirred as I reached towards it. I searched the cops' faces for clues. *Have you read it? What do you know?*

Neither man gave anything away. In fact, they gave the impression that they very much did not want to be there at all, which was not helping the negative voice in my head. They made me feel that this – that I – was a regrettable waste of time. *Oh God, I am wasting not just their time, but the time of Charlotte and Emma and Max. What do I think I am doing?*

'Do you mind if I . . .?' I asked, motioning towards the printout. Nobody minded. I skim-read the letter – 'Alright bitch?' etc., etc. It all came back as I read it again. I cringed. I wish I had felt compassion for the young woman who wrote it – she was so confused, and in such pain. But sitting there, with those policemen, and all the other people I had gathered in my righteous anger, I hated her. I hated her weakness and her folly and her fawning need to explain. *Grow the fuck up*, I whispered to her in my head. *Stop fucking whining. This is embarrassing. Worse things happen to people. Far worse. Stop crying. Go the fuck home.* How quickly shame slips into self-hatred. Or perhaps it's the same thing.

I wished I hadn't read it. Now I had to convince these bored policemen that something that had happened to me was worth investigating, and I just wanted to hide.

'I'd like you to investigate,' I said eventually, exhaling slowly – a beach ball with a puncture. Had I not been breathing before?

'Investigate?' one of them checked.

'Yes. To investigate, please. Because I reported a crime against a high-profile person and details of that crime ended up in the tabloid press. And you have access to emails and stuff, don't you? Perhaps my name was mentioned somewhere by executives at News International? Perhaps the electronic communications will tell us something. Isn't that what your remit is?'

The officers looked at one another. They puffed out their cheeks and shook their heads. One of them said, 'That's going to create a lot of work.'

I nodded.

'Not much chance we'll be able to give you answers. Loads of people worked on that case.'

I nodded again, feeling the anger I had turned inward starting to outface again. 'Yes. But only five people knew all the details, apparently. I have their names.' I tapped my notebook. 'And the name of their boss. And the name of a cop who is engaged to one of the reporters who wrote the articles that contained my private information. Confidential information. That I had only told to the police.'

Still, they tried their hardest to put me off. I became irritable. 'Sorry, if there is corruption in the Met Police, don't you want to know about it? Don't you want to stop it happening again?'

The cops exchanged glances once more. They gave me nothing. Finally, the older one said, 'We'll come back to you.' They nodded at us by way of a goodbye and Emma found someone to show them out. We thanked them for their time. When they had gone, she shook her head at me, and . . . did she whisper 'Dickheads'? Or is that merely what I was thinking?

Max offered to pay for Charlotte to stay on the case and I said I'd think about it. But by the time the bus had deposited me at my stop, I had emailed him to turn down another of his kind offers. I had a different plan. Whatever happened with the dickheads from *Tuleta*, I felt I couldn't trust them to help me. I was going to complain. And I could do it myself.

49

A few days later, I finished work at a production company in east London and made my way to Shoreditch police station, which happened to be the nearest, to meet two members of the Met's Directorate of Professional Standards (DPS). It is worth mentioning that the DPS is a department within the Met Police, made up of cops from the Met Police. It is not in any way an independent investigative body. Nevertheless, I was willing to put my trust in the system one more time; I had no choice.

I had been called in the afternoon to let me know that I would be meeting one member of the DPS and another cop who I was told was there because he was trained in dealing with sexual violence. 'I won't be talking about sexual violence,' I had said, 'and as a woman who was hurt by men, I would not feel comfortable talking to a strange man about it on a random Tuesday after work, whatever his training.' *WTF are you thinking?*

I was met by the two men. The Met Police can be *so bad* at listening.

I gave the two cops the lowdown on everything that had happened . . .

I reported a crime
the perpetrator was famous
details of my allegations were printed in the Sun *newspaper*
four days later.
Tabloids,
predominantly those owned by Rupert Murdoch,
continued to print articles
containing accurate confidential details about my case.
I was sure they shouldn't have known what they knew.
I became paranoid
I stopped trusting my friends and family
I became certain my house was bugged and
my phone line tapped.
Ultimately, I stopped talking to the police
Because I didn't know who I could trust.
The charges against the man who hurt me
were dropped.
I lost my chance at justice.
I trained as a journalist
to try to get to the bottom
of how this had happened.
When I first heard about
phone hacking
I thought that was the explanation.
But the PI at the News of the World *hacked the wrong person*
with the same name as me,
and anyway, the kind of information the paper had printed
could not have been contained
in a voicemail.
I have come to the conclusion

that someone in the Met Police
either gave or – worse – sold my private information
to the tabloids.
And I would like to know the truth, please.
So that I can move on.

I asked them to look into whether The Letter or a transcript of my police interviews had been shared with tabloids, and when, where and how leaking of my allegations could have otherwise happened. I gave them the names of the men I had been told were in the Gold Group, and I walked out of there feeling like maybe Dorothy Gale had bossed the Yellow Brick Road. This, surely, was the beginning of the end.

Jasp and I caught the Eurostar to Paris for the weekend and, in a beautiful square in Montmartre, with a timeworn theatre at one end and an even older accordion player at the other, he asked me to marry him.

50

Missing Milly Dowler's voicemail was hacked by News of the World

Once again, a *Guardian* article, written by Nick, brought me bumping back to earth.

Milly Dowler was a thirteen-year-old girl who went missing on her way home from school. The nation held its breath as her hometown, a sleepy, leafy, suburban part of the South East, was searched and searched again. There was footage of her leaving the train station with her friend. She texted her dad that she would be home in half an hour. She never arrived.

Letters were found in Milly's bedroom suggesting she had considered running away and appeals were made by her family for her to come home. A week after her disappearance, the police force investigating stated that she probably hadn't been taken by force.

'Don't know why they said that, but the newsrooms went crazy,' a source told me when we met in Soho for coffee to discuss Nick's story. 'The tabloids wanted to find her first. They wanted to beat each other, and the police, but – we all just wanted to help find her. The message from Rebekah was: "Get whatever you can on this."' Then she went on holiday to Dubai, but my sources recalled faxing updates to her.

'Did you take "Get whatever you can" to mean phone hack?'

'I don't phone hack.'

'No, sure. But . . .?'

'They always used figurative language, like "get whatever you can", but who knows what she meant.'

When pushed, the source told me he thought Brooks was genuinely worried about Milly and they should use all the tools in their toolboxes to try to help find her. It didn't necessarily mean she wanted her voicemail to be hacked.

A second source told me that when Milly's voicemail *was* hacked, a message was picked up from a recruitment agency somewhere, inviting her for a second interview at a factory. 'They must have just got the wrong number, but everyone who listened to the voicemail thought she might turn up at that factory. There was a reporter from every tabloid outside before the end of the day.'

A third source said, 'The police knew we were all hands on deck. They knew we were hacking phones. They welcomed our help. At first.'

In June 2002, three months after Milly disappeared, the *Sun* offered a £100,000 reward for information that would lead to her return.

Some of Milly's voicemails were deleted, leading her parents to cling to the hope she might be listening to them. They continued to leave messages and send texts, telling her they loved her. Begging her to come home – all of which, it is safe to assume, were listened to by tabloid reporters. When it was revealed, by Nick and *Guardian* colleague Amelia Hill, that journalists had hacked Milly's phone, it was presumed they were also the ones doing the deleting. This was common practice, to stop rival newspapers getting information. In fact, Milly's phone automatically deleted messages every seventy-two hours when the mailbox was full.

In September 2002, Milly's decomposed body was found in woods near to her home. She had to be identified using dental records. A mass murderer of women and girls was eventually arrested for raping and murdering her.

Milly's name is etched into the national psyche and into our hearts, along with the names of a handful of other women and girls whose lives were ended by male violence. We all so much wanted the worst thing in the world not to have happened to that little girl. So, when Nick discovered that while everyone else was searching for her, the tabloids' method of doing so involved invading her privacy and that of her family, potentially compromising the police investigation, the nation finally took notice. There was a national outcry.

This was the moment 'phone hacking' became a household phrase. This was the moment a story became a scandal. The average person doesn't care too much about a celebrity's voicemail, understandably. But everyone cared about Milly Dowler. In the end, it was the stolen secrets of a child, an innocent victim of crime, that demolished the *News of the World* house of cards.

Three days later, Rupert Murdoch announced the closure of the paper. I was alone in a hotel room, readying to film on location, when I saw the news. Inanely, I photographed the TV screen and sent it to Becky and Nia and the others on the *Dispatches* teams, even though they would of course have known. As with Coulson's resignation, to me it felt momentous. Huge. *Our work has made an impact.*

That photo flashes up in my social media timelines every year: a TV screen, a news reporter, the words on the tickertape: *News of the World to close.*

I spent a long time sitting on the edge of the hotel bed, staring at the wall. I couldn't work out if I was happy or sad. I felt sorry for all the brilliant reporters I had met, who would now need to find other work. I hoped they wouldn't get blamed. But that newspaper, run by bullies, had bullied us all. That newspaper, run by bullies, had humiliated me and now . . . the slingshot had knocked Goliath clean out. *Surely, that could only be good,* I thought.

Peeling myself away from the rolling news, I found a piazza, ordered myself a beer and closed my eyes to the warmth of the sun. *Surely, surely, surely, that can only be good.*

Now there will have to be a reassessment. An inquiry. Now there will have to be some conversation – about power structures, use of private information. Prosecutions for those who steal secrets, or give them away. Invasions of privacy. Surely.

That evening, still trying to absorb as much news as possible, I wrote in my notebook, 'The *News of the World* can bully no one now', and felt such a rush of adrenalin I was once more dizzy. It was like that moment when Ripley runs to the shuttle with Jones and the *Nostromo* explodes. *Got you, you son of a bitch.*

51

Rupert Murdoch and his son James, bespectacled head of News International in Europe, expressed contrition. They dropped their bid to buy a greater stake of BSkyB, the feared attempt at monopolisation. They agreed to sit before the same media-focused parliamentary select committee that had summoned Nick and the *Guardian* editor after the July 2009 article. No longer could they argue that the *Guardian*'s reporting was designed to mislead the British public.

I went to Parliament that day, because I found it hard to believe it was happening. The hearing was at Portcullis House, a modern extension of the Palace of Westminster, located across the road, just off Parliament Square. There is a lot of glass at Portcullis House. It has a large atrium which contains both a coffee shop and actual trees. Stairs and lifts take you to the committee rooms and offices that run around the edges, over multiple floors.

A queue of journalists, camera crews and gawkers like me snaked around the block from first light. Suddenly, everyone gave a shit. I couldn't help but smile.

We all had to get through security and scanners. Many had recording equipment. It took hours. I just had my notebook, but by the time

I made it to the committee room, it was full. I spied Nick's leather jacket in the rows immediately behind where the Murdochs would sit. I waved. He shrugged apologetically for not being able to get me in, then I felt a tug at my elbow. It was Cath, another close friend from my journalism training. She had moved to Paris a couple of years after we graduated from City and had come back to London to report on this story for the French TV channel she worked for. Cath, Kris and I had bonded over our ability to get work done well at City, despite not being as expensively educated or confident as most of the others. We had ended up laughing a lot then, as we tried to negotiate our way out of various pickles. We still laugh a lot now when we meet up, which is not nearly often enough. It was great to see her.

Cath grabbed my hand and tried to sneak us into the main room even after others had been stopped, but we were spotted at the last minute and ushered into one of the spillovers. There, we were told to sit down, stare up at the projector screen, and wait.

It would be another hour before Rupert and James arrived, with Rupert's then-wife, Wendi. When they did, Rupert's performance was jaw-dropping. This didn't get enough coverage at the time, in my opinion, so surprised was everyone that he had turned up at all, but his behaviour was extraordinary. This billionaire media tycoon, this tormentor of prime ministers and presidents, this tyrant, oppressor, bully – the most frightening man on earth. This autocrat, with the power to influence democracy, behaved like he belonged in a care home. His opening gambit, delivered in the faltering manner of a sweet elderly gentleman who could barely function, was, 'I just want to say, this is the humblest day of my life.'

His hands shook, he cupped his ear to hear, he paused 'to think' for longer than I believed humanly possible. Cath and I exchanged glances and the giggles started to bubble up.

'What is going on?' I whispered.

'He thinks we're stupid,' she replied.

After a long while, in which nothing much was achieved by any of Rupert's interrogators, Cath groaned in pain. 'This is embarrassing.'

I felt it too. This was not someone filled with remorse. We were being openly mocked.

Suddenly, there was commotion. I saw Murdoch's wife, Wendi, leap from her seat. People started running for the doors. 'What's going on?' Cath was in the corridor before me. The Murdochs and the MPs were safely escorted to a back room. Security had caught hold of a young man with long hair and were pinning him to the floor right next to us.

'He had a cream pie,' a bemused man to my right said, some of the cream attached to his ear.

'Why?' I asked. Nobody knew. 'Why?' Cath and I shouted at the young man with the hair.

No response. Most people were laughing with nervous shock. I realised I was now standing next to Nick. He was not laughing. In fact, he was mouthing 'Wanker' at the cream pie thrower, who looked a little put out. 'We're fucked,' he said when he turned to me. 'We'll never get that man back in a room to give us answers now. We're fucked.'

Nick was right. That poor, contrite, elderly gentleman did not return. And we never really found out why the doofus threw the cream pie either. It was something to do with the BskyB bid. What we did discover, shortly afterwards, was that though Rupert had closed the *News of the World* over the hacking of Milly Dowler's voicemail, he had registered the *Sun on Sunday* domain name just days later. Such contrition. There is no getting that son of a bitch.

52

The day after the announcement that the *News of the World* would close, Andy Coulson was arrested, by appointment. He reportedly agreed to attend a south London police station for the formality. *Was it where I was interviewed about The Letter?* I wondered, *the place I decided I could no longer trust anyone enough to pursue my case.* He was questioned in connection with allegations of corruption and phone hacking.

As with the closure of the *News of the World*, my emotions were mixed. *He isn't ultimately to blame.* If my sources were to be believed, he wasn't the only editor who must have known. He wasn't solely culpable.

As Roy Greenslade taught us at City, people must draw their own moral and ethical 'red lines', especially when the rule of law is relevant and it hasn't been fast enough to draw them for us, or it is being allowed to be ignored. It's true, Coulson had favoured self-interest and generating profit for Rupert Murdoch over respect for people like me, and over the public interest. But it wasn't personal. What Andy Coulson was was a very efficient member of a team. A cog in the machinery that powers Rupert Murdoch's news factory.

When I returned from my shoot a few days later, questioning, as I lugged the camera kit back in, why I had bought a flat with so many stairs, I was very ready for wine and chips. Rachel lived in Essex by now, but two old friends who lived nearby were around, I had checked, as was my smart and gentle flatmate, Jess.

Jess and I opened a bottle and did a little dance as I threw my *Tabloid Editors* and *Tabloids General* ring binders in the bin. Rosa, a uni mate, and Lotte, another best friend from the bar days, met me for Turkish food on Church Street, the road that runs through Stoke Newington – by this point quite zhushy and not what it was in the Bar Lorca days at all.

'Do you feel happy?' Rosa asked, as she shared out the rosé. We had a table by the window, humous, flatbread, falafels, the last tendrils of summer still just about holding on.

'I think I feel relieved,' I told her, 'but . . .'

She gave me a look as if to say, *Give yourself a break*, and raised her glass for us to cheers. 'This is a huge achievement, Jen. I know you are going to say it's not just yours, but it is partly yours. The truth is coming out. That is huge. And we love you. And we say, "Cheers."'

'Yes, we do,' Lotte added. We clinked glasses. 'Go on then, what was the "but"?'

'I still don't know exactly what happened with my case.' I suddenly thought I might cry.

'What do you think it might feel like if you never find out?' Lotte asked.

No one had yet asked me that, and it brought the tears I was suppressing closer to the surface. Finding out still felt so important. The Met had stepped up and made arrests at News International. It had only done so when backed into a corner –

but it had done it. Now I needed it to step up for me. I needed the DPS to properly investigate what happened and to hold someone to account. So much of my self-worth was riding on it. Too much. Would this organisation that I had trusted in my most vulnerable moment, because I had had no choice, finally pay me the respect that that deserves?

We ate, we drank more wine, we danced in my living room. The following morning, as I left for a cemetery run to clear my pink-wine head, I saw that a neighbour had put a note through the door asking us to stop singing Lionel Ritchie quite so loudly. This was a surprise. I'd say we were in more of a Beyoncé phase.

53

That week Sir Paul Stephenson, the commissioner of the Metropolitan Police – the big boss – resigned. His links with Neil Wallis, Coulson's deputy, had been more extensive than the PR job and the hotel. He had met with News International representatives twenty-four times during his tenure, despite having sixty-nine press officers available to take those types of meetings. Sir Paul had even met with Wallis when the first phone-hacking investigation was being carried out. To be clear, the commissioner of the Metropolitan Police *had dinner with the people his force was investigating, while they were under investigation.* In his resignation statement, Stephenson stressed his integrity and dismissed claims that it was compromised by his relationships with News International executives.

The following day, the Met's deputy commissioner, John Yates, also resigned. Yates. The guy who made the statement that Nick's allegations weren't substantive. Yates, who ran the Special Enquiry Team. Yates, who knew everything about me.

The previous week, answering for his decisions around phone hacking to a parliamentary select committee, Yates had expressed regret at not re-opening the case when Nick's July 2009 article was printed.

Just as the Press Complaints Commission had blamed the Met for its decision not to robustly investigate, Yates blamed the decisions he made squarely on News International, claiming, as the PCC did, that he was deliberately misled:

> *It is a matter of great concern that, for whatever reason, the* News of the World *appears to have failed to cooperate in the way that we now know they should have with the relevant police inquiries up until January of this year.*
>
> *They have only recently supplied information and evidence that would clearly have had a significant impact on the decisions that I took in 2009 had it been provided to us.*

'*What?*' I said to Jess, as we sipped tea and watched my laptop. 'He just took their word for it, did he? Aren't the police supposed to *investigate* rather than just take the word of the people they are investigating that there's "nothing to see here"?'

'Apparently, that is one of the police's specialisms,' was her ever-dry response.

Jasp was cooking for us. It was our last night in my flat – we needed to sell it to make alterations to his. Then we needed to sell his to combine our money to buy a house.

I was devastated. It was the only place I had lived in my adult life that had felt like a proper home. But I also had a sense that I hadn't landed yet. That my future held a husband, a family. That to really come home would be to resolve my betrayal by the police, my humiliation by the press, and to settle into a different life.

54

Jasp and I got married a year to the day that we met. We didn't mean to, it just happened that way, because my grandpa was dying, and we wanted him to be there.

Granny and Grandpa, Mum's parents, had moved to be near her when Will died, and had become central to our lives. Every time I went home, Mum and I spent the Sunday with Granny and Grandpa and a roast chicken. They'd share the cooking. We'd listen to Elaine Paige on Radio 2 in their little cottage kitchen. Grandpa would dance, sometimes with me, and he'd sing. Afterwards we'd eat home-made trifle and play Scrabble. The winner got a star drawn by their name, the person who came second, a boot (sometimes a leg), the person who came third was the fly. Occasionally, beside the unfortunate who came fourth, a poo was drawn for the fly to buzz around. It is a family tradition from way before my time and no one can remember where it came from.

Though many of those years were spent with hearts heavy with grief for Will, there was much love and joy at Granny and Grandpa's. He began to die of heart failure just as I met Jasper. As the only man in my life, he had become incredibly important and I am grateful they met, but it's a little heartbreaking they didn't get to know one another better. Grandpa was Danny Kaye silly, Peter Ustinov funny. Jasper would have loved him. When we realised he might not make a wedding the following year, we decided just to do it. I thought, *If I can produce a* Dispatches *in eleven days, I can organise a wedding in three weeks.*

We invited people by text message, secured the time of a registrar by the skin of our teeth and got married in the Angel, a boutique hotel in Abergavenny, twenty-one days later. As with all the best things in life, it was a group effort: a little rough around the edges, full of goodwill and love . . . and with the best Motown and Soul band around, who we got only because I rang up the second after a last-minute cancellation.

Rosa was maid of honour. Rachel agreed to read a poem. Lotte came early to help us make the reception look beautiful, as did my former flatmate Bob with his partner and their new baby. Lu and Charlie of the 'True Colors' wrestled their toddlers into formal wear despite the fact I was wearing slippers beneath my dress. I had looked into holding the reception at a pub near the hotel. When we were teenagers, the entire youth community drank in that pub, which was at the bottom of the car park that otherwise held the market. It was called the Wine Bar, but I am 100 per cent sure it never sold a glass of wine. You went to the Wine Bar to drink lager, or snakebite and black (cool cool), to dance to The Prodigy or The Pogues and to score cheap hash from a dude whose name was Tokey or Smokey or something. He used to rummage around in his boxer shorts for it while we waited. God.

To my disappointment, the Wine Bar had become a Chinese restaurant by the time I was getting married, and it didn't cater for weddings, so we settled for a church hall a short walk from the hotel.

The wedding was a celebration of Jasp and me and the love we had found, but it was also a celebration of friendship: a profound thank-you to all those who had got us through our respective trials and pains. I have so many brilliant, beautiful friends, who matter so much and who I have not named in this book, because it would be impossible. But I want to thank you all. You know who you are, and I love you.

One of my favourite moments of the wedding, which was caught on camera, was the giant double hug I got from Cerys and Rhi, our neighbours growing up. Their mum, Sue, who had worked the markets with Mum, had had a stroke and survived. Her kids were having to adjust to a new version of her.

Cerys and Sue had been the first people to get to Mum when Deb had told her that Will had died. It was a summer's day. Mum had been in our garden, Cerys and Sue in theirs, and they ran when they heard her scream.

Life had been so hard on us all since our family first moved in, two doors down from them, twenty years earlier. But here we were, me, Cerys and Rhi, still holding each other up. Then we were singing and dancing and sharing a moment of joy that we had well earned.

55

By the time the DPS at the Met delivered its report into my complaint, I had been married for two years, bought a cat, Cwtch, and moved from London to Bristol, to be near Joe, my surrogate brother, and to Mum and Deb, whose husband was ill. Jasp and I were a couple of years into trying unsuccessfully to have a baby. We have 'unexplained infertility': an agony like no other.

In the interim, the Leveson Inquiry, a statutory review of news-gathering practices, ended in the recommendation that an independent regulator be established for newspapers, in the style of OFCOM. Max Mosley tried to fund it. Newspaper proprietors were outraged. It does exist, in the form of Impress, but it is voluntary for newspapers to sign up and no major publications have yet done so. Not even the *Guardian*, which did so much work in exposing wrongdoing and corruption in journalism.

Evidence has since emerged, via employment and breach of privacy litigations, that suggests that many tabloid journalists, executives and editors outright lied under oath at Leveson. There has been no consequence for this.

Leveson Two, the second part of the inquiry, was meant to examine corruption: the secret links between the press, PIs and the police. The first part had only been able to conclude that there lacked evidence to question the integrity of the senior police officers involved. It was Leveson Two I was most personally interested in, of course. As, I suspect, were the Dowler family and all other crime victims who found themselves the focus of the tabloids. To what extent was the relationship corrupt? How often did it interfere with justice?

We are still waiting – the next Conservative government cancelled it. Culture secretary at the time, the unfeasibly successful Matt Hancock, ignored calls of 'Shame' from the Labour benches to declare, 'It's clear that we've seen significant progress, from publications, from the police and from the new regulator,' and it therefore wasn't needed.

I had occasionally been sent an email by the investigating officer at the DPS, expressing his regret at his report taking so long. Sometimes I just thanked him. Sometimes I replied with polite questions. I rarely got a straight answer.

> On 17 Jan 2012, at 11:11, [redacted]@met.police.uk wrote:
>
> Jenny
>
> Please find attached the terms of reference and investigation plan which have been approved by the IPCC.
>
> As stated below I have obtained the case papers for the the [sic] investigation of the allegations against [The Famous Man]. This covers all the allegations and there is a large amount of material. I am continuing to review that material.
>
> If you have any queries do not hesitate to contact me.
>
> Regards

From: Jenny Evans
Sent: 20 January 2012, 09:41
To: [Redacted] – DSPP DPS
Subject: Re: Update Regarding Complaint Against Police.

Hi [Redacted],

I've had another thought. Would it be worth asking Glenn Mulcaire where he got Rachel's name from? The name of the journalist who commissioned him to hack my voicemail was redacted when I saw the papers, for a reason I still don't understand, but if you can see it, it would be worth asking. If I am allowed to know that name ever, I would like to.

What do you think?

From: [redacted]@met.police.uk
Sent: 26 January 2012, 10:14:45 +0000
To: Jenny Evans
Subject: RE: Update Regarding Complaint Against Police

Jenny

Thanks for your response to my email. As with all investigations I will review it as it progresses and assess what other actions are required. At present I am working through the actions in the investigation plan I sent you. I will keep you updated with progress.

If you have any queries in the meantime please contact me.

Regards

From: Jenny Evans
Sent: 30 January 2012, 10:03
To: [Redated] – DSPP DPS
Subject: RE: Update Regarding Complaint Against Police.

Thanks [redacted], I understand. In light of the new info' available re Data Set 3 (in today's Guardian), I wonder if it's also worth checking what emails were sent about me in 2003, after you've worked through the list, as you describe. Getting the redacted name from my Mulcaire papers would help with that too. Will you let me know when I can know who that was?

Sorry if I am being a pain! It all matters to me a lot.

I didn't get an answer at all to that one. My fawning tone is cringeworthy. I was still so afraid. Instead of apologising, I should have asked more questions. And I should have kept doing so until I got an appropriate response.

I wasn't given any warning when the report was finally complete. Nor that it would land on my doorstep one morning in late November 2013, shortly before Andy Coulson and Rebekah Brooks were due to go on trial.

The brown A4 envelope was moderately heavy. I made tea and took it to bed with the cat and my laptop. My safe place.

Any hope I was feeling sank into my stomach as I opened page one. The tone was defensive of the conduct of the Met. It was offensive in relation to me, implying I had courted press attention when I made the allegations.

I had specifically requested The Letter be compared to the final *News of the World* article, but I had asked, beyond that, if The Letter was not the source of the information, the Met assist me in working out who was. I had given the DPS the name of the journalist whose fiancé was a Met officer, for example.

I skim-read the report for mention of investigation into these matters. There was none. It entirely ignored my request that potential leaks beyond The Letter be investigated, stating that my case was not considered exceptional enough for phone records to be recalled. Why not? *You are not important enough.* The shame at my core was stirring. It did not mention the reporter engaged to the cop at all.

Grateful, as always, for Cwtch's little heartbeat – a lifeline in moments of distress – I stroked her stripey head, then took a glug of tea for courage. 'These cunts,' I whispered to her. 'These cunty cunts, Cwtch.' I had trusted them yet again, and they were not going to help me. They were going to cover it up.

I read on. The report was almost entirely focused on my question as to whether The Letter had been released to the press, which was categorically not the agreed remit of their 'investigation'. It concluded that The Letter had not been leaked and the reason given, which made me gasp, was that if it had been, the tabloids would surely have printed every salacious detail it contained. The cop drew attention to the element of The Letter in which I tell my friend that I had slept with women. He suggested, surely disingenuously, that as the tabloids hadn't printed that fact, The Letter could not have been disclosed to them. *What is going on here? Is he trying to humiliate me?* It was working. I wiped away hot, angry tears.

This cop had to know that this was an illogical conclusion. If the *News of the World* had printed that 'salacious' fact, it would have revealed without doubt that the journalist who wrote the article had The Letter. Which would, in turn, have revealed the link to the police, and burned for the reporter a clearly very valuable source. It would have been an incredibly foolish thing for any reporter to do. And if my research, for Nick and for Channel 4, had taught me one thing, with absolute clarity, it was that tabloids are not run by foolish people. Ruthless people, yes. Possibly some very damaged people. But highly intelligent, professional, efficient, fast-thinking, slick-operating, ruthless, possibly damaged people. This report, I was concluding, was what is known as a 'whitewash': lacking depth or quality, used to cover up.

Towards the end, the report did reference officers from *Operation Elveden* interviewing *Sun* and *News of the World* journalists in relation to corrupt payments made to police officers on my case. I didn't know they had done that. I focused, reading the extract multiple times. But no matter how many times I did so, it told me nothing.

Expenses records seen by Operation Elveden show that prior to writing the article the journalist met with a 'police contact' regarding [The Famous Man] investigation.

The journalist was arrested and interviewed by Operation Elveden. He has denied obtaining information from police sources. The person he referred to as a 'police contact' [in the article] has not been identified.

No further action has been taken against the journalist.

The report did admit there had been one leak from the Met. It was attributed to a press officer, 'a member of the Directorate of Public Affairs (DPA)'. It said he had been suspended for telling journalist sources which police station The Famous Man had been taken to. *Okaaaay.* I sat back to take this in. *Not a detail I am at all concerned about; not my allegations. Not my trauma. I mean, all leaks are bad, but this is – not relevant, surely?* The report named the press officer, then claimed that his file had accidentally been deleted, and that he had since died, so the DPS could not help me further with this. 'Wow,' I said to Cwtch, who stretched out her paws and purred loudly, as if she was having the best day of her life.

The report concluded,

> *The comparison of the article against the letter and subsequent [police] interview strongly suggests that the author of the article published on [date redacted] was not in possession of a copy of the letter or a copy of the interview. The article does not refer to the existence of the letter.*
>
> *However it is clear that the author of the article was aware of why criminal proceedings were halted. It is not possible to establish how the author obtained this information. It has been established that a member of police staff working in the [Directorate of Public Affairs] (DPA) did inappropriately pass information to the media regarding [The Famous Man] investigation. However it is not clear whether he was still working within the DPA when the letter came to light or whether the DPA were made aware of the letter.*
>
> *The possibility of persons within the [Met] having disclosed the reason why proceedings were halted to the media can not be discounted. Similarly the possibility that the extensive investigative journalism being undertaken could have established this also can not be discounted.*
>
> *Having considered the available evidence on the balance of probability it is concluded that Metropolitan Police Service staff did inappropriately disclose details relating to the investigation of an allegation of indecent assault made by you in October 2002. The complaint is upheld.*

> There is no evidence to support criminal proceedings against any member of the [Met].
>
> There is no evidence to support misconduct proceedings against any member of the [Met].
>
> Whilst reaching my conclusions on this investigation, I have also considered whether the performance of the officers involved was satisfactory, i.e., have they done their jobs to the standard expected of them. Having weighed up all of the available evidence, this matter is not one of unsatisfactory job performance. I therefore intend to take no action under the Unsatisfactory Performance Procedure.
>
> I have considered whether there are any opportunities for individual or organisational learning. I have not identified any such opportunities.
>
> You have the right of appeal in relation to this investigation to the Independent Police Complaints Commission (IPCC). You have 28 days within which to make your appeal to the IPCC. You are advised to post your appeal in good time to ensure it reaches the IPCC before the end of the 28th day. The 28th day is 25th December.

Merry Christmas.

No apology. The 'no opportunities for individual or organisational learning' made me wince. The message was, *Something minor occurred here, there is nothing that can be done, and you are wasting our time. Close the door on your way out, Ms Evans.*

I googled the dead press officer. One article had been published about his suspension at the time it had happened. He was let go months before the *News of the World* article that tipped me over the edge was published, so 'it is not clear whether he was still working within the DPA when the letter came to light or whether the DPA were made aware of the letter' was an easily provable . . . lie? What other word is there?

Even if the press office had been made aware of the letter, and this leaky man was therefore party to the kind of information that was in the article, *it still couldn't have been him who leaked it because he had already been suspended.* 'He thinks I am just going to slink off with my tail between my legs,' I told Cwtch, who smiled. She wasn't getting it.

The suggestion in the report that my allegations and other deeply personal details could have been obtained via journalistic rigour is similarly misleading. Much of what was in the article was information I had only ever told the police. I *might* have then discussed some of it with Katie and Lizzie, or with family, but that would have been at home, probably with taps running to avoid bugs picking it up, because I had become so paranoid. If bugs had done so, that was not legitimate journalistic enquiry. Surely it was a form of unlawful information gathering, with no public interest defence. Nothing in the report about that.

A broadsword of winter sun cut through the curtain. I needed to get out. To walk. To think. *What next?* I was at that time recovering from an ectopic pregnancy. It was the only time an embryo formed by Jasper and me had clung on, but it got stuck in the wrong place and had had, the previous day, to be aborted. The needle had bruised me like a kick. I felt I had shattered. I didn't know how to put the pieces of myself back together. So, I wasn't in the best headspace to fight the Met.

The truth is, I am not a natural fighter. It is something I have had to learn. When you are looking for the truth and the people who have it keep changing the rules as to how you find it, you begin to understand the battle.

I had been given a short timeframe within which I could complain to the Independent Police Complaints Commission (IPCC. Now IOPC). It is the body responsible for investigating the behaviour of the police, and it is staffed mostly by ex-coppers, or it was then. So, it's not wholly independent, but it's all we've got. After I had dressed in jeans, a jumper, thick socks, hat, scarf, driven to Ashton Court, a stately home near our house, and stomped about gnashing my teeth and swearing, I sat down at my laptop and complained to them. Still bleeding.

The remit of the IPCC was not to reinvestigate my complaint, but to evaluate whether the Met had carried out a sufficient investigation into itself. Whatever. I would complain.

56

A few months later, following an Old Bailey trial, Andy Coulson was found guilty of conspiracy to hack phones and sentenced to eighteen months in prison. The *News of the World*'s chief reporter, Neville Thurlbeck, and news desk editors Ian Edmondson and Greg Miskiw pleaded guilty to the same charge before the trial started and were jailed for a few months each.

Rebekah Brooks was cleared of conspiracy to hack phones as well as conspiracy to pervert the course of justice when her secretary removed seven boxes of her notebooks from the News International archives. A journalist's notebooks or tapes, or both, are her footprints; evidence she has walked through and around a story. We keep them because they are often very helpful if information we have gleaned is challenged. Also, to remind us of the facts after the passing of time; it is so easy to forget the detail, so it is helpful to preserve the evidence. Sometimes, I guess, evidence can potentially be unhelpful too.

It emerged during the trial that Brooks and Coulson had a six-year affair during their editorships of the *Sun* and the *News of the World*. They denied ever discussing the detail of their work during this time, which the jury clearly believed. The period of their affair covered the time the articles were written about me.

I was not in court. Sources who were there hypothesised that the discrepancy in the verdicts was unsurprising when you consider the proof – or lack of it. Brooks presided over – and pushed for – an extensive deletion of company emails, something I was warned was happening when we were investigating but could not get close enough to.

In a 2010 email sent by Brooks to a member of the legal department, titled, 'Framework for email deletion', she clarified that the purpose was:

> ... to eliminate in a consistent manner across News International (subject to compliance with legal and regulatory requirements) emails that could be unhelpful in the context of future litigation in which a News International company is a defendant.

Counsel representing News Group Newspapers in the litigation in which this emerged said the insinuations were unfair, adding, '[Email deletion] is a very complex topic'.

In a *Prospect* article in 2024, Nick temporarily came out of retirement to report on newly released court documents in relation to this.

> How Murdoch's company magicked away 31 million emails

... is quite the read. Thirty-one million emails that could be unhelpful for News International 'in the context of future litigation', deleted. Most, in the five months after Sienna Miller issued her threat to sue;

> *all the emails and the hard drive of Murdoch's UK chief executive, Rebekah Brooks, were destroyed or lost; some evidence was removed from a room in Murdoch's HQ in east London where police had stored it until they had time to examine it; and other evidence was hidden in a secret underfloor safe in Brooks's office.*

Private Eye reported on some of this during the trial, highlighting that,

> *An HTC mobile phone, three BlackBerrys and at least one iPhone, all apparently used at [Brooks's] Cotswolds property [to send emails] during 2010–11, remain unaccounted for.*

The judge in her trial ruled the jury could not be made aware of the fact that one of these was replaced by an identical model on the same day that News International handed over the new evidence of phone hacking, which prompted the Met to launch *Operation Weeting*.

The line from News Group Newspapers has always remained that the destruction of the emails, paperwork and hard drives was routine, nothing to do with concealment of crime, and the timings coincidental.

57

When my IPCC response arrived, it echoed the Met's own report into itself:

> *The [police] investigation has been unable to identify the member of staff who may have leaked the information. The available evidence, however, suggests that a member of police staff, [the press officer], is the most likely suspect in this case. Unfortunately [the press officer] has retired from the Met and is now deceased, which would make progressing the investigation further very difficult.*

It said it would not be proportionate to investigate whether any corrupt payments were made 'given the number of suspects', ignoring, as the Met itself did, the fact that only five people in the Gold Group were meant to have known the kind of detail that made it into those articles. It added that it was unlikely that the legal requirement could be met to obtain personal, financial details from all potential suspects for the same bogus reason.

It said that my request for assurances that the Met has systems in place so that this doesn't happen to anyone else again 'would not be appropriate' because the 'most likely suspect is deceased', ignoring the fact that the press officer was suspended before the final article was written – and wasn't in the Gold Group anyway, so wouldn't have known the kind of details that either the *Sun* or the *News of the World* printed.

The report stated that there was no case to answer for misconduct or gross misconduct because 'no officer or member of police staff has been identified as responsible for leaking the information'. I wanted to scream, 'BECAUSE NO ONE HAS PROPERLY LOOKED FOR THEM, YOU PIECES OF SHIT.' Instead, I picked up Cwtch and tried to teach her the word 'Kafkaesque'. She purred.

The IPCC concluded that the Met's own report was adequate and that taking no further action on the force's part was proportionate. It agreed that the case should not be referred to the CPS on the same basis. I was not surprised. Neither was I ready to give up.

I needed a big hitter. Someone who knew the media. Someone who would confront the police. Who would not be afraid to take this on? The only person I could think of was the lawyer I had tried and failed to contact when I had first worked with Nick.

Tamsin Allen was head of media law at human rights-focused firm Bindmans. She had many high-profile clients, most of whom were famously liberal, or left wing, and who had been bullied by the right-wing press. Tamsin had been mentioned to me many times as a feminist and a badass. If she would represent me, there would be a warrior standing in between me and the 'fucking patriarchal fucking structures and fucking bullies I am absolutely sick to the back fucking teeth of, Cwtchy'. Cwtch looked delighted. Once again, I reached for my laptop.

I had been too afraid, when Nick and I were first investigating, to put into writing any of my secret agenda. Now, with the *News of the World* closed and the truth of press abuse in the public domain, I felt free to tell Tamsin everything.

I realised as I pressed 'Send' that I kind of expected nothing back. Tamsin was probably busy. I hadn't ever managed to get hold of her before. I was probably insane to think I could get to the bottom of this. *Who do I think I am? What am I doing?* The old spiral.

So it was genuinely hard to believe my eyes when I saw her name heading an email in response, just minutes later. She suggested we talk and added, 'I think you have a claim.'

A claim for damages is what she meant. For the damage caused to me by the Metropolitan Police. For giving, or selling, my secrets to the newspapers.

I took the train to London. I had finally become used to the cold sheen of top law firms and Bindmans was no different. Tamsin – brown bob, sparkling eyes, big jewellery – was reserved at first. Perhaps practised at flashing her core of steel in a professional context. I thought, *I wouldn't want to be your opponent in any kind of battle.*

But she wasn't my opponent. She was my ally. And I was soon to discover that Tamsin is anything but reserved and cold. She is smart and she is formidable. She is also warm and funny.

We shared Turkish food at a place near her office and caught up on 'the phone-hacking scandal' so far. A couple of her high-profile clients were senior politicians.

'It's on the public record who most of them are,' she said, as if she knew I was itching to get my notebook out. I was, but I replied, 'Obviously we're off the record. I'm not here for that.' She smiled and offered me a falafel. I don't know why I was so touched that she was prepared to share food with me like this: ripping the flatbread to give me half, telling me the vine leaves were good, encouraging a bigger dip of the humous.

Despite all that had happened, all I had achieved, part of me was still embarrassed that this woman knew how vulnerable I had once been. She knew I had been disrespected and mistreated, multiple times, by many powerful men, and she was still willing to show me she felt we were equal. To show me respect. Perhaps that is why she did it.

'The hacking of some of my clients' voicemails would be considered a breach of national security,' Tamsin went on, thanking the waiter for my sweet mint tea and asking for a cup of her own. 'It is eye-watering that the Metropolitan Police did not think it was their duty to inform them.'

Tamsin had been on a train when she read Nick's 2009 article headed *Murdoch papers paid £1m to gag phone-hacking victims*. As had I. She had never heard of phone hacking either, but it occurred to her that it might explain some of the gaps in her clients' knowledge as to how tabloids seemed to know so much about their lives.

She, too, was amazed when John Yates claimed to have reviewed all relevant material just one day later and had been able to determine that there was nothing substantive enough to re-open a criminal investigation in that short time.

'What was he talking about?' She laughed, though she was not at all happy at the time. 'How could he possibly know? *How was that decision made?*'

She laughed again as she told me that it was at a Murdoch-funded drinks party, sipping his champagne, that she and barrister Hugh Tomlinson had concocted a plan to request a 'judicial review' (JR) of the Met's decision-making; 'God knows why Murdoch invited us.'

A JR must be requested, and a judge persuaded that it is in the public interest for a member of the judiciary to spend time reviewing whatever decision-making is in question. Tamsin had based her argument for a review of Met decision-making around

Article 8 of the European Convention of Human Rights, Right to a Private Life. It was granted on the basis that her clients – any of those whose privacy was breached – had a right to be notified of that breach. She corralled other media lawyers and spearheaded the work, with Tomlinson making representations in court.

As a result of this legal action, the Met was forced to admit that it had failed . . .

> . . . *to take prompt, reasonable and proportionate steps to ensure that those identified as potential victims of voicemail interceptions were made aware of:*
>
> *(a) The interference with their right to respect for private life that may have occurred;*
>
> *(b) The possibility of continuing threats, where such threats had been identified;*
>
> *(c) The steps they might take to protect their privacy; and*
>
> *(d) Following the conclusion of the criminal proceedings against Glenn Mulcaire and Clive Goodman, the identity of those whom the police believed to be primarily responsible for the interception.*
>
> *Such steps should have included informing the public generally, by announcements in the media, through the mobile telephone companies, or otherwise (and should have included, where appropriate, individual notification).*

Tamsin had released the following statement:

> *The legal obligation to warn victims of privacy violations in the phone-hacking case has now been made clear. But at the time of the first investigation into phone-hacking, instead of warning the hundreds or thousands of victims of voicemail*

> *interceptions, the police made misleading statements which gave comfort to News International and permitted the cover-up to continue. If the police had complied with their obligations under the Human Rights Act in the first place, the history of the phone-hacking scandal would have been very different.*

Thank God I had found her. A woman who was, and is, entirely unafraid of nailing Goliath's feet to the floor. In fact, who relishes it.

'Why do you do your job?' I asked, feeling something like ambition stir in me. *Could I do it?* I wondered, sipping my tea. *Could I make people feel as worthy as she makes me feel?*

'I think because I'm quite combative,' Tamsin replied. 'I'm politically motivated and litigation suits me because it's about fighting, and I like that . . . it is hugely satisfying to represent an individual against a monolith.'

I think about the word *monolith* a lot: a seemingly immovable and impenetrable blockade that will hurt you if you run at it too fast . . . but will not move. You have to take care to bring down a monolith. You have to look for detail, find a fissure, work diligently to crack the facade. Tamsin is right – it is hugely satisfying when you manage that, whatever your profession, because there is a unique frustration to playing by the rules, only to discover that those who make or enforce the rules don't play by them at all. To find that, in fact, they use their access to power to change the rules to suit their whim – or their bank balance, or the bank balance of their friends – and not only lock the rest of us out, but attempt to hide it.

Lawyers can sometimes use the rule of law to challenge such unfettered power. Journalists too. This is why wealthy businesspeople and politicians with something to hide attack us so regularly and so vehemently. Gratifyingly, we can be a threat. Sadly, though, more often than not, as I was having to accept with my case, the corruption has been so swiftly and efficiently swept from view, getting to the truth of a hypocrisy or a betrayal can be impossible.

'I will never know which policeman sold my secrets to the press, will I?' I asked Tamsin. She thought about it.

'Probably not,' was her answer, her tone matter-of-fact, but her eyes searching mine for pain.

'Or why,' I added, almost to myself.

Tamsin was still watching my face. 'It's the same with all corruption,' she said gently. 'Sometimes, public inquiries can prise the truth out of the hands of the people who want to bury it. But very often, before the right questions can be asked, records are destroyed, jobs and job titles changed, departments renamed. The truth becomes – undiscoverable. But you can still seek justice – civil justice, at least. And an apology.'

Tamsin was clearly familiar with the staff at the restaurant, chatting politely as she paid the bill. The light over London seemed ashen to me, as we emerged into it. White. A blank page. She hugged me before she left, looking reassuringly into my face once more. We didn't speak, but she nodded when she saw resolve in my eyes, before heading back into her firm, to rejoin the fight.

I bought a hot chocolate at Paddington, in honour of Will, and sipped it as my train left the station. It was the same route west I used to take when we still lived with Mum. I had taken it the day after The Famous Man incident, when I had had to bite my fist to pee, because I was in so much pain. It was another moment to reflect on the shape of the journey I had taken to get here. I was no longer that girl. It seemed now as if that experience, and what came after, wrought me from myself. Now, I was returning. *No place like home.*

58

'Apology – of sorts.'

Tamsin handed me an A4 envelope with a letter inside. I saw the Metropolitan Police logo at the top of the paper and my heart stopped. An *apology*.

We were standing in the Bindman's foyer, but I opened it on the spot. I found I was crying. Then I was laughing. What a cop-out. Literally.

> *Dear Ms Evans,*
>
> *I am writing to you with regard to the public complaint you made in [date redacted] and your letter of claim [date redacted]. Your complaint resulted from an investigation conducted by officers from the Metropolitan Police Service into an allegation of serious assault made by yourself which occurred in [date redacted]. You alleged that officers inappropriately leaked details of the investigation to the media.*
>
> *As you are aware your complaint was investigated by officers from the Directorate of Professional Standards-Specialist Investigations. Their investigation upheld your complaint and concluded that staff working within the Metropolitan Police Service did inappropriately pass details of the investigation to the media.*

> *I would like to apologise unreservedly on behalf of the Metropolitan Police Service for the conduct of the passing of information to the media.*
>
> *I am very sorry for the distress caused.*
>
> *I would like to thank you for bringing your complaint and concerns to our attention and thank you for your cooperation throughout the investigation.*

The Met had managed to congratulate itself for blaming the dead press officer and did not mention that it had otherwise failed to investigate anything at all. It summed up the way the most privileged operate so perfectly: a sheen of pompous self-congratulation, a sprinkle of obfuscation, an on-the-record readjustment of the truth. Suddenly they are protected from having to admit to anyone – least of all themselves – that they can be criminal too.

I had become used to such reputation laundering while investigating this story, which was really an exposé of the machinations of the power elite. The greatest irony of the phone-hacking saga was that those at the centre, presiding over the covering up – tabloid executives and owners, politicians, police – had built their reputations, and in some cases their millions, on exposing the shit out of everyone else.

Tamsin shrugged. 'Classic MPS,' was all she said. Then she took me into a side room and told me she had negotiated a sum of money from the force, by way of 'damages' – compensation for how I had been treated. 'Better than that shitty apology,' she added, smiling as she watched my eyes widen.

The Met neither admitted nor investigated the extent of the corruption in my case, which I still hoped at that time the second half of the Leveson Inquiry might uncover. But Tamsin had secured from them tens of thousands of pounds for me, by way of recompense for how carelessly my deepest secrets were shared. *How incredible*, I thought, *to be able to force powerful institutions to apologise ... and to pay ... for their mistakes, even if they won't admit them.*

I have witnessed in filmmaking how validating it is for some people to have their story put into the public domain. Journalism can return power to those who have been silenced or mistreated, gaslighted or spurned. I have seen the positive effect on my sources of being really seen, really heard, and it has had long-lasting implications for their well-being and sense of worth. It is the most rewarding aspect of the job. But using the rule of law to gain them not just recognition, not just a voice, but an apology when they have been wronged, a sum of money to help them set their life back on track – that was life-changing stuff. That was real power. Idly, every now and then, I would google 'train to be a lawyer', deciding each time I did so to wait just a little longer – Jasp and I had been 'trying' for a baby for three years at this point, and each month I thought I might get lucky. I might need the money for maternity leave.

Instead, I bought Jasper a new computer, and a second-hand car, which I gave to him one Christmas morning, having put the keys in his stocking. I paid our bills for a while. In the end, we spent the rest on IVF. It would take four more years, five 'rounds' and eight 'embryo transfers' to get the positive pregnancy test we had craved for so long, and hoped would last. After seven years of 'trying', nine months later, we met our little boy.

In the interim, Tamsin had taken on the newspapers, several of which agreed to pay damages to me, none of which admitted liability. With that money, I renovated the kitchen of our new house to the spec that Jasp desired – he is a massive person who likes to have space, and a very good cook.

We had another embryo, which had been formed during the same round of IVF as Leo. Putting aside enough money to ensure we could afford the embryo transfer – we ended up having treatment at a clinic in Barcelona, so it cost a lot – in 2020, I enrolled to study law. One day, I hope to be someone else's Charlotte Harris or Tamsin Allen.

Having Tamsin on my side felt like having a force field. I felt protected, truly safe. Maybe I truly was safe, for the first time since The Famous Man grabbed my throat. It should never have taken that long.

Postscript

As a result of my allegations, and his own actions and reactions in their wake, The Famous Man lost his career. I discovered from the DPS report that forty-nine women came forward to accuse him of sexual assault at the same time as I did, yet only my allegations were considered credible enough to press charges. Many others have since reported him for sexually violent crimes. The criminal burden of proof has to this day not been met.

And though naming him might keep other women safe, in warning them he is someone to stay away from, I can't do it. As the press intrusion and my subsequent paranoia led me to stop talking, and the charges to be withdrawn, if I name The Famous Man, or in any way identify him, he could sue me for libel. Insult to fairly serious injury. To be clear, he could still decide to sue if he feels that, despite my anonymising him, he is recognisable in this book, but it would be a gamble for him; he'd have to surrender the anonymity I've given him and put his hand up as one of the men accused of this violence. As truth is a defence to a libel action, he'd need to be confident that a court would, on the balance of probabilities, conclude that I had decided to lie about what happened. I am prepared for this, if that is his choice, but there are other things I would prefer to do with my time and energy.

Many women who have spoken out about sexual violence have found themselves on the wrong end of an aggressive legal action, especially if they have attempted to name their attacker/s. Luckily, brilliant legal minds like Jennifer Robinson and Keina Yoshida's are working on this:

> *The fact is that parliament and the upper echelons of both the media and the legal profession have been, and still are, dominated by men. This matters . . . it can be seen in laws about gender-based violence and the laws regulating women's ability to speak about it. It can also be seen in media coverage of gender-based violence, and in the laws regulating the way the media can report it. And it affects the way these laws operate in practice to silence women.*
>
> *How Many More Women*, Robinson and Yoshida, Endeavour, 2023

But maybe I don't want to name him. This is not about him. This is about naming the institutions and organisations, 'boys' clubs' all, that treated my terrible experiences with such disregard. They betrayed and traumatised me and, I suspect, many other women who have been treated in the same way. I write this for them, for us, at a time when women's rights worldwide are being curtailed in terrifying and damaging ways.

In connection there is community, in community there is belonging. In belonging, we shed shame. We begin to heal. Those of us who have experienced violence can feel so alone; all of us Dorothy Gales, blown off course, looking for a way back home. But we are not alone. There are millions of us, and we have each other. We belong.

And the message I want women, especially young women, to take home when they read this story is that, if you feel you have no power at all, there is some power in simply asking questions. Trust your gut. Self-advocate. *Ask questions.*

No one will help you if you don't, but if you do, the people who will answer your questions truthfully are going to help you get somewhere. And the people who won't should be asked again. Because they may be hiding something that you – and others – need to know. *Ask them again. Ask questions.* It is easy once you start, but women, socialised to understand that 'good girls' take supportive roles, supress 'negative' emotions, placate, are too ready to second-guess our instincts.

'Are you proud?' is the question Mum asked when the payment came in from the Met.

I thought about it. 'Well, I still don't know who sold me out, exactly, and I haven't yet worked out how I am going to expose what happened, but I suppose I did slay some dragons.'

It was true. I had helped expose illegality at the newspaper that so offended and humiliated me, and seen it closed. I helped reveal its corrupt links to politicians and, perhaps more seriously, to the police we have no option but to trust when we are hurt. 'Maybe.'

Mum looked at me and said, 'I am so incredibly proud of you. And Will would be too.'

We held back our tears, I don't know why. We shy away from showing each other the pain of the loss of Will, I think. It is so deep. I did a few dance steps on his grave before we left; I always dance on his grave, he'd have liked that. I elected to walk home across the river meadows that border the town. The meadows Will and I had walked with Dad and Teggy so many times, and where Dad's ashes are scattered.

I do sometimes feel proud, I thought, looking out at the river, hoping for a kingfisher, *but not always*. Violence is bewildering and recovering from violence is a slow process. Looked at another way, this story is a tale of many lost years. For a long time, I still had symptoms of trauma; I could be crippled by shame, hypervigilant about dynamics I might miss, or rooms I might misread. I feared being too visible, which affected my life choices and my filmmaking career.

The final chapter of this book pays respect to that trauma. If you balk at reading about other people's therapy, I totally get it – look away now. But to me it felt disingenuous to name your memoir *Don't Let It Break You, Honey* and not address the moment that you broke. Or – it felt more like melting.

It happened after this part of the story was over, when I was beset by another tragedy: the death of my daughter. I include my meltdown, and recovery, to show those young women for whom I write this book, who hopefully are even now noting down all the questions they want to ask everyone, that there is strength in breaking. You can rebuild.

Beautifully, when I did so, alongside this writing, Maya Angelou re-emerged, stronger than ever, as the guardian angel I had always needed. That is why it is named for her.

> You may write me down in history
> With your bitter, twisted lies,
> You may trod me in the very dirt
> But still, like dust, I'll rise.
>
> Maya Angelou,
> *Still I Rise* (1978)

Epilogue: Rupture and Repair

Rupture

Twenty years after The Famous Man and The Wolf assault, following the stillbirth of my daughter, Lula – one catastrophe too many – I began to uncontrollably leak tears. Unaware for a short while of what was happening to me, I tried to carry on as normal.

Lula was stillborn in February 2021. In a work meeting on the second anniversary of her death, I felt blamed for something that wasn't my fault and humiliated by a team member. I usually quite enjoy a creative tussle in what TV calls a 'development' meeting – a brainstorm in which you attempt to create or refine an idea. This time, the experience took my breath away. My mind blanked. Feelings of shame surfaced that I hadn't felt in a very long time, and I found I could not recover.

I assumed it was grief that caused this response. In Ariel Levy's incomparably beautiful description of the pain she felt after her own baby loss, she says,

> *Grief is a world you walk through skinned, unshelled. A person would speak to me unkindly – or even ungently – on the street or in an elevator, and I would feel myself*

> *ripping apart, the membrane of normalcy I'd pulled on to leave the house coming undone.*
> *The Rules Do Not Apply: A Memoir* by
> Ariel Levy, 2017

I know grief. I thought it was that. But this just would not pass.

I began to leak sorrow. I felt as if I could not tolerate one more sad thought in my head. As if the depth of my pain connected from the centre of my being to the core of the earth and into every atom of every thing there is. I was sadness and sadness was everything.

I could not stop crying. I thought endlessly of dying. I was not coping.

It was Mum who first described it as trauma. She had driven me and Leo to the Hay Festival – the same place she had taken me to see Maya Angelou so many years before.

Leo was four, a bundle of blond curls and fart-joke energy in blue stripey leggings. He was asleep in his bunk bed in her spare room. Mum and I drank cold wine on a warm evening and talked about him, which is exactly what Jasper and I do when we've finally got him to bed too.

'You look tired,' she said.

You're always tired when you have a four-year-old, but it was true. I was bone tired. I could not escape it. At any point, I could have lain down on any floor and slept. A few weekends before, another night Leo and I had stayed over, Mum had sent me back to bed first thing in the morning, assuming I was ill, because I looked so truly awful.

'It's happening a lot,' I had told her. 'I sleep for a full night but when I wake up, I look and feel like I haven't slept at all, and I'm not sure that I have.'

I opened up a little about how stricken I had been feeling. I do try to protect my mum, most people, from the deepest horror of grief, but I was a little frightened by the power of it this time. Of its capacity to overwhelm. I couldn't hide this in the way I had become accustomed with other grief; it was like my armour no longer fit.

I now understand that is because it was trauma that was leaking out of me, not grief. And the trauma of losing Lula opened a channel to unresolved sexual trauma I had no idea was still there, which is why feelings of being blamed and shamed in that development meeting became intolerable.

I expect I quietly cried as we talked. I couldn't seem to stop myself from doing that. I told Mum that, for the first time in my life, I was aware of feeling intensely anxious; that at times my heart beat in my chest as if it might grow wings and escape.

I told her how desperate I was to have another child. How I felt like somewhere inside me I was always silently screaming, as if I had never actually stopped giving birth to Lula. As if I was stuck in those last few moments, when you roar as you tear to make room for your baby's beautiful head. How, if the last baby's head I held to my face was destined to be Lula's, tiny and ice cold, I might never recover. When your baby dies, your instinct to mother does not. In fact, it becomes stronger. This is the thing that those who tell you, believing it to be compassionate, to 'maybe just stop trying' do not understand.

When I got up in the morning, Mum told me, gently, I had Post-Traumatic Stress Disorder (PTSD). It was bewildering, but a sense of relief swept through me like rain; this was different from grief, she might be right. And that meant someone out there might be able to help me.

She had been researching and gave me the contact details of a therapist who specialises in working with baby loss and infertility. Her name is Miriam. With great patience and skill, Miriam began to truly return me to myself.

I could tell from the moment I picked up the phone to her that she knew her shit. I could hear her intelligence, feel her compassion, sense her competence. I could sense in her too that core of steel I have come to recognise in so many impressive professionals. Another warrior.

'Trauma is rooted in shock,' Miriam explained. 'You have received shocking, life-changing news and experienced shocking, life-changing violence more than once.' Each time it had sent my body into survival mode. We can't process memories properly when our nervous system is overwhelmed. 'That is why those memories glitch, sometimes they flash back. I can help you . . .'

I. Can. Help. You.

I didn't hear the end of the sentence.

I asked her if she was sure it was OK to potentially need to talk about the sexual violence. Her stated specialism was perinatal work; it felt like such a lot to put on a person. Miriam told me that working with women means working with sexual trauma. She said, slowly, as if her instinct for empathy understood that I needed her to slow down for me to take it in, 'It's OK to bring that here. You can bring it here.'

It was August and we had to take a break while we both went on pre-planned holidays. I wrote that sentence down and reread it every time my heart tried to break free from my chest. Every time I was overwhelmed with distress about my daughter. Every time I got an email from the company I had felt so shamed by. Every time I felt fear about that shame. I read it about a hundred times a day. *It's OK to bring that here. You can bring it here.*

Would I be able to find the words once more? Would I finally be able to let this go? The attack by The Famous Man and The Wolf had flickered at the edge of my vision for so long: a candle flame I dare not look at, a dark zoetrope of fear. Was it possible to blow that candle out?

Miriam suggested we use EMDR therapy to release the traumatic memories. EMDR stands for Eye Movement Desensitisation and Reprocessing. Snappy. The idea is that using bi-lateral stimulation – moving your eyes, for example, or tapping your body on consecutive sides – while guided by a professional to think or talk about what is causing you pain, the neural pathway that contains the traumatic memory is able to release it. To process it. To file it away with the other memories, those that were not formed when your nervous system was in a state of panic, so that it no longer has the power to physically affect you.

EMDR is highly specialised, dependent on a strong relationship of trust between therapist or psychologist and client. This is true of all therapy, and I have had counselling before, but it was nothing like this. It felt like, when processing my trauma using EMDR, I was at times as exposed and vulnerable as I had been during the incidents; I felt sensations I had felt, or supressed, at the time, even smelled the smells. My feet instinctively tapped at the same time as my hands, because, I understand, when the men trapped me, I so much wanted to run. This is why you need your therapist to be as badass as your lawyer: totally unshockable, exceedingly skilled. You are back in the high school biology lab and you are letting her tend to your wounds.

Repair

If a rape falls in the forest, and there's no one around to hear it, does it make a sound? Miriam theorised that I remembered Ken, that taxi driver, so well because he was the first person after The Famous Man attack who really saw me. Ken seeing me made it real.

In this context, the context of abuse, so often shielded from view by a cloak of shame, to be witnessed is to exist. I hadn't thought about it like that before. How lucky I was to have a brain like hers focused on helping me understand.

The *Barbie* film had just come out when we were having these sessions, and Miriam joked that it was hard to picture Ken as anyone but Ryan Gosling, 'Taxi Driver Ken'. I loved that. It was such a relief, to find a moment of light in the relentless dark of this distress.

She did check – 'Is that OK?' – but she knew it was, or she wouldn't have said it. What expertise, to be able to see in your client a coping mechanism such as this, of combining horror with humour in order to survive, and to use it. She knew I would laugh.

To be witnessed is to exist.

With the jaws of denial firmly shut when I began my work with Miriam, I struggled at first to connect to the traumatic memories. The Famous Man incident, in particular, often flickered in my peripheral vision, but I was unable to look at the images. Unable to accept them as real.

She asked, 'What does it mean about you if these things did happen?' Heat crept up my face. I could not answer. I had to fight the urge to run out of the front door and never stop running. Partly, because that was what I wanted to do at the time, I think. Partly because the words in my mind were, 'If this really happened, it means I am not worthy of respect', 'It means I do not matter', 'It means I cannot make myself safe'.

I did not want to face the truth that I felt those things. I could not say them. Miriam worked patiently and compassionately to help me, if not to say them, to accept I felt them and let them move through me. Let them go.

Once, she asked if there was anyone we might insert into the most traumatic moments. Someone who could be a protector, who, if I'd had a magic wand, could have got me out of there. Knowing my love of her poetry, she suggested Maya Angelou.

'Maya?' I laughed.

Miriam nodded and smiled encouragingly. It didn't seem like a crazy suggestion to her. I felt a pull in my chest as I thought, *Oh God, it would have been amazing if Maya Angelou had arrived and got me out.*

So, she did. That's what Miriam helped me formulate. That's who we 'tapped in'. Now, Maya arrives in every traumatic memory I process, leading me out of there, straight backed, kind and stoic, saying, 'You're safe now. I've got you, honey. Let's get you out.' Maya Angelou, my guardian angel.

As Miriam and I worked – an exchange of trust and knowledge, guesswork and feeling – the sadness of the truth that these *were* experiences that *did* happen slowly rose to the surface. Gently holding this emotion with me, she sat there as I wept. Once, through a thick veil of tears, I apologised to her that she was having to spend her Friday morning doing such intense work. She looked at me with deeply kind intent and sincerity and said, 'There is nowhere else I would rather be.' Then, I wept for her kindness. I had needed to do this for so long.

Miriam looked thrilled one session when I told her I had fought The Famous Man and his friend 'like a raccoon'.

'I LOVE that.'

She asked the same question, 'What does that say about you?'

I thought.

'It says I have some fight in me?'

I had been looking away when I said that, but I glanced back at a moment Miriam wasn't expecting me to and caught her looking genuinely delighted by what I had just said. 'You *have* got some fight in you. Yes, you have. Let's tap that in.'

I tapped my shoulders, as I had been shown, and remembered myself attempting to fight them off. Why should tapping be able to work such magic? I didn't know, but I had absolute trust in this beautiful and compassionate woman. The pain woman. The woman who sits with other women, in the deepest throws of their sorrow and distress, and helps them to heal. What an incredible woman to be.

Have there been versions of this woman throughout history, I wonder. The archetype of the matriarch; using whatever tools or tech available to her in the time she finds herself alive, to help other women in their distress: in childbirth, in parenthood, in recovering from male violence. Women must have been helping women like this since the beginning of time.

Around the time I lived down The Well, and met the 'True Colors' friends in the bar, Irish poet and philosopher John O'Donohue published *Anam Cara*. It is a book of philosophy, poetry and spirituality based around connection and friendship, and I bought it, at the time, for Evan.

'Anam Cara' is a Gaelic expression. It means 'soul friend'.

> *In the Celtic tradition, there is a beautiful understanding of love and friendship . . . Anam is the Gaelic word for soul and cara is the word for friend. So anam cara in the Celtic world was the 'soul friend.' . . . With the anam cara you could share your inner-most self, your mind and your heart. This friendship was an act of recognition and belonging . . .*

Originally, I related to this in respect of my brilliant, life-affirming friends and family, my original copy thick with dog-eared pages, underlines and exclamation marks. Working with Miriam, half-remembered passages began to come to mind and I returned to the book, drawn to the notion that there can be more than a little of the anam cara in the therapist–client relationship, too. It is not friendship in the same sense, but their job is to be a friend to your soul:

> *[Anam cara] originally referred to someone to whom you confessed, revealing the hidden intimacies of your life . . . you are understood as you are without mask or pretension. The superficial and functional lies and half-truths of social acquaintance fall away, you can be as you really are. This love allows understanding to dawn, and understanding is precious. Where you are understood, you are at home. Understanding nourishes belonging. When you really feel understood, you feel free.*
>
> *The anam cara perspective is sublime because it permits us to enter this unity of ancient belonging.*

We all need to feel we fit in somewhere. It is a cruel trick of the traumatised mind that in order to make us hide – to keep us safe – it convinces us that we are cast out and cannot belong; pain unmoors you, shame then steals your boat.

Don't let it break you.

You are not alone.

Afterword

Rupert Murdoch's News Group Newspapers (NGN) has reportedly spent over £1 billion settling legal claims against the *News of the World* and *the Sun*. These settlements have been reached outside of court, with recipients required to sign Non-Disclosure Agreements (NDAs) as part of the process.

In one sense, this suggests the UK's civil justice system is functioning as designed: preventing lengthy trials, reducing court backlogs and sparing claimants the emotional toll of legal proceedings. But there's a catch. If a claimant refuses a reasonable settlement offer, they risk financial ruin – forced to pay not only their own legal costs but also those of their opponent, even if they win. The sums involved can be staggering.

It's a system that, as I discovered first hand, has a fundamental flaw: those with power and money can make their problems disappear. The wealthy can pay to keep their secrets buried, ensuring that even those who begin with the strongest resolve to uncover the truth are eventually worn down. Hugh Grant, when settling his case against NGN, put it bluntly:

'I don't want to accept this money or settle. I would love to see all the allegations they deny tested in court. But the rules around civil litigation

mean that if I proceed to trial and the court awards me damages that are even a penny less than the settlement offer – an enormous sum of money – I would have to pay the legal costs of both sides.

My lawyers tell me that that is exactly what would most likely happen here. Rupert Murdoch's lawyers are very expensive. So even if every allegation is proven in court, I would still be liable for something approaching £10m in costs. I'm afraid I am shying at that fence."*

Grant, at least, found a way to repurpose his settlement – donating it to campaign groups like Hacked Off, which emerged in the wake of the 'phone-hacking scandal' to push for greater accountability in the press.

I write this just days after Prince Harry and Lord Watson reached their own settlements with NGN. Harry did, at least, secure a rare concession, described by his lawyer as: *'a full and unequivocal apology [by NGN] for the serious intrusion by the* Sun *between 1996 and 2011 into his private life, including incidents of unlawful activities carried out by private investigators working for the* Sun . . . *[and] for the phone hacking, surveillance and misuse of private information by journalists and private investigators instructed by them at the* News of the World.'†

It is, I think, the closest any victim has come to securing an admission of liability, though in legal terms, it remains just shy of one.

And so, with this final case settled, the door to the truth swings shut. At least for NGN and the Mirror Group, which also quietly settled all cases. The other tabloid owner in the UK, the Daily Mail and General Trust (DMGT), which owns the *Daily Mail* and *Mail on Sunday*, faces litigation later this year.

---

* *Guardian,* 17 April 2024
† BBC News, 22 January 2025

In respect of the others, we may never fully know the extent of the wrongdoing, who was involved, or how high the knowledge went. In the end, Murdoch bought his privacy in a way that the rest of us simply cannot. Let's pause a moment for the irony to fully seep in.

This is why I felt it necessary to include in this book the raw material I gathered while investigating this story. In any normal circumstance, these claims would need thorough verification before being published. Certainly, neither the *Guardian* nor Channel 4's *Dispatches* would have aired something that couldn't be definitively proved. But when I went back to my notebooks, I found a wealth of testimony: pages of credible allegations, given by people who were there. Information that the legal system might have dragged into the public domain – if not for the existence of these settlements.

As I explain in the Author's Note, it felt important to include this material – not as absolute truth, but as an insight into the breadth and depth of what was shared with me. Public interest matters when the power imbalance is this stark. Where possible, I have verified information, but I haven't been able to do that for every anecdote or allegation. It is not how I would normally operate, but to omit this information completely would be to erase the reality of what I uncovered, and the path it led me down. It needs to be included, for me to be allowed to tell the truth of this story.

Acknowledgements

It is a great privilege to have been given the opportunity to write this book. To have cautiously asked, 'Does this story seem important?' and for the answer to have been 'Yes' means such a lot. The first person I would like to thank, therefore, is Jemima Hunt at the Writer's Practice: fearless friend and advocate, talented writer, laser-focused editor, powerhouse agent. Thank you for believing in this and in my ability to conquer it, for never giving up, for saving me from my inner Adrian Mole.

Thank you also to Emma at Little, Brown: gentle, unflappable, fiercely intelligent. You commissioned a story that is difficult to tell on many levels and did nothing but fight for it. I am so incredibly grateful. These thanks extend to Tamsin and the rest of the team at Little, Brown/Hachette whose kind support helped make this exposing process a little less utterly terrifying.

Nick Davies, Charlotte Harris, Tamsin Allen and all others who feature, who helped me. Thank you. I would also like to thank my very private family for allowing me to include you, and the friends who permitted the same: Cerys, Rhi and Sue Jones, Lyz Jones, Emma Lewis, Rachel, Lucy Baker-Swinburn, Charlotte Nowosad, Katie Woods, Evan Maloney, Nick Pincombe, Neil Wilkinson,

Lizzie Hodge, Joe Fisher, Bob Donald, Catherine Norris-Trent, Kristina Cooke, Becky Read, Jess Watts, Rosa Allday, Lotte Friedrich, Luke Ritchie and Eleri Lynn (Lel, sorry to have had to cut the description of us reading *Under Milk Wood* to each other endlessly when we were teenagers. Cool cool cool.)

Life is so much more beautiful with all of you in it. How lucky I am to have you.

Tom Dennis and Ben Addis: two very important, very funny, endlessly supportive and loving flatmates, with whom I lived during some of this time - sorry that you were too boring to make the cut. But thanks for the many hours of taking bets on the *Antiques Roadshow*, the roasts, Ben's perfect sandwiches, the dancing in the living room. I love you.

Don't Let It Break You, Honey originated as an article. Or, two articles. The first, which was published anonymously, I would like to thank Emma Jones and Graham Johnson for helping me with. You have done nothing but help me, endlessly, and I am so grateful. The second, which became this manuscript, was initially shaped with the patient support of the brilliant Rebecca North, who helped me distil the essence of the story and my reasons for telling it. I gave it to David Modell next, who offered insightful and gentle feedback. Later readers, whose journalistic or storytelling instincts – or both – helped shape a narrative that was entirely new to them, learning crazy new stuff about me along the way and dealing with that with extreme grace, were Florence Wildblood, Jim Nally, Clare Bradbury, Jack Simcock, Jaine Rubin, Claire Riviere, Yvonne Beckett, Hannah Livingstone, Jo Potts and Sue Roderick. Thank you. I am so appreciative of the time each of you gave to this.

Special mention must be reserved for the friends who read early drafts of the manuscript. I took this to be an expression either of deep love, or sincere support, or both. Because who wants to read the same book twice, ever? So, thank you, and deep love back to Kate Evans, Poppy Goodheart, Jacqui Honess-Martin, Ben Addis, Rachel Greenwood, Victoria Hollingsworth, Penny Compton, Kelly Paull, Vicky Walker-Love, Emma Shaw, Joel Ross and Abbie Hickson, and to later, pre-publication readers. You know who you are. Also, to Miriam, The Badass With The Big Smile™, whose gentle strength is so moving and inspiring. Thank you, all, for not trampling all over my soul in big boots, for your tender, honest and constructive opinions, and for the many hours of your precious time.

There are a number of people I trust and respect – some mentors, some friends, some both – to whom I have over the years disclosed aspects of the events described in this book. Grief and trauma are a lot to ask people to hold and I never do so lightly. I would like to offer heartfelt thanks to those of you I trusted with some of this, who held it and did not judge me. Rather, who treated me gently and with extreme kindness.

So, for deep chats, or dances on tables, or both, I am very grateful to Natalie Triebwasser, Jojo Martin, Rupert Hill, Jenny Platt, Sarah Brodbin, Laure Filho, Steve O'Connor, Colette Bacahlau, Kam Kandola-Flynn, Heidi Donald, Zara Hayes, Kate Cook, Bruce Goodison, Siobhan Sinnerton, Ramita Navai, Ali Chivers, Fergal McGrath, Anne Henry and last through the door, but no less wonderful, Anna Lichtensteiger.

Also, to my mate, Bill Dare, who died in an accident days before the book was announced. He would have been (probably quite sarcastic and) massively encouraging and proud.

To Juliet Grayson, whose kind and gentle support helped me first start talking, and to Sophia Gazla, who helped me continue.

To those who knew me very young, and for whom I could not find all the words, but who knew and who were older and did things like feed me and encourage me to leave the house and try to have some fun. Among them Kevin Allen, Rhys Ifans, Coleen Spencer (and beloved Si – both of you geniuses), Mike Jones, Virginie Balthazard, Ming Brookes, Lorraine Statham and David Cooper. Thank you so much for your time and compassion, for the laughs – and for the food.

Also to Ali B, who sent me and Neil on holiday to Greece after the criminal case collapsed, in an act of jaw-dropping generosity I don't feel I have ever managed to adequately thank him for.

Speaking to the grief towards the end of the book, for Lula. I would like to make a special mention of my 'Mum friends', who have graciously accepted one among them whose second baby died, and who cries at Christmas again now. The love of Stella Fisher, Sophie Herrera, Amy Pope, Kelly Paull, Gemma Farrar, Naomi Randall, Minia Alonso, Rachel Coombswood and Helen Viner stands out, among the kindnesses of many. As does the community at The Worst Girl Gang Ever.

I would also like to thank again the friends who have been a major part of my life but are not featured in the book, either because I couldn't reach you to ask permission, or because of where the narrative turned. Again, you know who you are and what we mean, or have meant, to each other. Gill Stark (née Atkinson) is principal in my mind. As are Helen Evans and Lucy Rivers, treasured friends since primary school. I love you so much. As well as Rhiannon Hopkins, Ali Matthews, the rest of the Regent Street, Aber' and Soho loves of my life, and to wider family. Thank you for being you and for helping make me, me.

Thank you to L, whose mantra, 'It is what it is' truly is a profound philosophy. And to Grace and Rosie and others with whom I have worked. You are an inspiration.

Finally, I would like to thank the brave whistle-blowers and anonymous sources, whose courage in sharing their life experiences has allowed me to ask the right kinds of questions and to get to the bottom of a few of the issues that I think matter. Especially those who helped with the story this book tells. I – we; journalists, authors, lawyers – are nothing without you. I am in awe at your courage. Thank you.

All.

May your tea always be the perfect temperature. May your taxi driver always be Ken.